IMAGES
of America

LAKE JACKSON

ON THE COVER: The first barber in the city was Tom Vaughn. Dickie Frerking is receiving a cut while Captain Brown waits in the early 1940s. (Courtesy of the Lake Jackson Historical Association.)

IMAGES
of America

LAKE JACKSON

Harry Sargent

ARCADIA
PUBLISHING

ISBN 978-0-7385-8479-9

Published by Arcadia Publishing
Charleston, South Carolina

Printed in the United States of America

Library of Congress Control Number: 2011926332

For all general information, please contact Arcadia Publishing:
Telephone 843-853-2070
Fax 843-853-0044
E-mail sales@arcadiapublishing.com
For customer service and orders:
Toll-Free 1-888-313-2665

Visit us on the Internet at www.arcadiapublishing.com

*This book is dedicated to the creative and driven citizens
who have made and continue to make Lake Jackson
a unique community in which to live our lives.*

Contents

ACKNOWLEDGMENTS

I appreciate the staff of the Lake Jackson Historical Association—Jennifer, Angela, and Ande—for willingly putting aside their work to assist me in the search for photographs and background information for this book.

Unless otherwise credited, the images are from the archives of the Lake Jackson Historical Association.

INTRODUCTION

The city of Lake Jackson was named for a lake on the former plantation of Abner Jackson, one of the early settlers of the area who began a large agricultural operation. Jackson began purchasing land along the lower Brazos River in 1842. He had married Margaret Strobel, a wealthy widow in South Carolina, and they owned more land in Georgia. Jackson's motivation to come west was most likely to find better soil for agriculture. He accumulated about 3,000 acres adjacent to the lake where he ultimately raised sugarcane and cotton. He had about 285 slaves and three plantations. He traveled back and forth many times before his wife moved to Texas. Each trip resulted in another child until there were four. His last son was born in Texas.

After Abner's death in 1861, his son John contributed to the story when he returned from the Confederate army to manage the plantations. He was 23 at the time and apparently very ruthless financially. He had relations with a housekeeper named Rosa, and thus began the line of African American Jacksons through a son, Frank. They now number more than 500 and gather for a reunion in June each year.

After the war, John attempted to pay the freedmen a small amount while providing clothing, housing, and food. This only delayed the demise of the plantation as a viable business.

John resented his only surviving brother George's return from the war and his request for his share of the land. The boys fought on two occasions during the next year. George went to court and won the rights to the Lake Jackson Plantation. In 1867, the final confrontation on the front porch of the main house resulted in George shooting John several times, which killed him. George was indicted, but apparently there was never a trial. George died in 1872 in Galveston at his sister's home. In 1870, the land was lost to taxes.

Ward and Dewey, businessmen from Galveston, added to the saga when they purchased the land in 1872 with a plan to lease Texas prisoners to operate the sugar plantation. The plan failed before the 10-year contract was completed, after 36 men came and two died due to poor treatment.

In 1900, the Lake Jackson Sugar Company attempted to reestablish the sugar business but the Galveston storm ended the effort with great devastation.

The plantation land remained unused until the board of the Dow Chemical Company, a corporation of Midland, Michigan, purchased land adjacent to Freeport and Velasco in 1938 in order to recover magnesium from seawater. The land included the Lake Jackson Plantation. A.P. Beutel was the first manager of the site. The project took on major national importance with the advent of World War II in 1941 and the need for magnesium and synthetic rubber.

Beutel knew that the quality of life was important. He worked with Alden Dow, a son of the Dow Chemical Company's founder, to establish a city to house the bright young people who came to build and work in the chemical plant. This project was one of the first designed communities in the country, with many curving streets to create an excitement of what was around the corner.

The downtown area was quickly constructed to serve the citizens. There were permanent buildings, of which most currently remain. There were also surplus buildings moved in to house shops.

Beutel established a park on the lake for picnicking and Saturday night dances. He also constructed a home on the lake and sold select lots around the lake to leading employees.

Lake Jackson was and is the size of a town in which an individual can personally know key citizens. Many consider this a privilege and advantage relative to larger cities in which one can get lost. The following are a few who impacted Lake Jackson, past and present.

The young town grew thanks to Jim Nabors, Jack Reid, Bob Franklin, Mac MacLean, John Stark, Bob Hackney, and many more.

Jim Nabors was a veteran of the Pacific War. He came to Brazosport as publisher of the *Facts*. He was a community leader and member of the Texas Historical Commission. He was also a key asset of the Lake Jackson Historical Association. He had the Lake Jackson Plantation site declared a state archeological landmark and arranged for the archeological study by Joan Few of the University of Houston at Clear Lake.

Jack Reid came to town looking for work as a bricklayer. He found work in the chemical plant. He built schools, businesses, and homes. When brickwork slowed, he was invited into the lumberyard business in Lake Jackson, which also sold home appliances. He ultimately had his own appliance store. A long-time supporter of the city, he provided the truck and watermelons for the Jaycees Fourth of July celebration several times and served as mayor. He was also known for free repairs for his customers' refrigerators when they were damaged during Hurricane Carla in 1961.

Mac MacLean, a Canadian Scotsman, came to Lake Jackson as the city manager in 1956 and served for 35 years. He brought a conservative financial plan for the city that kept the taxes low and the services high. Streets were constructed of concrete and parks were included in all subdivisions.

Bob Franklin came to town from Oklahoma, working for the government organizing the housing for the employees of the local chemical plant. A potential transfer caused him to set roots with his young family by entering the insurance business. He was a Mason and his office was on the ground floor of the lodge in 1953, thus providing income to help support the lodge. He was active in his support of the city and was a key leader in the Methodist church.

John Stark was a Dow Chemical Company construction engineer who also made an impact on the community by overseeing the building of the First Methodist Church, Girl Scout house, Salvation Army, and women's shelter. He made a point of completing the buildings without a debt service. This required strong requests of the local construction company owners. If visiting his church, one shook hands with John and his massive bear claw because he always welcomed people in the narthex as long as he was a member.

Bob Hackney came to Lake Jackson in 1948, as a physical education teacher after serving in the war and completing his degree from Southwest Texas State College. When the Korean War began, he returned to active duty with the Marine Corps. Unfortunately, he suffered major wounds that delayed his return to the city. He drove a school bus, established a swim instruction business, was a city councilman, and was on the First National Bank Board, as well as being a teacher.

Early social and service opportunities were provided for the citizens by churches, schools, the Masons, the Junior Chamber of Commerce, the garden club, and the Girl and Boy Scouts.

Later developments included Brazosport College, the Center for the Arts and Sciences, the Brazosport Regional Hospital, the Brazosport Rotary, a mall for southern Brazoria County, a bus system, Little League and youth baseball, girls softball, youth soccer, Lions clubs, Optimists, retirement facilities, a civic center, the Sea Center, the historical museum . . . the list continues to grow and compliment life in Lake Jackson.

The city has a relatively short history. The area evolved from an agricultural economy to a home for people involved in industry. Then, the nature of the city grew to a community of active, intelligent, upper middle class families seeking a quality of life for themselves and their neighbors. The following pictures and captions will tell this story.

One

Pre-city Highlights

Lake Jackson began life as an oxbow lake of the Brazos River a millennium ago.

The river moved west about 1,000 years ago and left a two-mile-long lake that was named Lake Jackson in the 1850s. This was an attraction for Karankawa Indians in prehistoric time. Coastal inhabitants left the signs of their existence with arrow points, pottery shards, and shell middens.

Lake Jackson was part of the original 1822 land grant by Mexico to Stephen F. Austin along the Brazos River. The motivation of the Spanish was proactive to prevent the settlement of Texas by the French and displacement of the Indians in the territory.

The Lake Jackson area was part of the Groce and Austin land grants from Mexico. Active occupation near the lake by settlers did not begin until 1842. Abner Jackson came from North Carolina and Georgia with slaves and a desire to begin a plantation. This was in response to news of the much-improved cotton production relative to the overused soil in the southern United States. Over several years, he accumulated three plantations with a total of about 15,000 acres.

The Lake Jackson Plantation included approximately 3,000 irrigated acres with about 85 slaves. Cotton and sugarcane were grown. The slaves made tens of thousands of bricks from the local clay found adjacent to the lake. From these they constructed at least eight buildings, which have been uncovered in recent archeological work.

This plantation began to fail financially with Jackson's death in 1861. After the Civil War, the failure was completed after attempts to transition to paid freedmen, family feuding, and taxes. The family lost the plantation in 1870.

The Lake Jackson Sugar Company bought the land in 1900. Unfortunately, the Hurricane of 1900 passed over the plantation and destroyed all the buildings and the hopes of the young venture.

The plantation lay dormant until it became the site of the future city. The Dow Chemical Company purchased it in 1941.

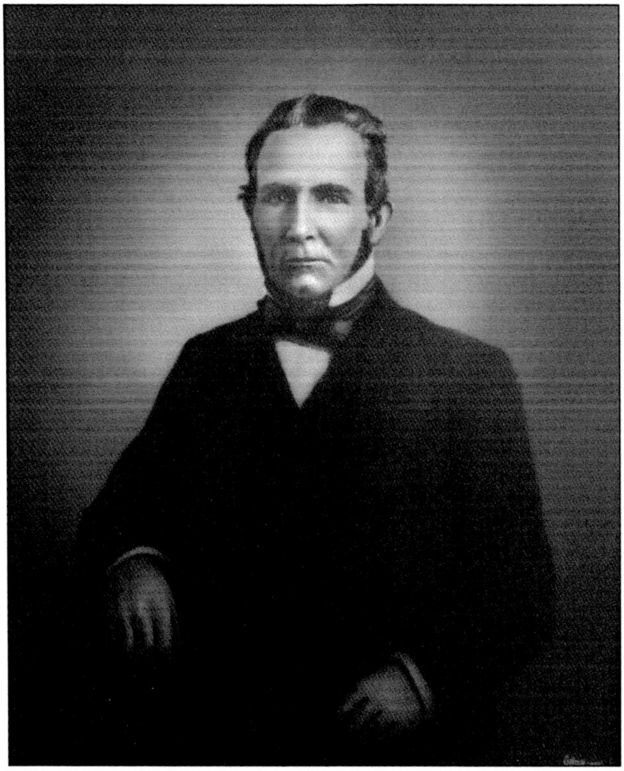

Abner Jackson was born in Virginia in 1809. He married a wealthy widow, Margaret Strobel, in South Carolina who had one son, Lewis. Jackson moved his slaves to Brazoria County in 1842. He purchased land for the Lake Jackson Plantation from 1842 to 1849, and acquired more land at Retrieve and Darrington Plantations, north of Lake Jackson.

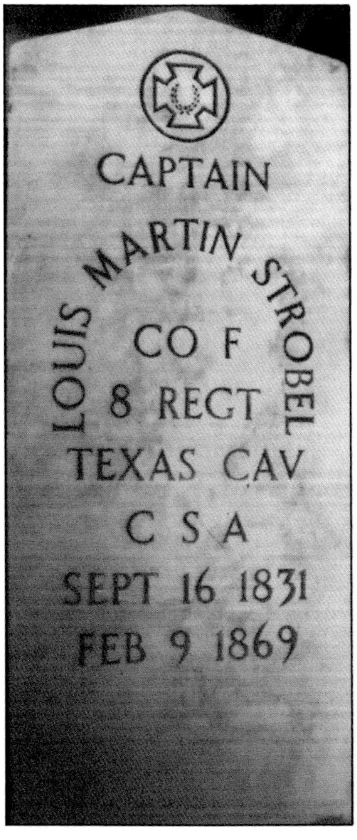

Louis Strobel was the stepson of Abner Jackson. He was the father of Abner Jackson Strobel who wrote a book about the old plantations and their owners of Brazoria County, Texas. Louis died in the Lake Jackson Plantation lake house. The stone indicated that he was buried with the Jacksons on the banks of Lake Jackson. No other grave markers are apparent and this stone was not installed until 1962.

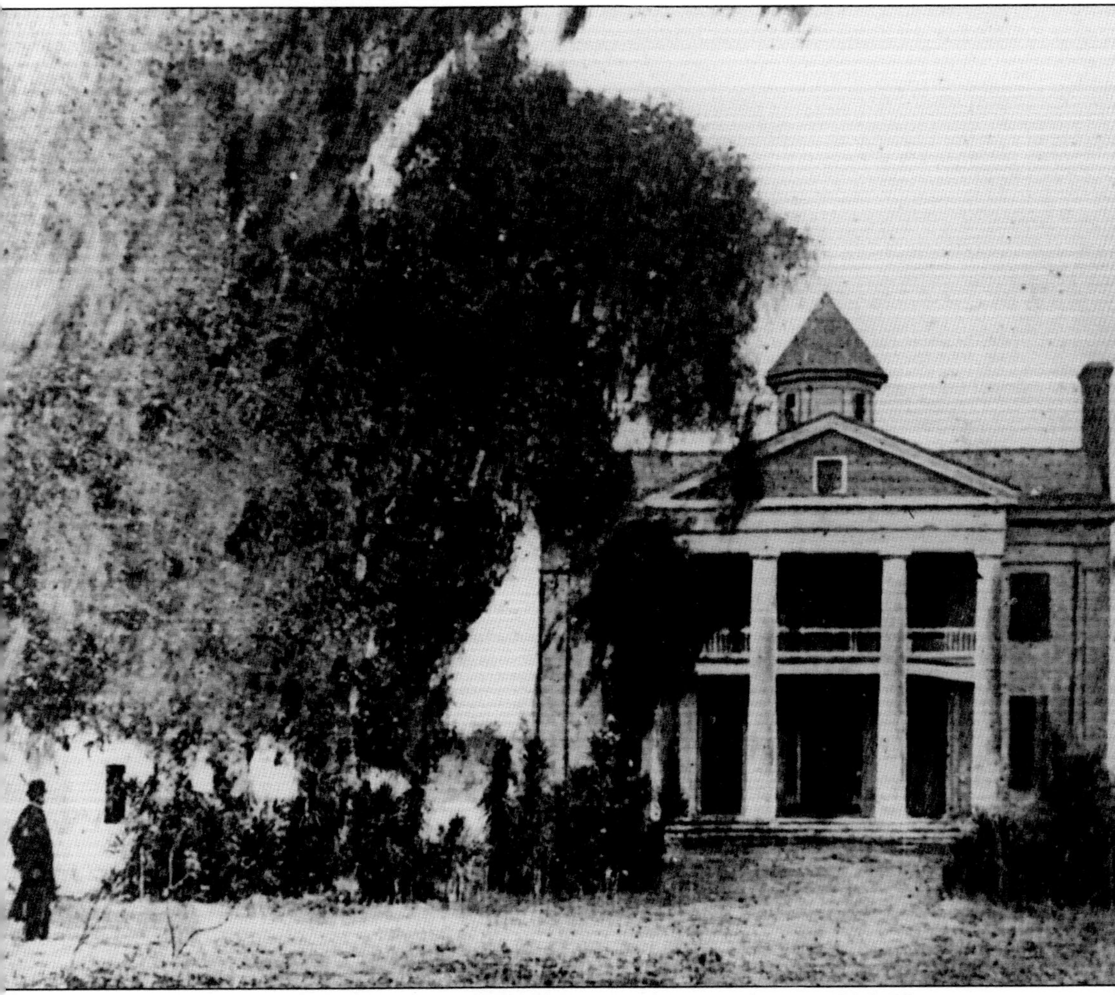

This picture is of the abandoned Lake Jackson Plantation house, taken in 1896. The man is unidentified. The house and land were purchased in 1900 by the Jackson Sugar Company. Architect Robert Glass and his family moved in to refurbish the house. They were present when the Hurricane of 1900, known for its damage to Galveston, came over the plantation and destroyed virtually all of the structures.

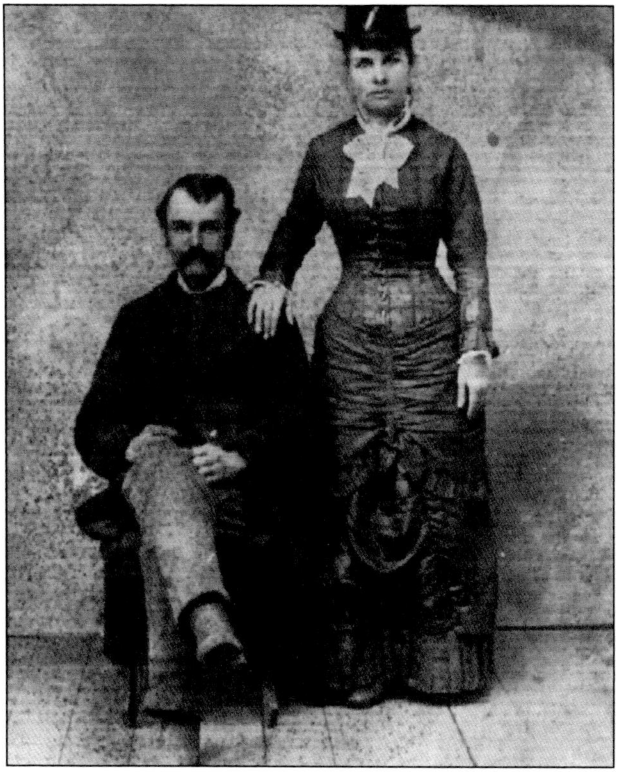

This is an early picture of Robert and Lillie Glass. They moved to Lake Jackson for health reasons. They still have heirs in Brazoria County. (Courtesy of the Brazoria County Historical Museum.)

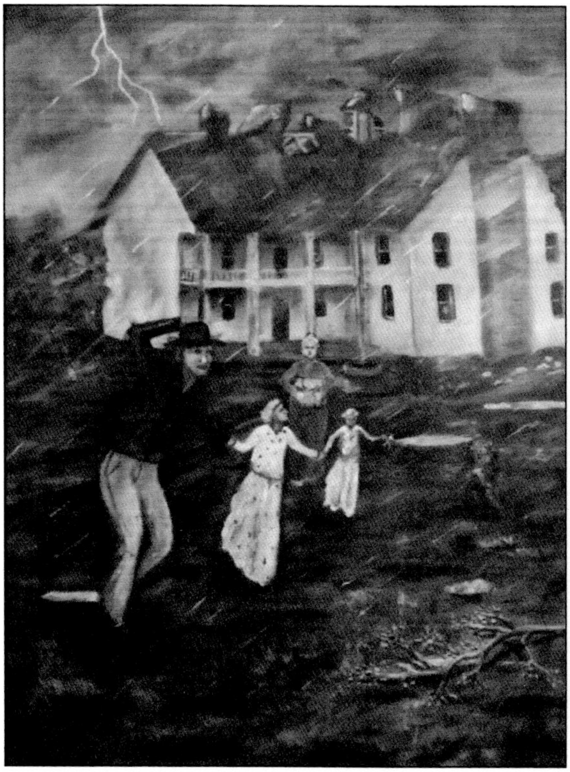

The eye of the storm of 1900 passed over the Lake Jackson Plantation. The Glass family realized the house would not withstand the storm, so they ran. The account of the evacuation was recounted in 1985 by the daughter. They found safety in a structure called the jail, which has not been found in the archeological process. This painting by the author is in the collection of the Stephen F. Austin Statue gift shop.

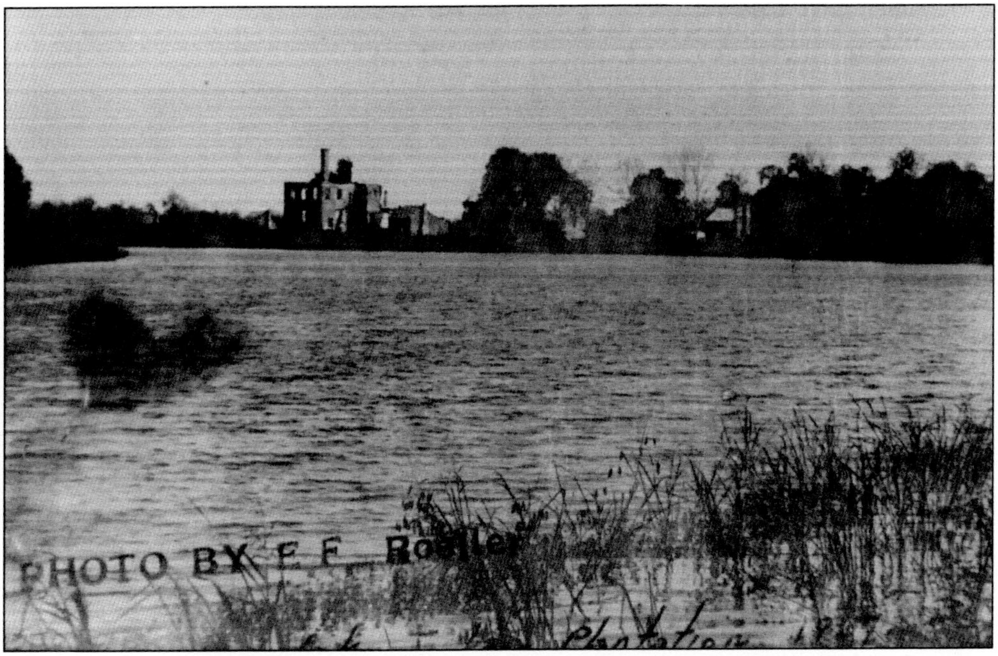

This is a picture of the Lake Jackson Plantation house and auxiliary houses in the vicinity taken in 1907, after the Hurricane of 1900. Archeologists studied the site from 1993 to 2002. Joan Few, archeologist instructor for the University of Houston at Clear Lake, wrote a book titled *Sugar, Planters, Slaves and Convicts*, providing an image of life during the plantation era.

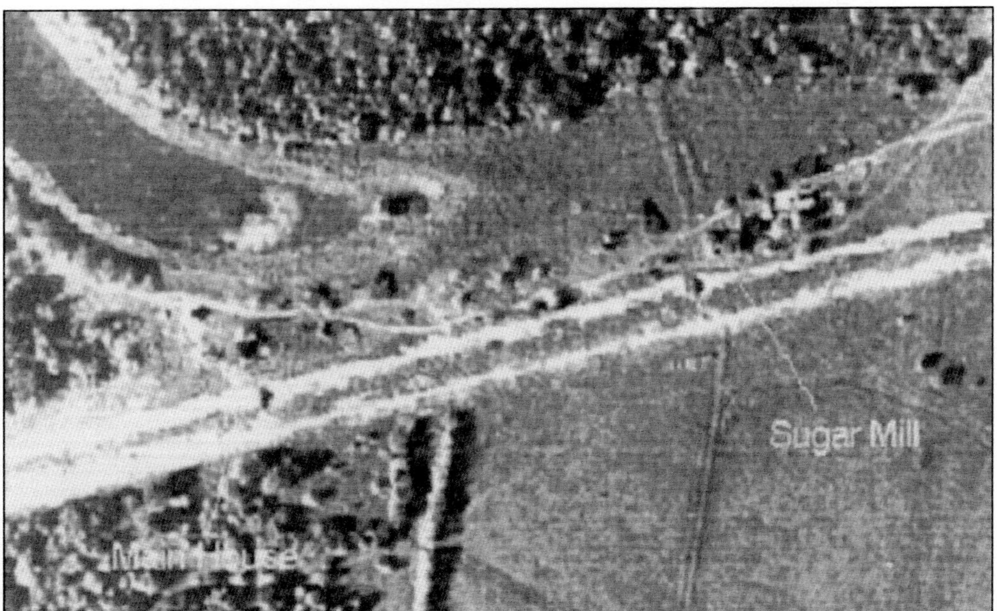

The Brazosport Archeological Society found this 1930 aerial picture of the Lake Jackson Plantation. The level of the lake was low relative to today. A road bed of some kind is seen going across the lake to where an overseer's house was located. The open fields can be seen; they grew sugarcane and cotton. A road at the edge of the trees led to the main house. The levee was built in 1929 in order to protect the new Freeport Harbor, which was the original mouth of the Brazos River.

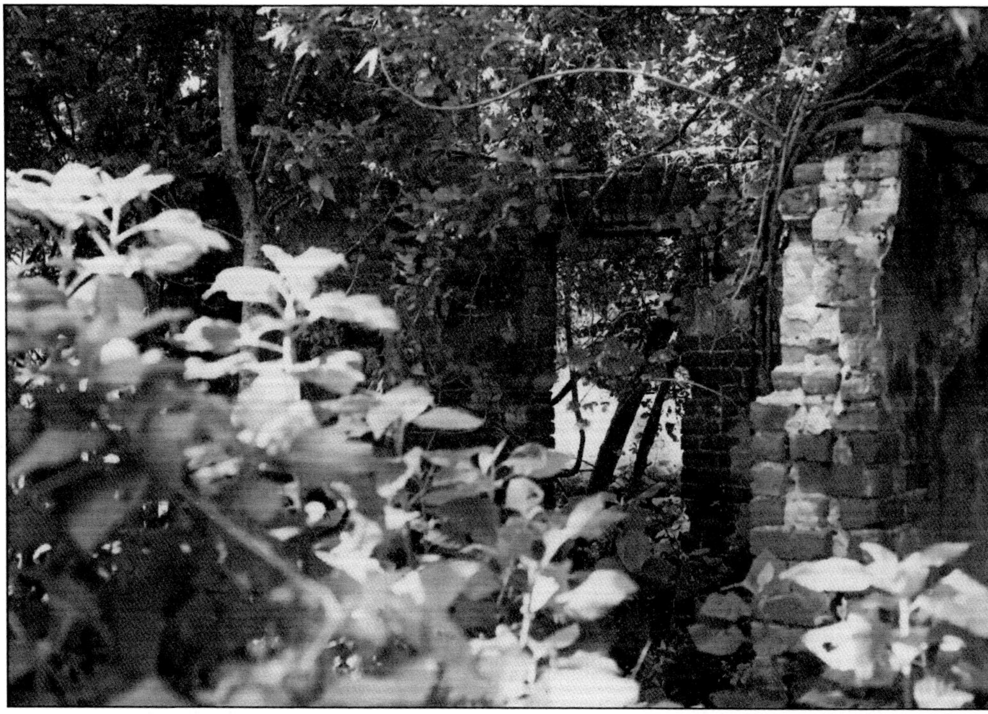

The construction of a Lake Jackson Plantation doorway shows the keystone brickwork over a metal beam. The walls were three bricks thick and the plaster on the interior wall on the right can be seen.

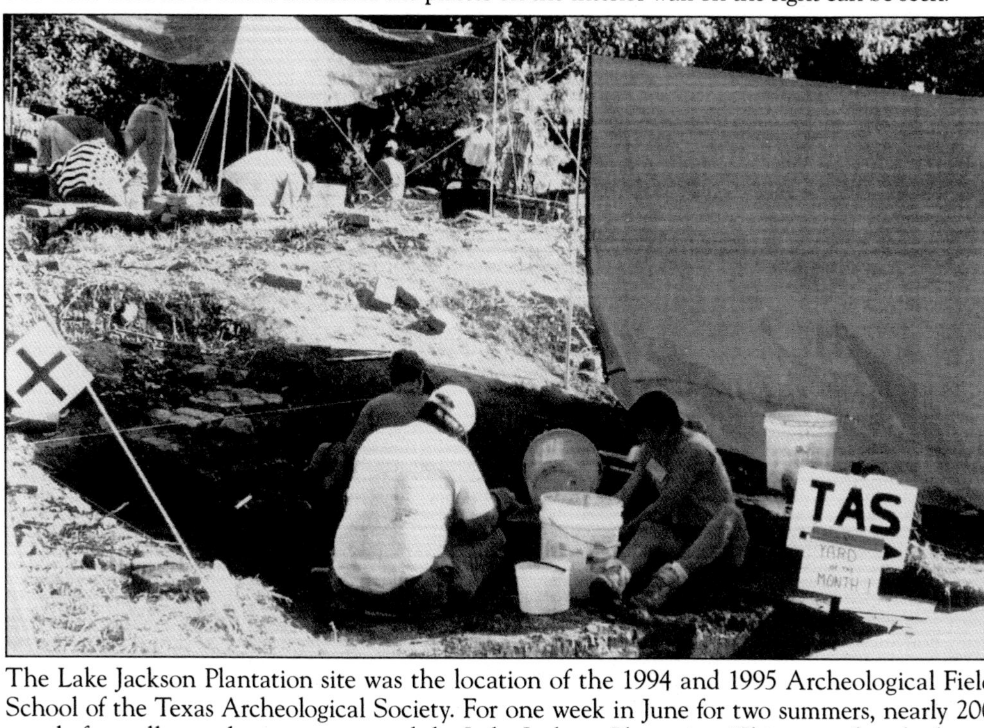

The Lake Jackson Plantation site was the location of the 1994 and 1995 Archeological Field School of the Texas Archeological Society. For one week in June for two summers, nearly 200 people from all over the state excavated the Lake Jackson Plantation. This area of study shown was the sugar mill.

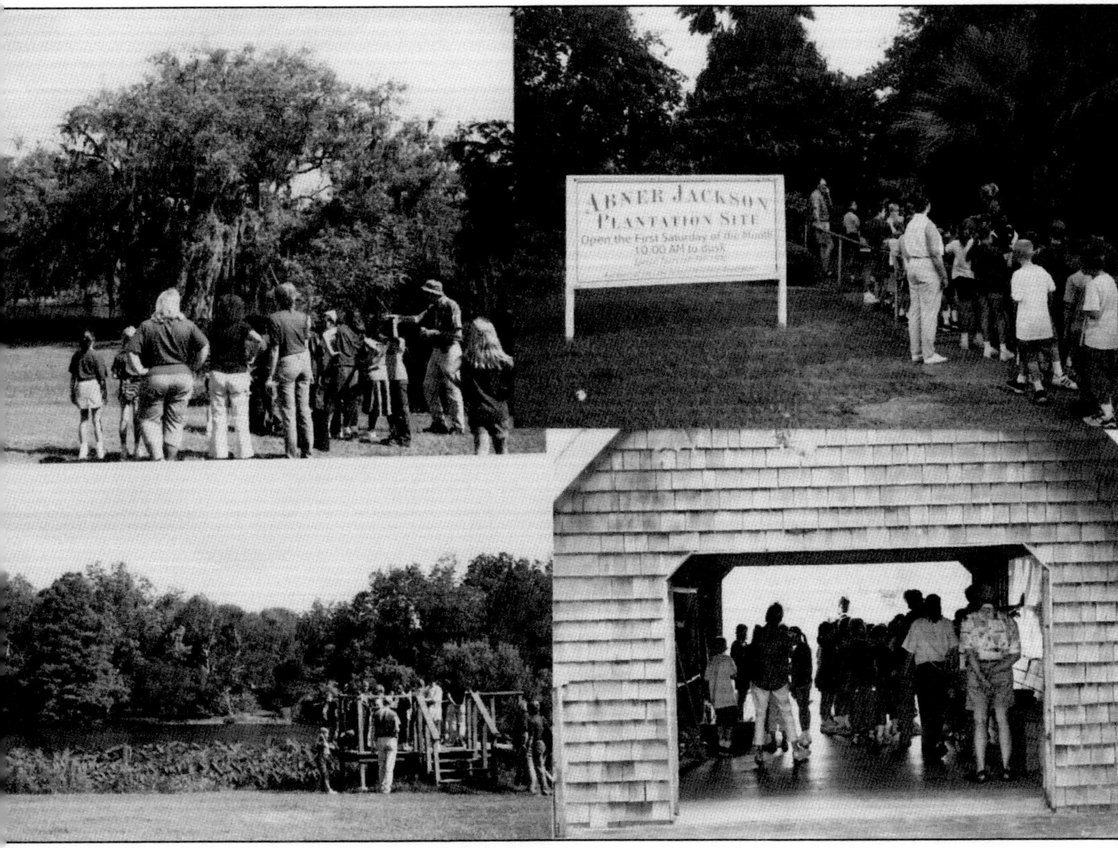

The Lake Jackson Plantation site has had several events inviting the community to tour the site. The upper left shows the Lake Jackson Oak—the source of the city logo—being visited by a group led by Harold Crone. At the upper right, the author gathers a group of youth entering the pathway to the site. Shown at the bottom left is Harold Crone telling a group about the road under the surface of the lake, and at the bottom right is a group being orientated before the tour in the covered bridge. The covered bridge had to be demolished in the summer of 2008 due to failure of the 1940s creosote supports.

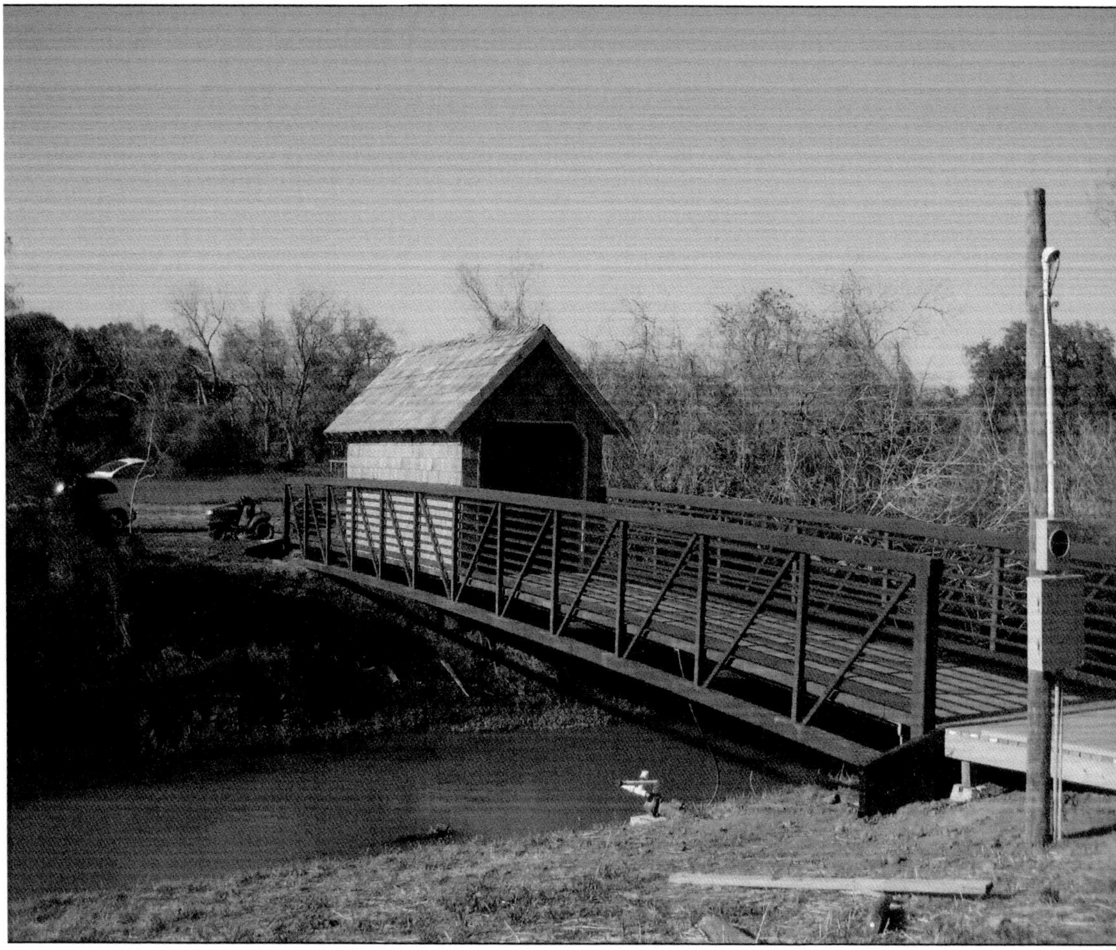

The Lake Jackson Archeological Site was reopened in 2011 thanks to a major contribution by the Brazosport Rotary and tireless volunteer work. The 70-foot truss bridge was constructed in Missoula, Montana, and shipped in one piece. The gatehouse structure was built to provide security for the site and shelter for volunteer docents.

Two

A City! Why Here? Why Now?

Development of southern Brazoria County was based on agriculture, proximity to the Gulf, and industry. The agricultural community primarily grew rice after a fungus decimated the sugarcane crops in the 1920s. There was also fig farming and even the collection of Spanish moss, which was used to stuff upholstery and mattresses.

The Gulf offered shrimp, shipping, and tourism. The mouth of the Brazos had been moved to provide a safer harbor in 1929. Tarpon fishing in the new river attracted many people, including Pres. Franklin Roosevelt.

Sulfur mining was well established and was a key to the Freeport economy.

Strange mounds in the area were known to be the result of salt deposits several thousand feet below the surface. This became an asset that attracted Dow Chemical Company in its quest for a Gulf Coast industrial site in the late 1930s.

Dow Chemical Company had a process for removing magnesium from brine. It sought a location to extract the metal from seawater. It also deemed the salt deposits as a feedstock for chlorine and caustic production.

Dow Chemical Company bought property on the peninsula opposite Freeport, downstream of the harbor for its first construction. The company ultimately added more land farther from the coast due to the risk of storms.

Construction was so intense that housing was in short supply. Beds in Freeport were rented to different people from day to night. The government was the actual financier of the new chemical complex. It brought in trailer houses in various locations, and it constructed a complex of prefabricated houses and buildings in 1942 called Camp Chemical as temporary housing for 12,000 people in 16-by-16-foot structures.

Seeking more permanent housing, Dow Chemical Company sought a location. Velasco, a historical town on the harbor, had limited space. However, land ownership issues and resistant residents forced the selection of a site in the old Lake Jackson Plantation holdings in 1941.

Thus, Lake Jackson was born in 1943 with no assurances of survival after the war.

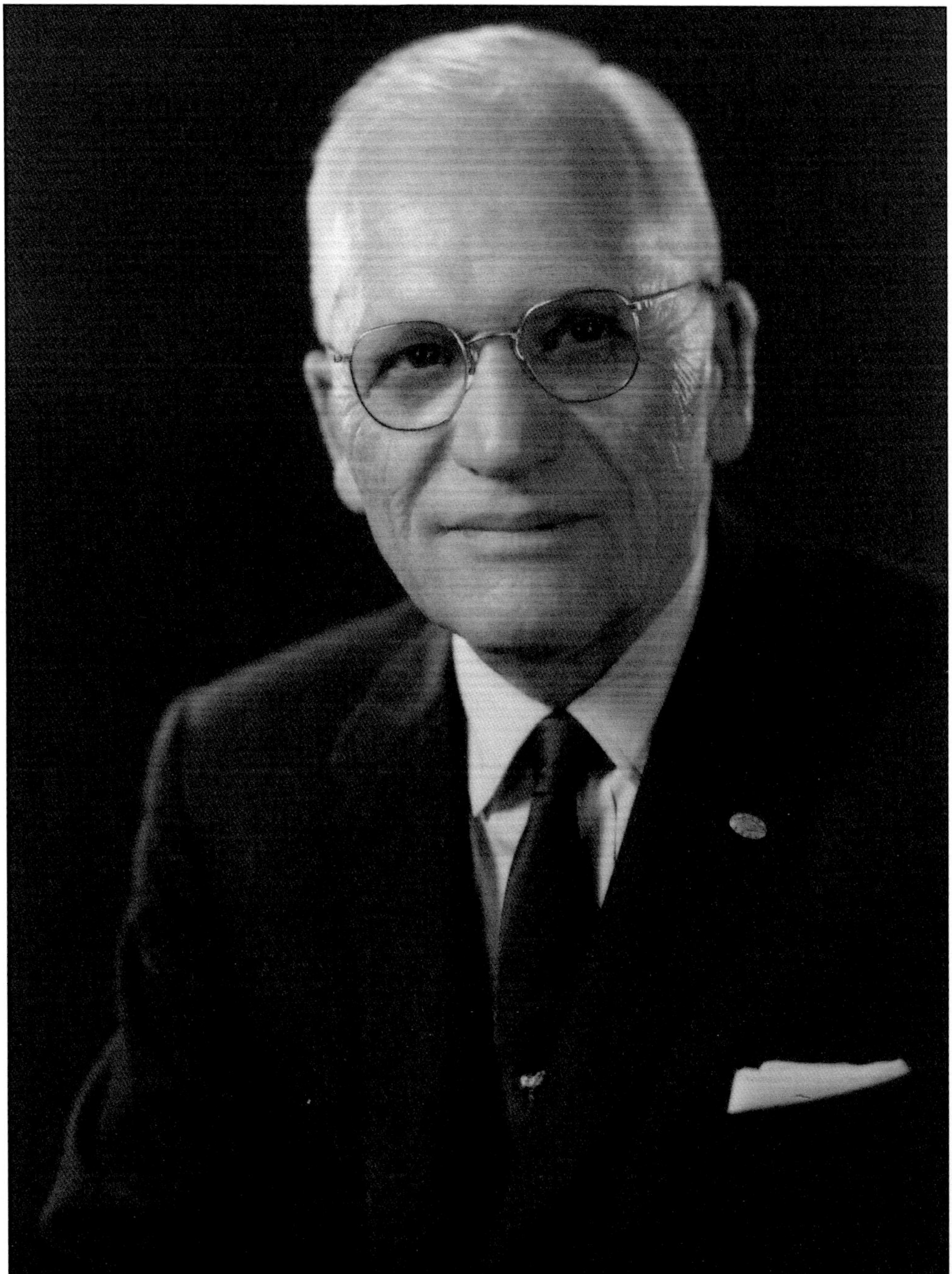

In the late 1930s, Dr. A.P. "Dutch" Beutel, shown above, and Willard Dow, president of Dow Chemical Company, were seeking a manufacturing location on the Gulf Coast. A major driving force was magnesium from the seawater. Corpus Christi and Freeport were the final two sites considered with Freeport selected due to the proximity of salt domes as a source of salt for chlorine production, the Gulf, a supply of workers in Houston, and a harbor for shipping. The company bought 800 acres close to the harbor and $18 million was authorized for the first production units. The first load of construction equipment arrived in Freeport by train on March 22, 1940.

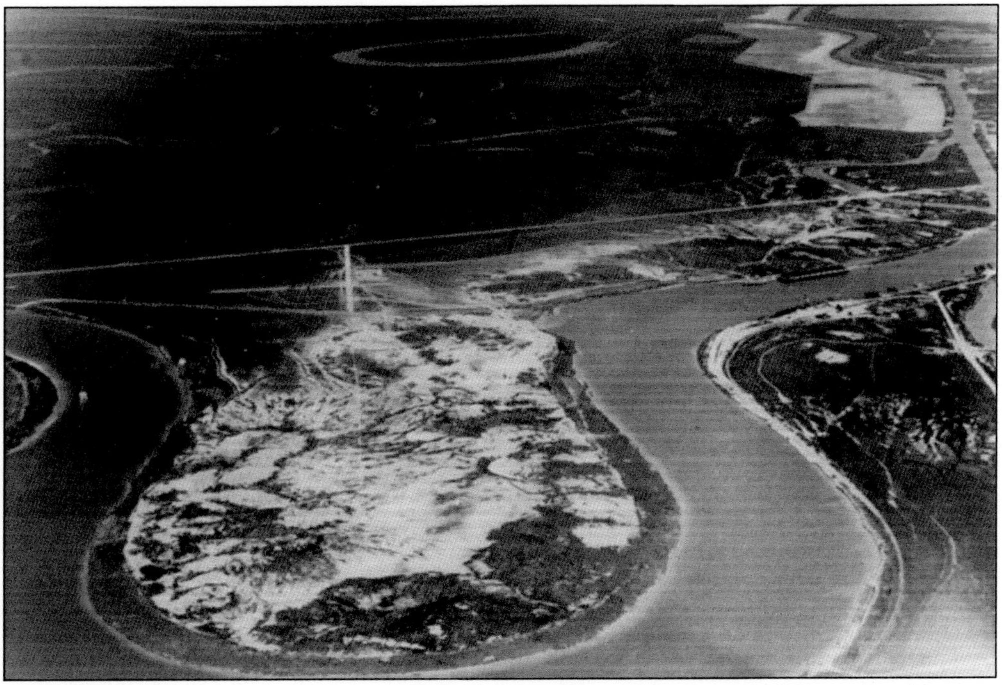

This was the site for the future Dow Plant A before 1940. In the distance, Oyster Creek's entry to the intracoastal canal can be seen with levees, ponding areas, and an alternate boat channel leaving the intracoastal canal.

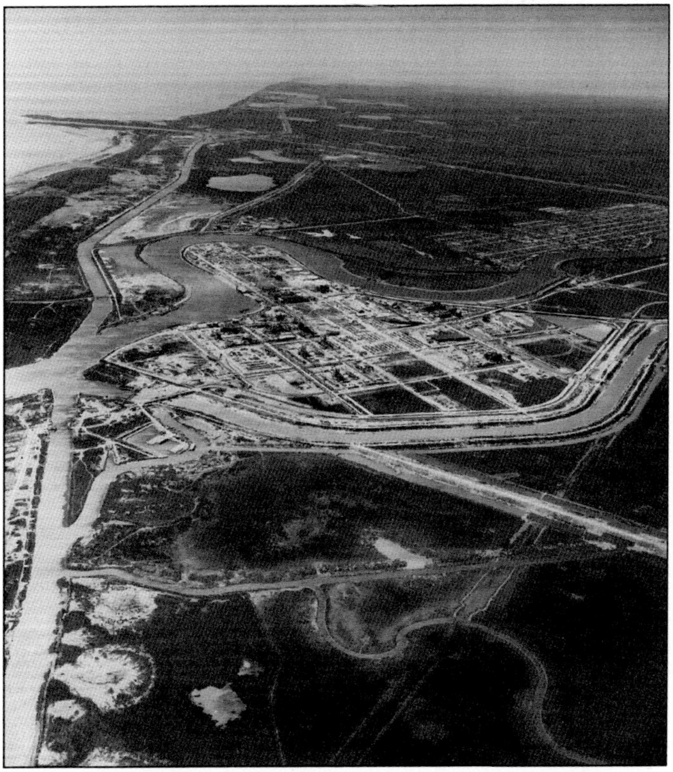

Dow's Plant A is shown with the Freeport Harbor passing the peninsula. These are the original 4 Dorr Ponds (a brand name) on the point to remove magnesium from the seawater. Hydrocarbon units are on the left, power production is in the center, and Ethyl-Dow—a joint venture, which extracted bromine from seawater—is on the right. A bridge across the intracoastal canal on the other side of the harbor has long been removed, as is the apparent waterway in the foreground coming from the intracoastal. The new mouth of the Brazos River, dug in 1929, extends into the Gulf in the upper left.

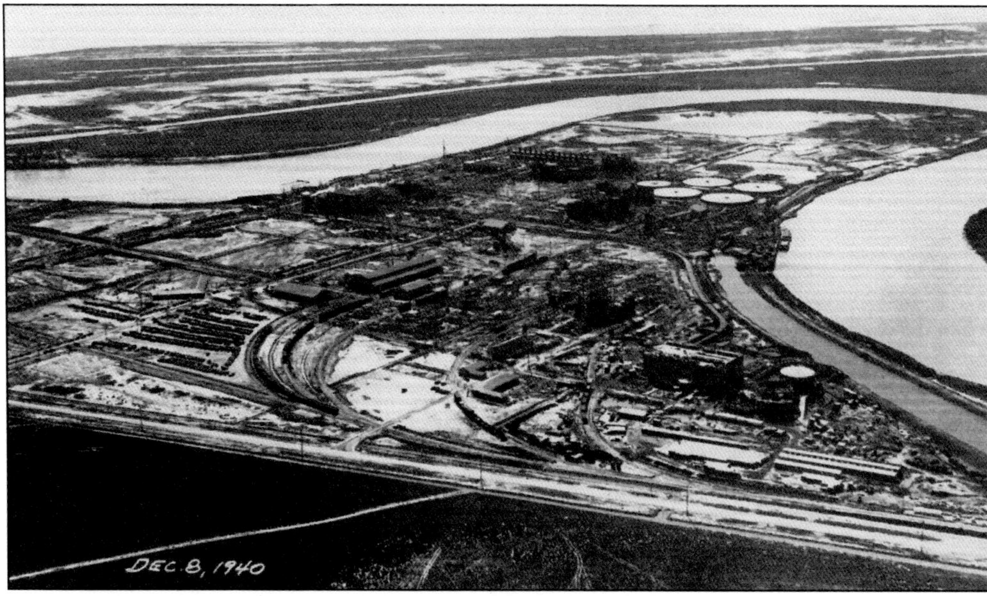

This aerial photograph taken on December 8, 1940, of Dow Plant A shows how the unit began to evolve. The V-shaped building on the left in the center was the administration building, which housed A.P. Beutel's office. The unit left of center with steam plumes was a gas-fired power plant. The far unit, including the round ponds, was the magnesium plant. The waterway paralleling the ship channel on the right was the spent water from the magnesium unit flowing to the Brazos River. Railroad entry had been established. The large building in the center was the machine shop. The plant to the right foreground was Ethyl-Dow. This entire site was across the river from Freeport where most of the workers lived.

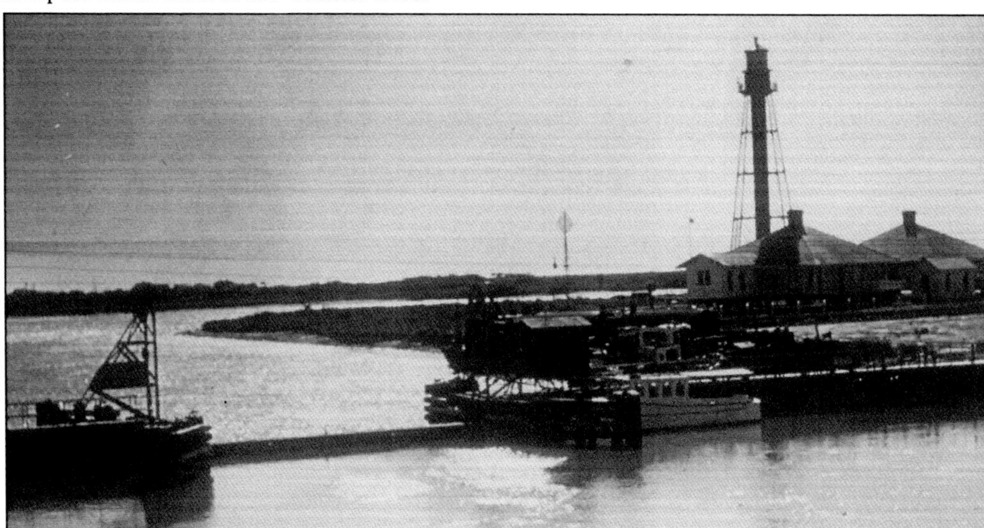

The Skimmer Gates in the foreground are the access to the barge canal to Dow Plant B. The Coast Guard station and lighthouse are shown on the ship channel. This was most likely in the late 1940s. The lighthouse was demolished in 1967. The structures were moved across the intracoastal canal on the east bank of the ship channel where they continued to serve along with a boathouse, which was added. The original Coast Guard buildings were reduced to one, which burned in the 1990s leaving only the boathouse. The boathouse was moved and became the Surfside City Hall.

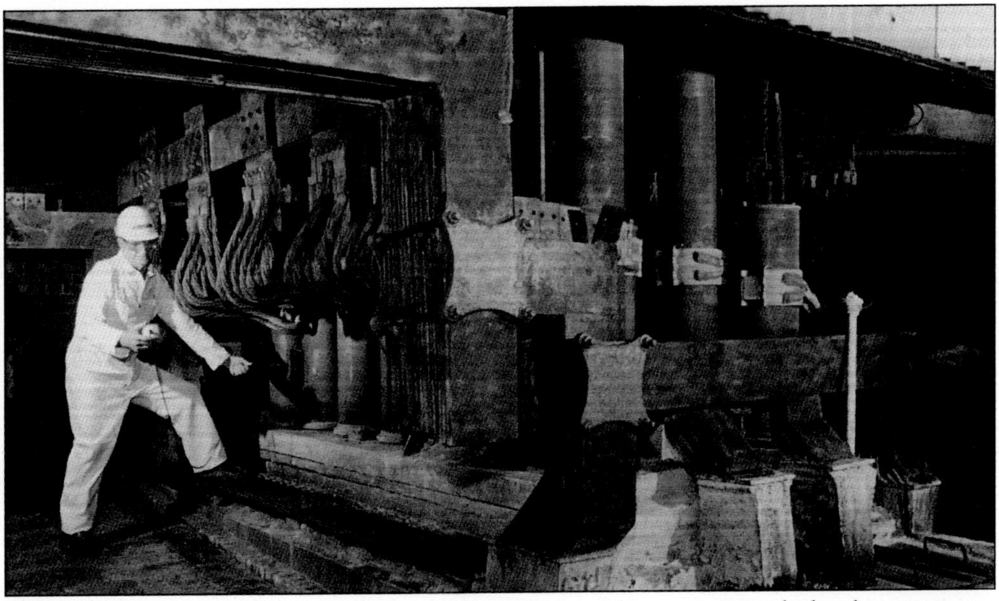

This is an early magnesium production cell. It was an electrolytic process with the electric current passing down the carbon anodes. The operator is measuring the current flow in the individual anode. The external area around the cells was between 130 and 150 degrees, making it a very uncomfortable work site. Molten metal was recovered from the front right of the cell. Dow Chemical Company discontinued production in the 1990s due to Russia joining the free market economy with a large inventory of magnesium.

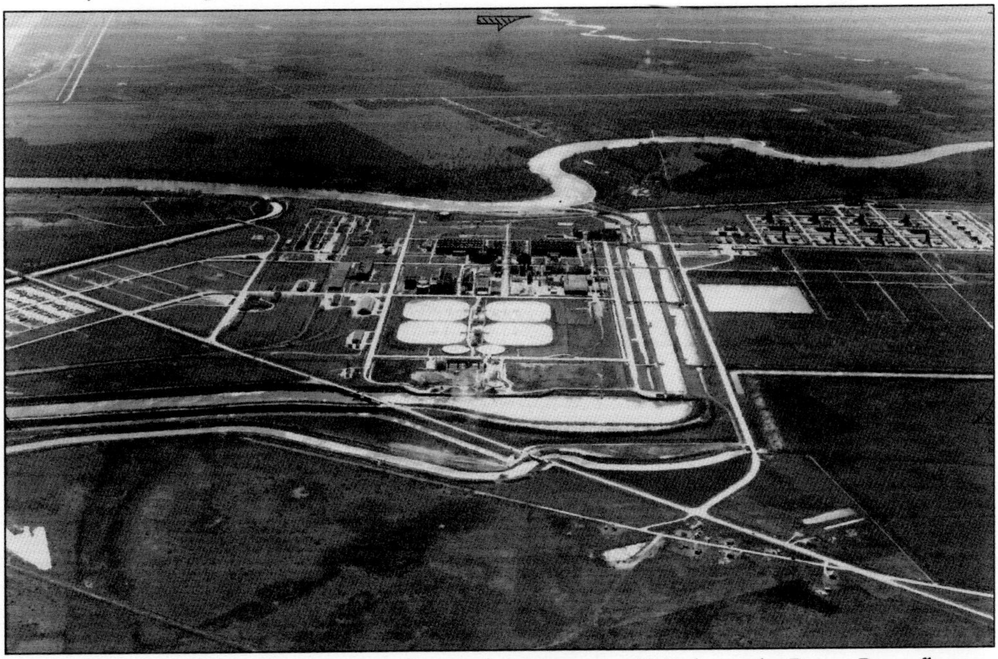

This aerial view of Plant B of the Dow Chemical Company in 1949 shows the Brazos River flowing from right to left. The chemical unit in the center is the magnesium plant. The units to the right are the styrene process. These units were constructed to provide some protection if bombed. They were physically well separated and bulk flammable products were bunkered underground.

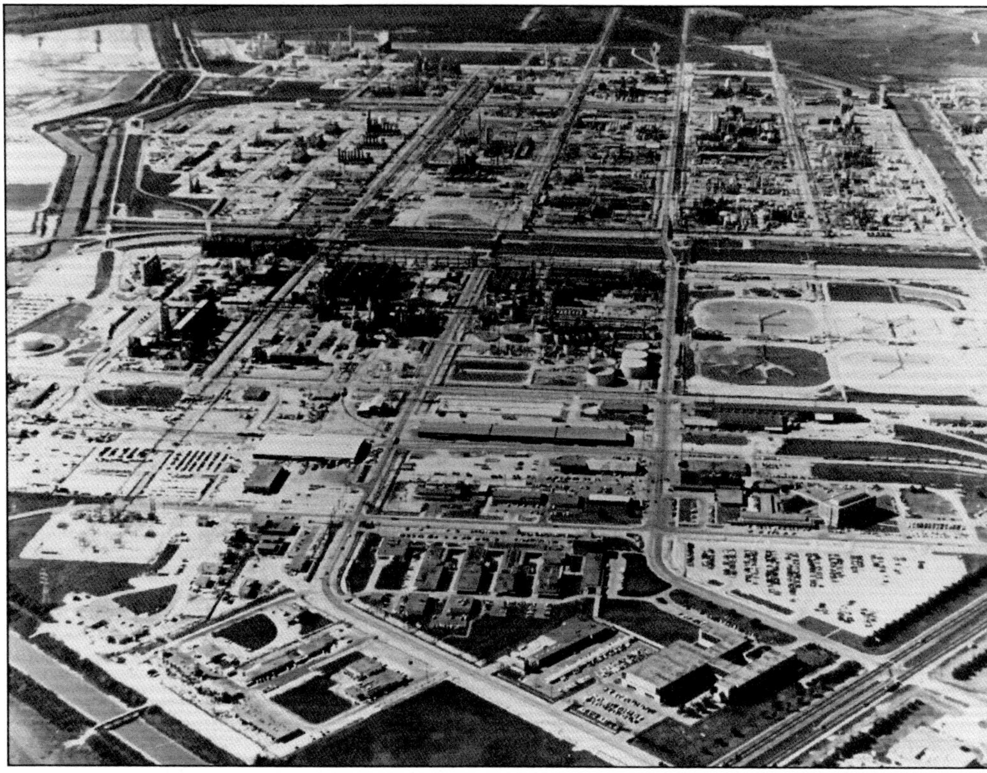

This aerial view of Dow's Plant B looks northwest. The administrative offices for A.P. Beutel are located in the building in the foreground. Across the parking lots from this building to the right is the Brazosport Community Hospital, an expansion of the old Dow Hospital.

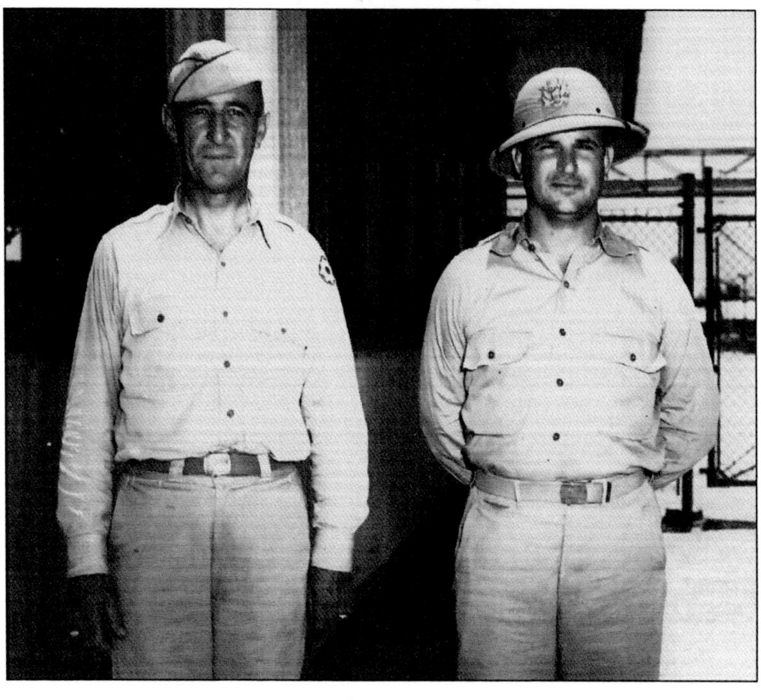

Military personnel were assigned to the chemical plant during World War II. There was great concern about coastal assaults from Germany.

Mildred is shown in her security uniform at the Styrene Plant Clock room in October 1943.

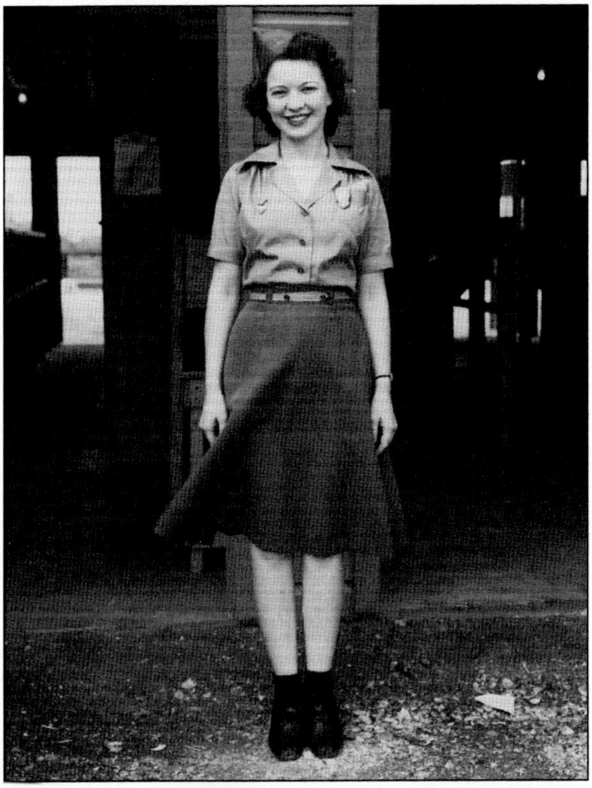

A Dow Chemical Company management meeting is being held around A.P. Beutel's famous desk that provided space for all the participants. Around the table clockwise starting on the left are Beutel, Nelson Griswold, O. Beutel, C.M. Shipley, Earl Barnes, ? Raebke, W. Raeshe, and L. Evans.

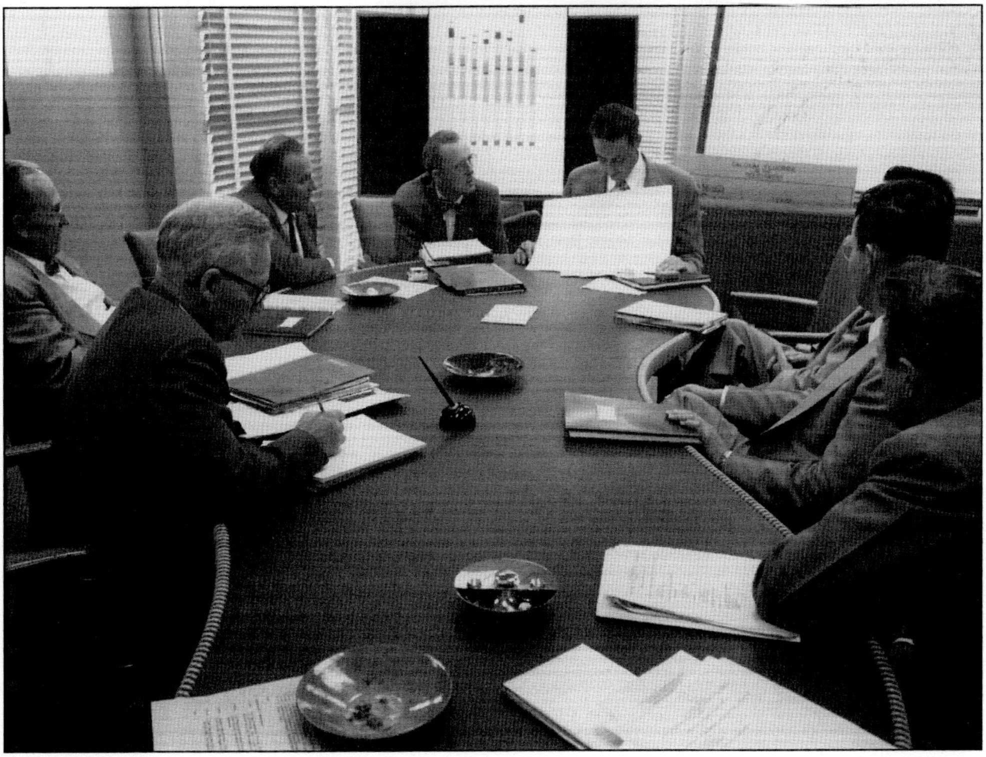

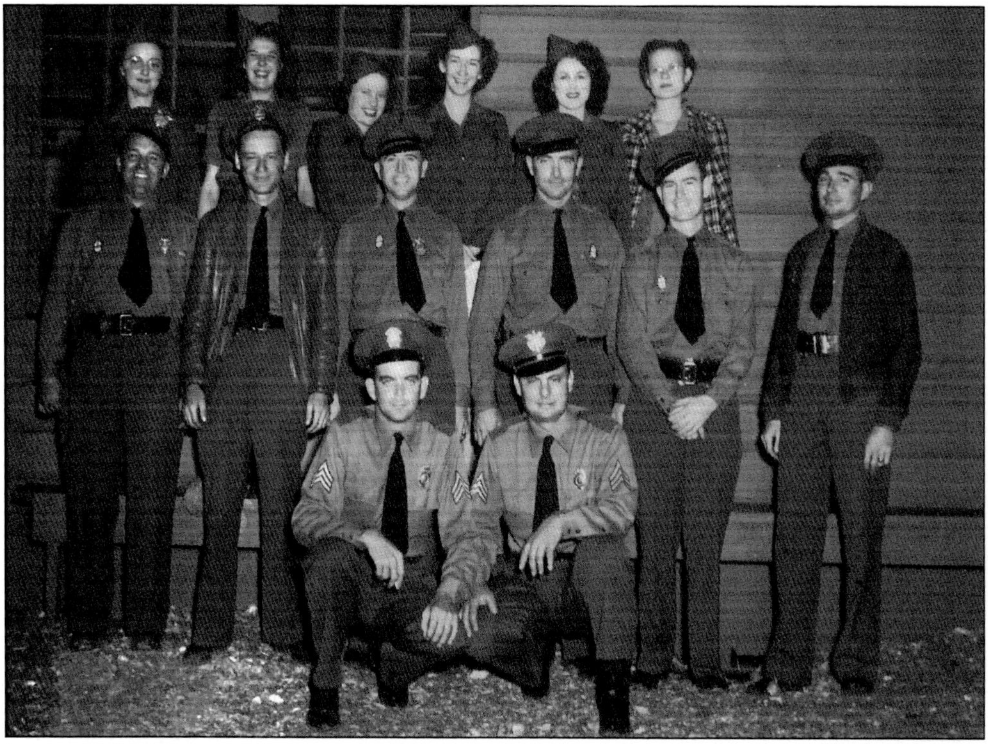

In June 1943, these were the plant security personnel. They are, from left to right, (first row) Hulen Fults, and ? Caldwell; (second row) ? White, ? Betterfras, Pete Fults, Johnny Scearii, ? Hess, and an unidentified supervisor; (third row) Elsie Emunans, Nadine James, Thelma Balentine, Beth Muelinud, Gloria Schnity, and Lousa Morgan.

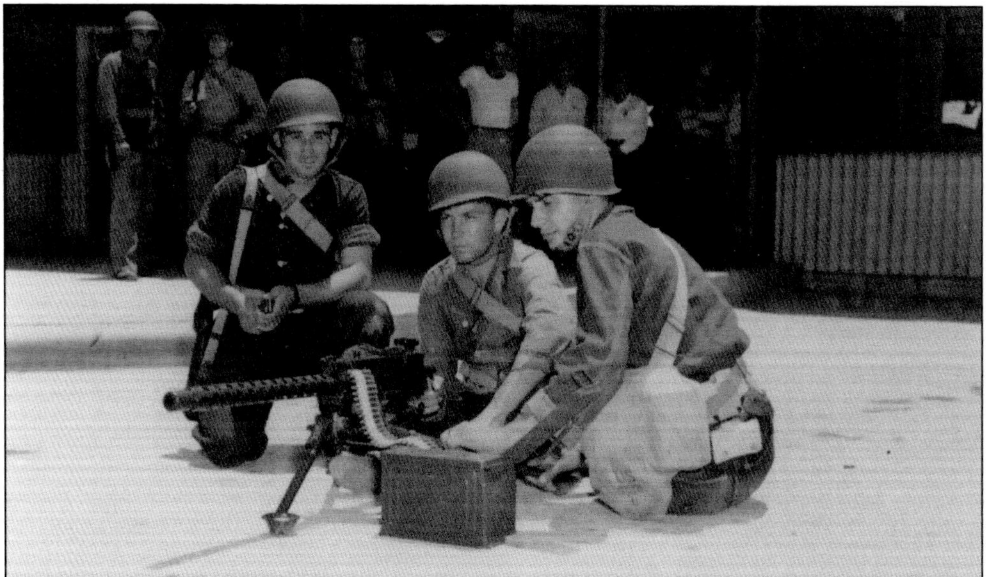

This Army group was assigned to the Styrene Plant Clock room in 1943. There was a fear of invasion and at least one German submarine was reported in the Gulf. Pictured here are, from left to right, Cpl. Joseph DelDonna, Pfc. Olen Goodnight, and Pfc. Daniel S. Bunze.

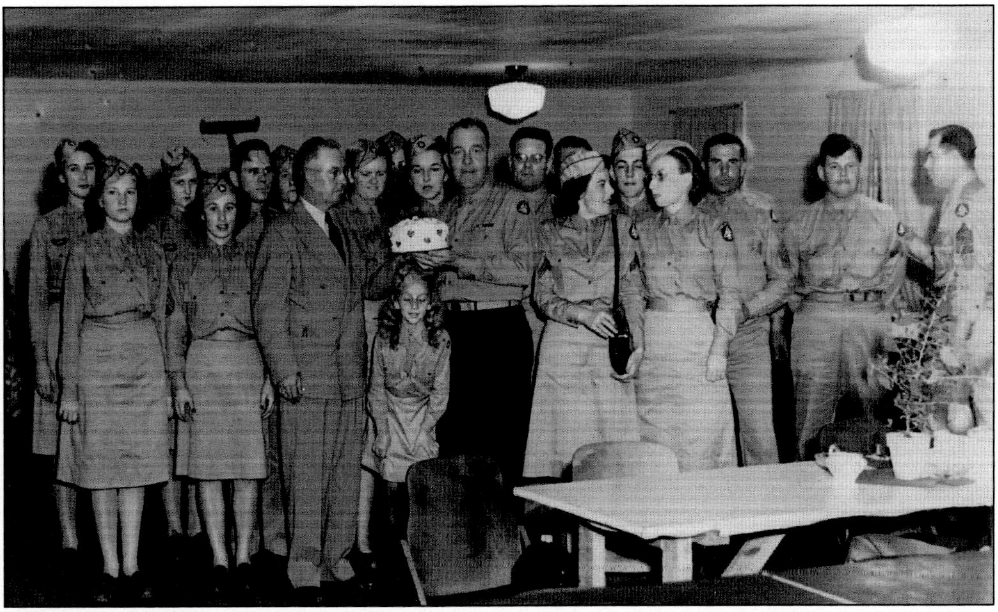

This group picture of the Civilian Aviation Administration reflects the war effort in coastal Texas.

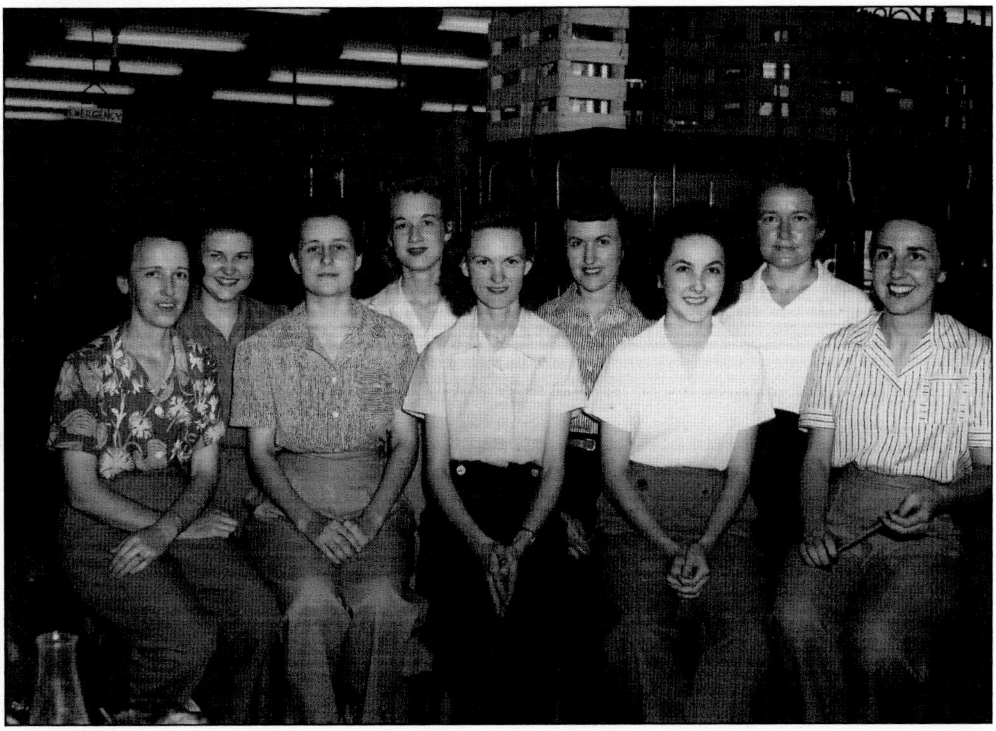

Pictured here are the first ladies employed at the central lab for the government's chemical plant before it became part of the Dow Chemical Company. They are, from left to right, Reba Roberson, Hazel Sledge, Ruth Hall, Margaret Owen Krenzke, and Cornelius Wetzel Marshall; (second row) Jo Gibson Shepard, Malveon Davis (secretary), Perk Gibson, and ? McCormick. The central lab provided chemical analyses to guide plant operations and to confirm product quality.

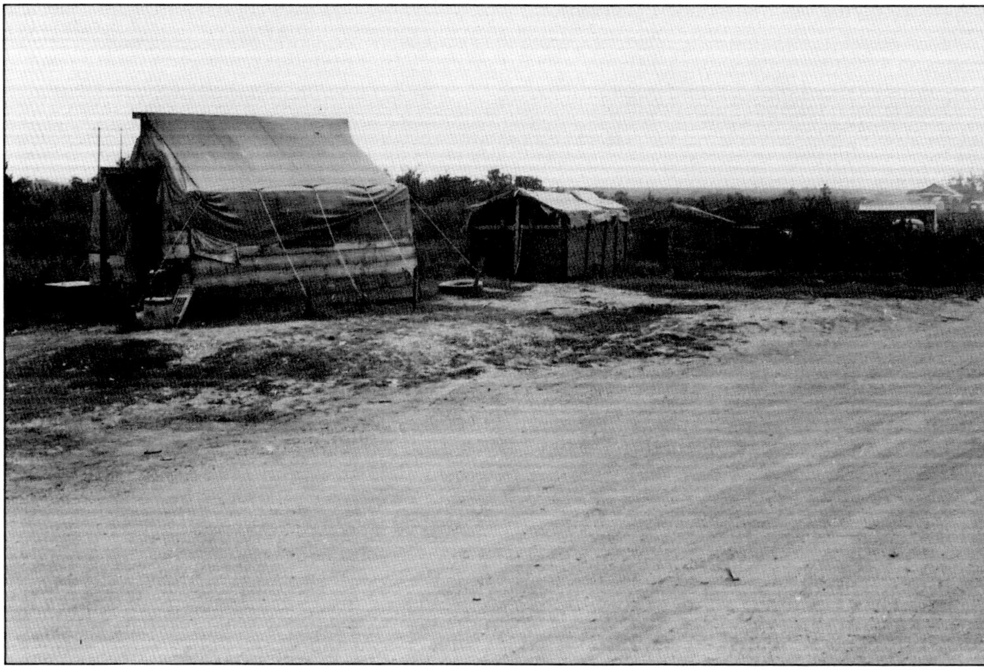

Housing was desperate for the thousands of workers needed to construct the chemical plants in 1940. The workers came from far away due to the country still recovering from the Depression.

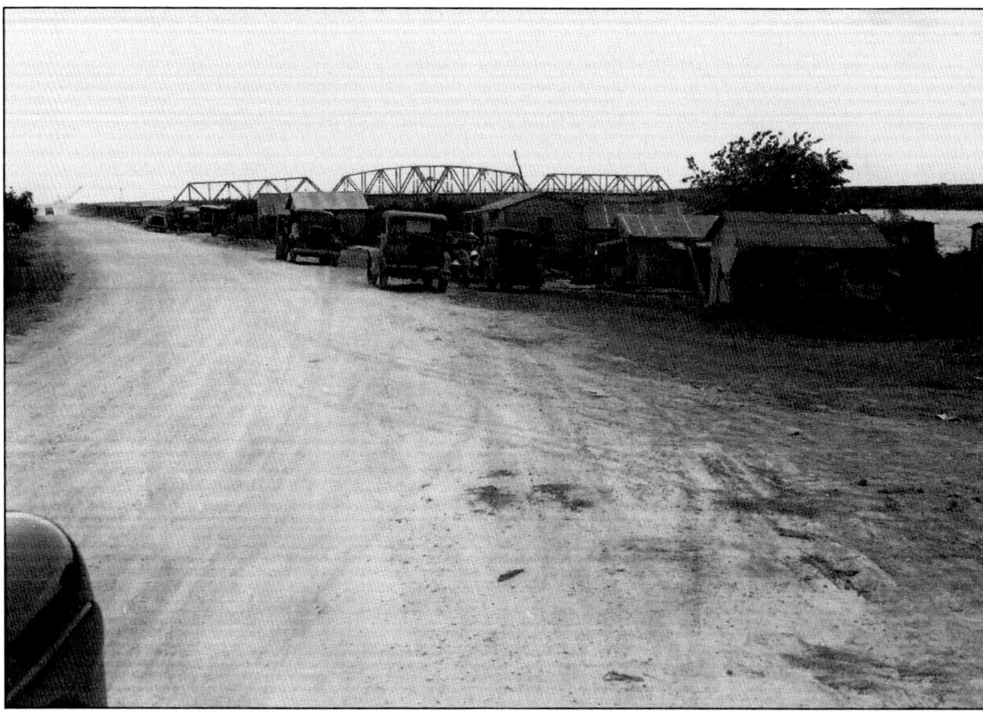

This construction housing had the bridge of Highway 36 in the background. Conditions were tough with mosquitoes, hot summers, and cold, windy winters.

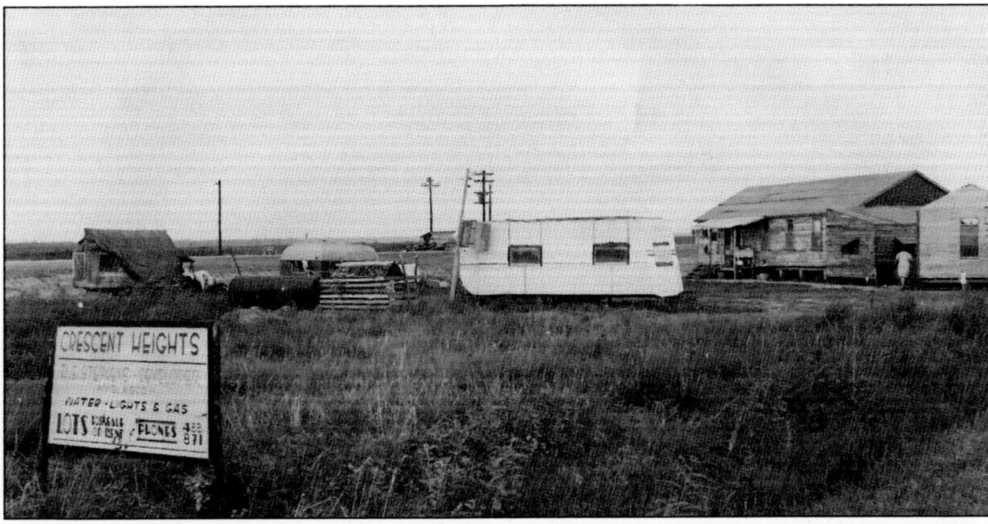

Crescent Heights provided all the conveniences and there are several clients. The camper on the left is homemade and sits on a truck.

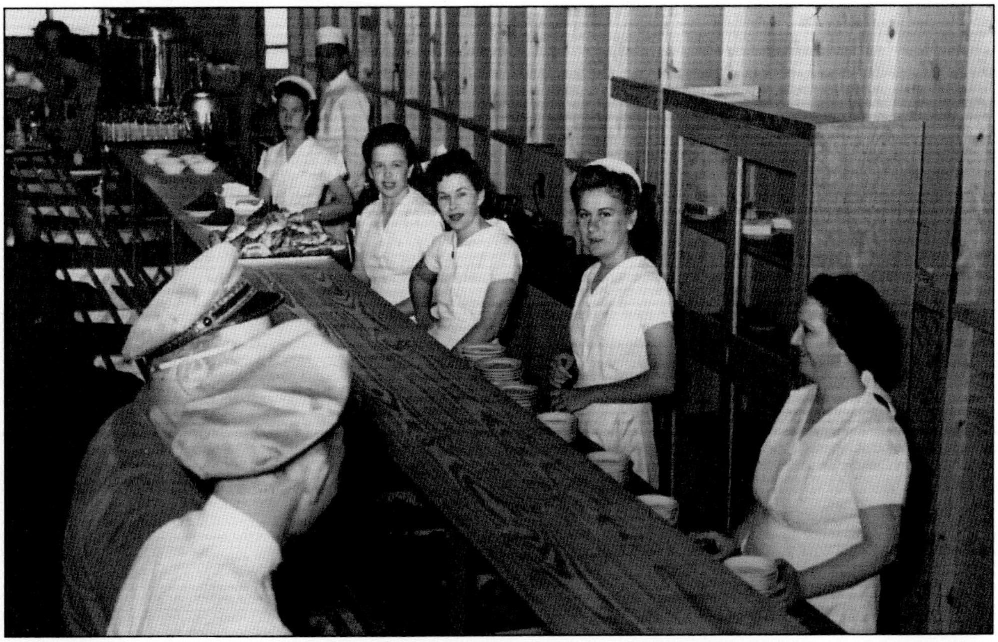
Before Lake Jackson could be planned and constructed, Dow Chemical Company executive A.P. Beutel organized the construction of Camp Chemical, a temporary housing area. At its pinnacle, Camp Chemical was the largest city in Brazoria County and home to more than 12,000 people. With help from the US government, which needed Dow Chemical Company materials for the war effort, construction of the housing began on February 20, 1942. It was completed in just 31 days. Designed by Alden B. Dow, Camp Chemical consisted of more than 2,000 one-room cottages for married workers and 46 barracks to house 120 men each. It also contained a cafeteria that could seat 1,000 people, a school, a large store, an entertainment hall, a ballpark, a firehouse, and a police station. Roads, sidewalks, running water, sewer lines, and electricity kept it going. Soon after World War II ended, Camp Chemical was torn down to make room for more plants at Plant B. This is a picture of the cafeteria serving line.

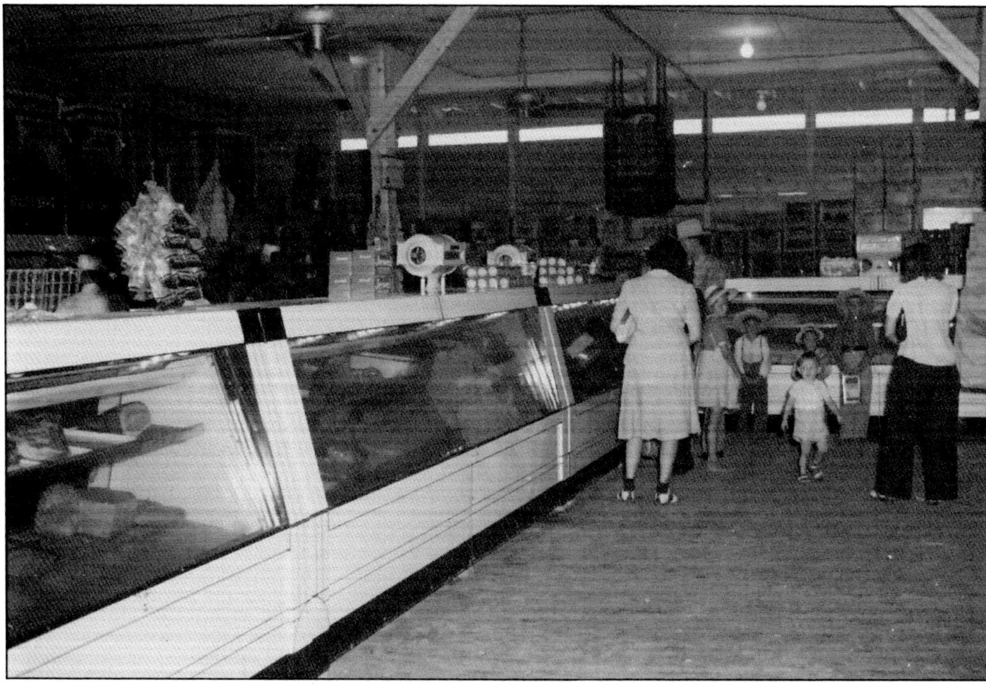

The commissary of Camp Chemical in 1942 provided groceries for employees. Everything was dispensed over the counter due to wartime rationing, such as lard and eggs, which can be seen on the counter. There were no shopping baskets, which are now typical.

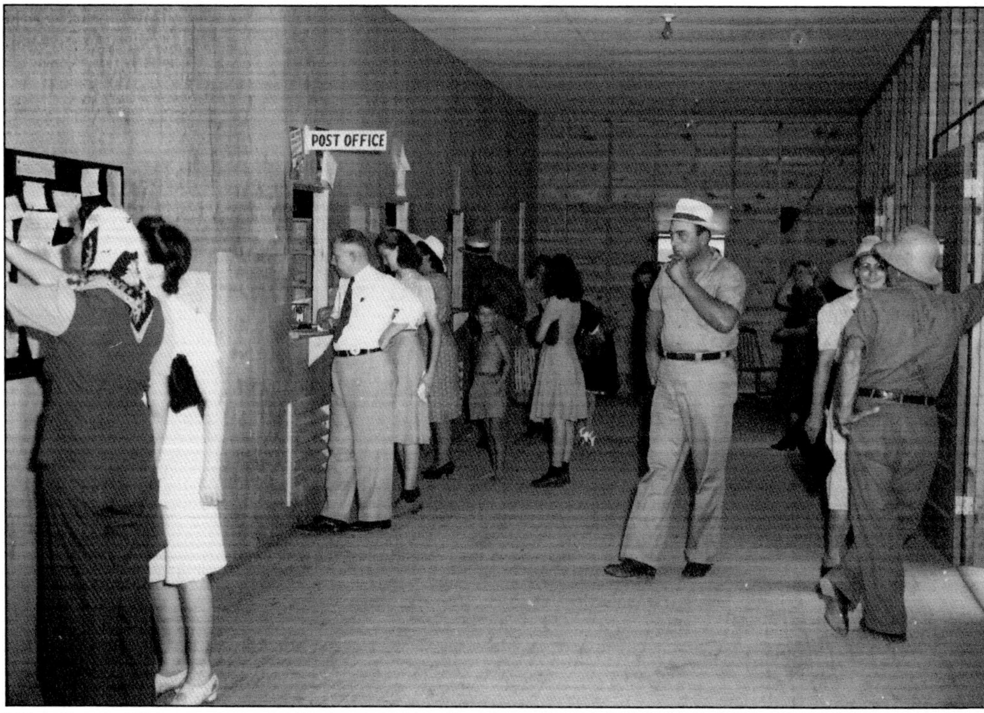

The Camp Chemical post office was busy, showing a variety of clothing. It was also austere with plywood walls and uninsulated outside walls. The bulletin board seems to be a popular attraction.

Three

How Do You Build a Town?

Herbert Henry Dow Sr., the founder of the Dow Chemical Company of Midland, Michigan, had two sons, Willard and Alden. Willard was an engineer who took over leadership of the company after Herbert's death during the Depression. Alden was an architect who followed the Frank Lloyd Wright model and interned with him in the summer of 1933. Alden was asked to design a planned community to house 5,000 people who worked at the Dow Chemical Company site in Freeport.

Alden and A.P. Beutel, manager of the Dow site in Freeport, chose a location in the heavily forested area adjacent to the dormant Lake Jackson Plantation fields. The initial layout of the city was drawn on a 1941 aerial map that was wall sized.

The layout included curving streets to add a special nature to the community and offer surprises around every bend. Alden designed duplexes adjacent to the designated downtown area and residential homes of five designs. He named the streets to and from downtown This Way, That Way, Circle Way, Parking Way, Winding Way, and Center Way.

Streets were initially prepared with lime sourced from oyster shells, but soon the streets were constructed of concrete. This provided aesthetic value, plus it lowered the cost of street maintenance through the years.

Dow Chemical Company was a strong, positive force in Lake Jackson. Early city officials worked for the company. Several key community members moved from working for Dow or the government to enter private businesses such as insurance agencies, banks, physicians' offices, concrete companies, and more.

The community was established in 1943, incorporated in April 1944, and received a post office in 1945. The first school opened in 1943 and was initially part of the Clute school district, which offered classes through the eighth grade. High school students attended Freeport High School. In 1944, area school districts voted to consolidate and form the Brazosport Independent School District.

It was controversial at the time, but Dow Chemical Company selected an African American family to begin integration of the city and its operations in 1963. The company hired a young chemist and family head and assisted him in taking up residency in Lake Jackson. This is another indication of the company guiding the development of the city.

Dow Chemical Company was a supporter and facilitator for the local hospital. The government expanded the unit in Freeport in 1947. Dow purchased the facility and gifted it to the community in 1961. A new building was constructed in 1966 that was adjacent to the Texas division headquarters.

The company donated land at the previous airport location and purchased the old hospital in 1983. In 1984, the hospital moved into a new, larger structure in Lake Jackson.

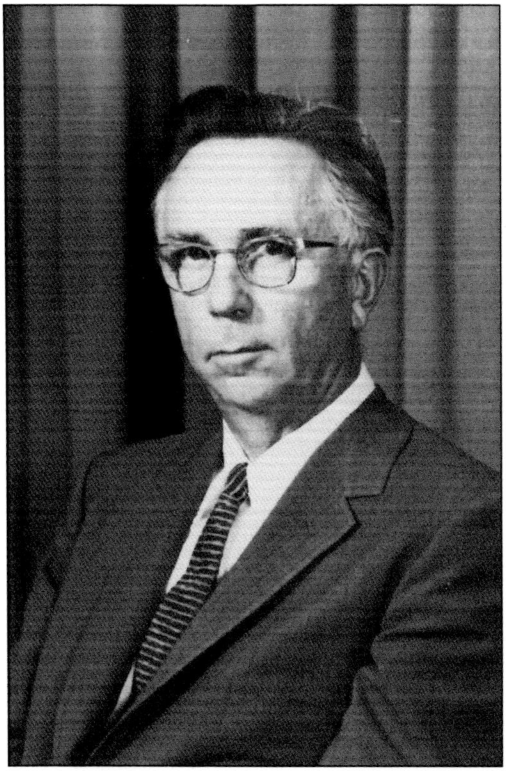

Alden Dow—son of Herbert Henry Dow Sr., founder of the Dow Chemical Company—chose a site west of Freeport that was formerly the site of the Lake Jackson Plantation. He made a point to save trees; however, he located the city within the trees rather than in the open cropland of the former plantation.

Alden Dow sits at his desk with secretary Mrs. Clyde Passmore in the early 1940s, with Frank Steves and T.J. Dunbar on the left. These men were key in implementing the city plan as Alden envisioned. It appears that the model behind Alden is an A-frame church design. This office was donated to the Lake Jackson Historical Association in 2008. It was remodeled to its original state and opened for tours.

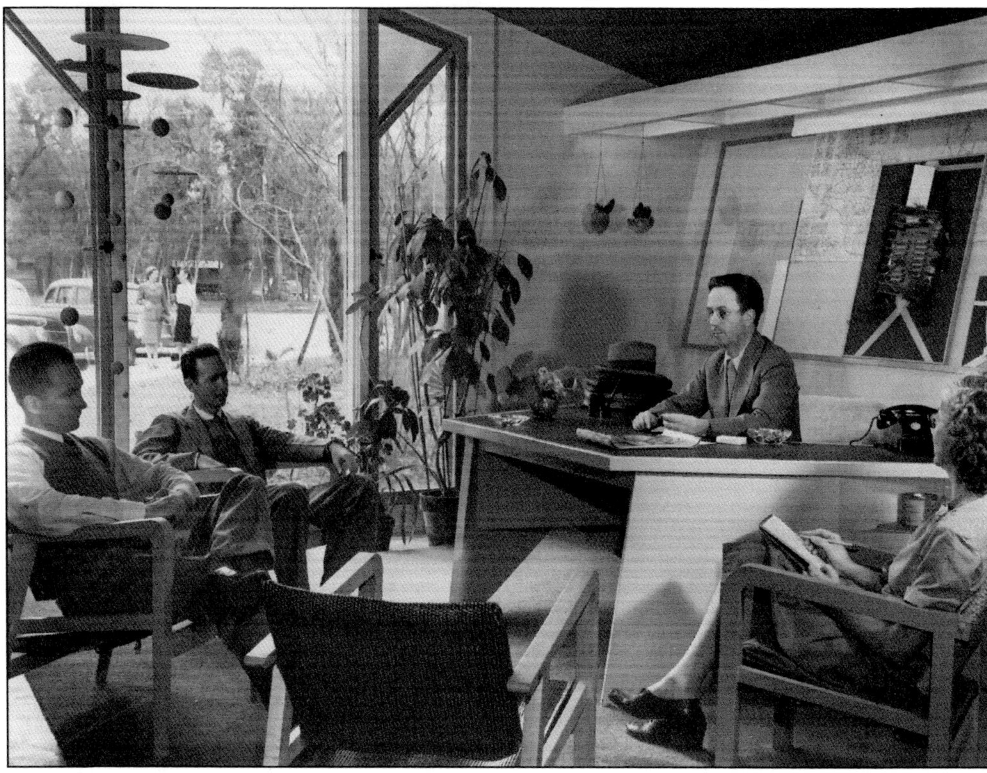

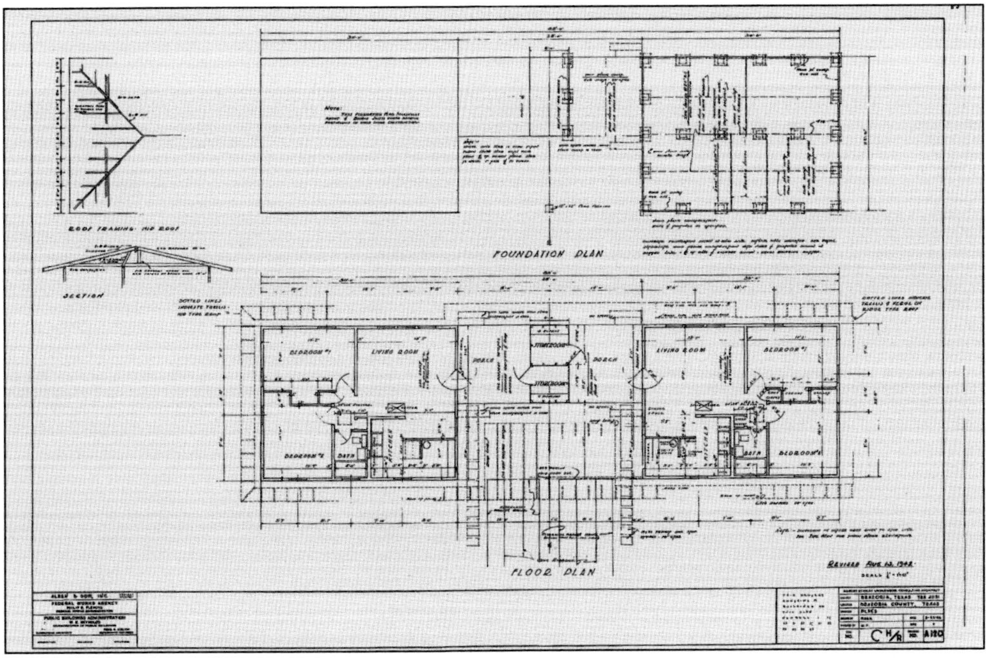

These are the 1942 plans by Alden Dow for some of the duplexes. These plans were for numbers 1, 19, 23, 31, 33, 57, 61, 82, 85, 89, and 92. This was Alden's effort to provide variety in the neighborhood. There are two bedrooms with separate additional storage on the breezeway. The living room dimensions are 15-by-13 feet and include both the front door and entry to the hallway.

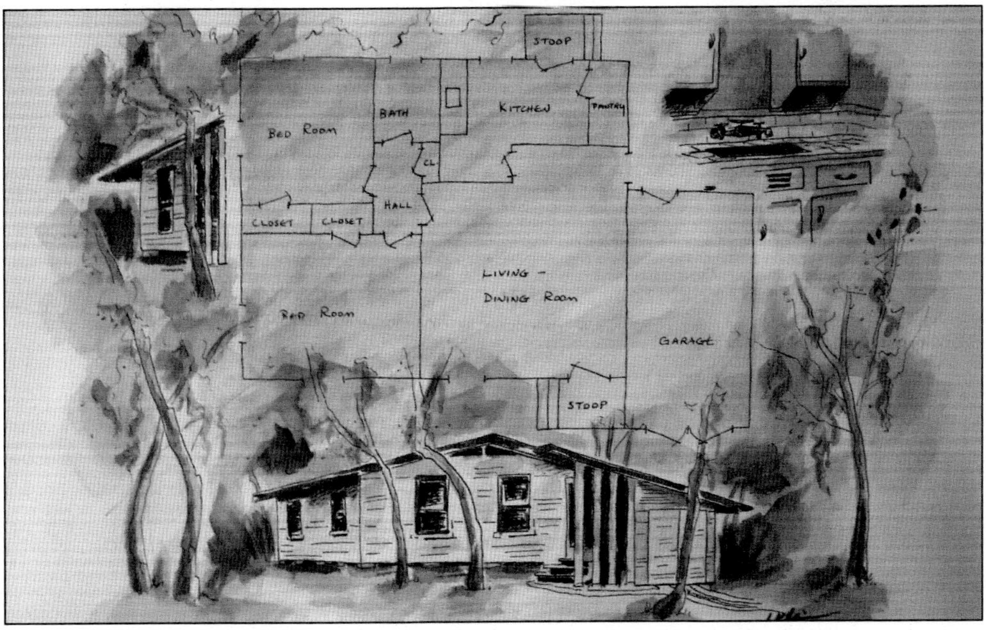

Lil' Anna Klein, a local artist and lifelong resident, painted this watercolor for the museum showing her home at 428 Winding Way. It was an Alden Dow design with two bedrooms, one bath, and a single-car garage. Many copies of this floor plan, or the mirror image of it, utilized frame construction on raised blocks in the early 1940s. Many of these homes are still occupied. These were considered one step up status-wise from the duplexes, but the biggest driving force was availability.

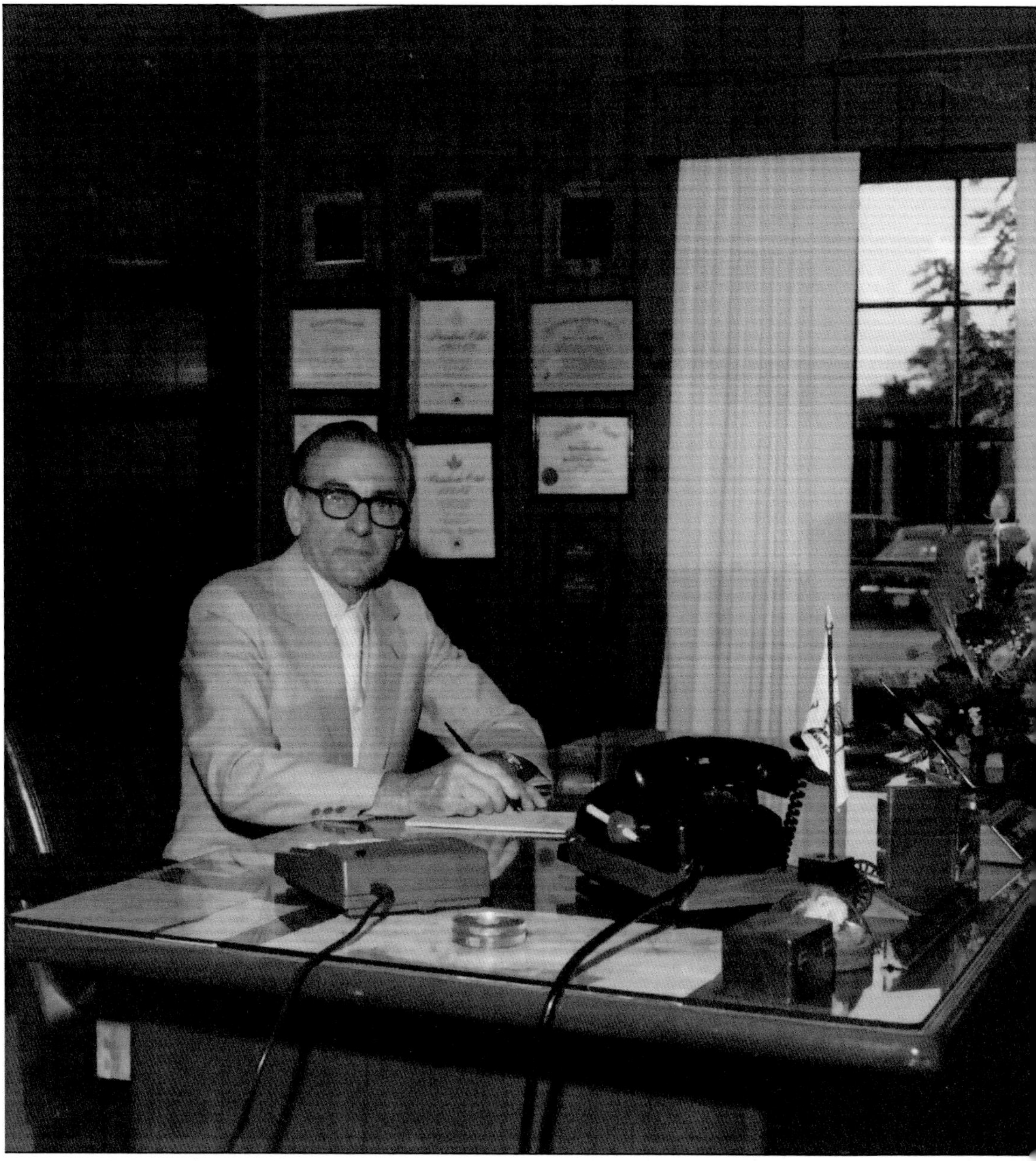

R.E. "Bob" Franklin was a successful insurance agent and active citizen. He was in charge of providing housing for the government in the early 1940s as the chemical plant was being built.

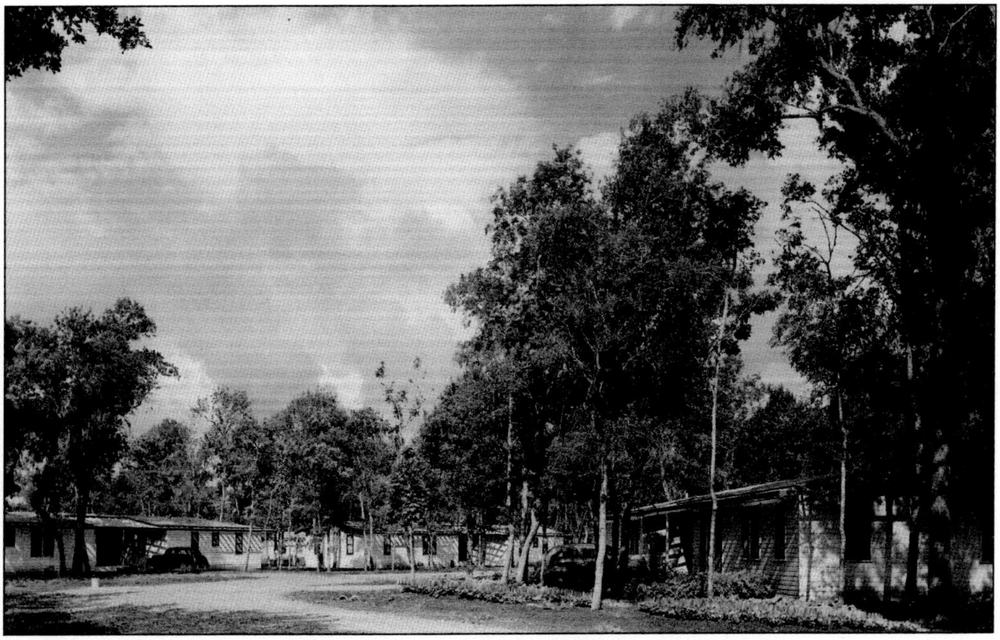

Trumpet Vine was the gravel street where the first duplexes were built. There were no garages and all the houses were the same design with a breezeway between the units.

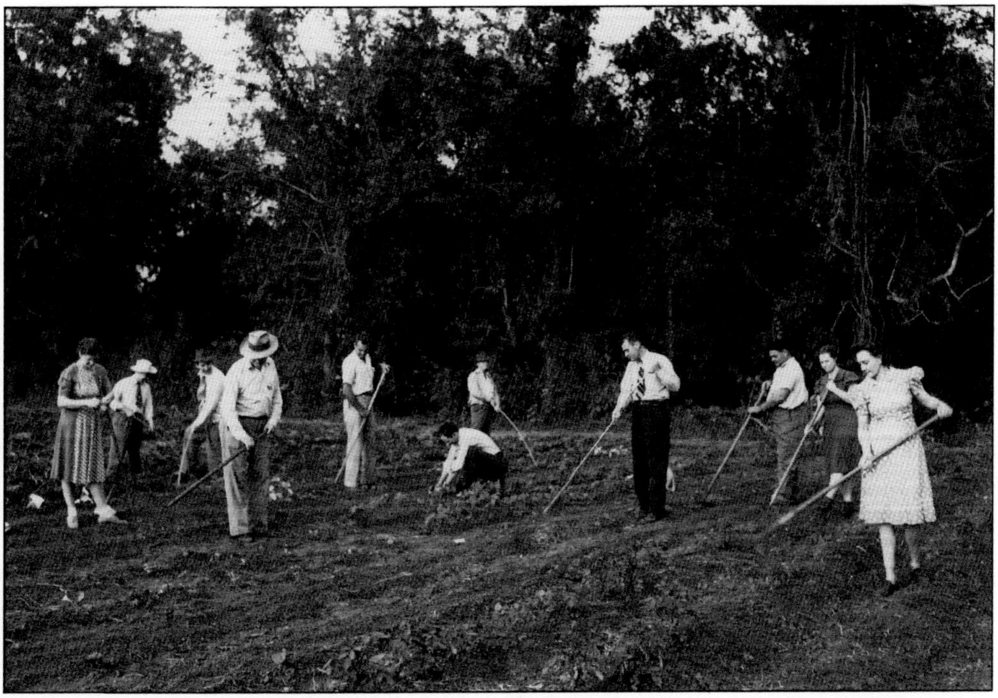

Men and women—dressed in their work clothes, which included hats, ties, and house dresses—work on a 1943 Victory Garden.

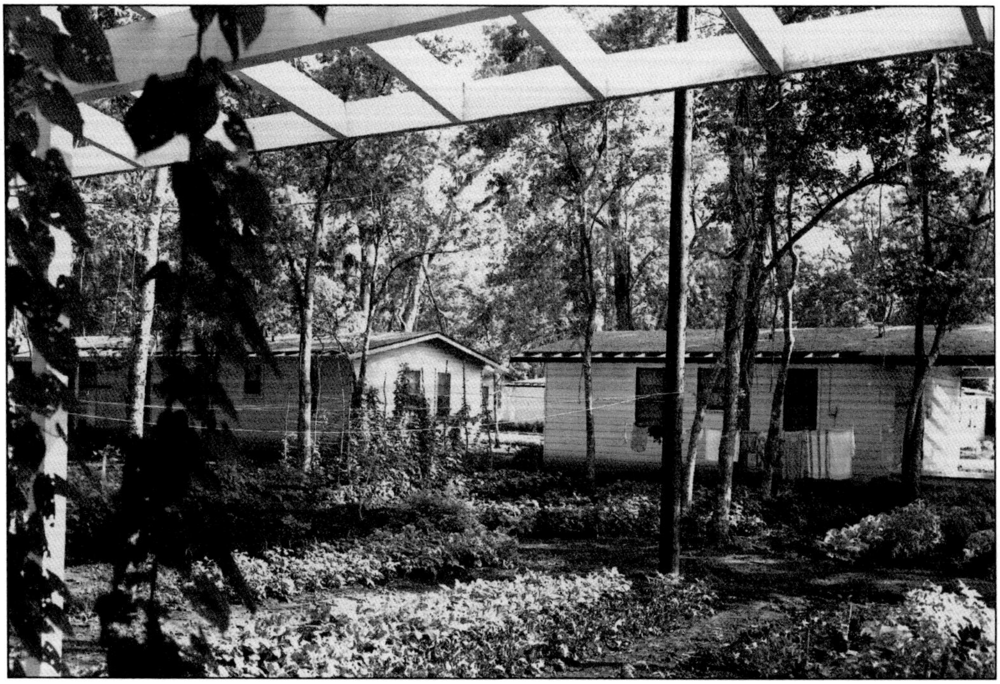

The early duplexes were designed by Alden Dow with distinctive eaves. Victory Gardens shared the backyards with clotheslines. Tar and gravel roofs were a modern design and were possibly used to saved lumber.

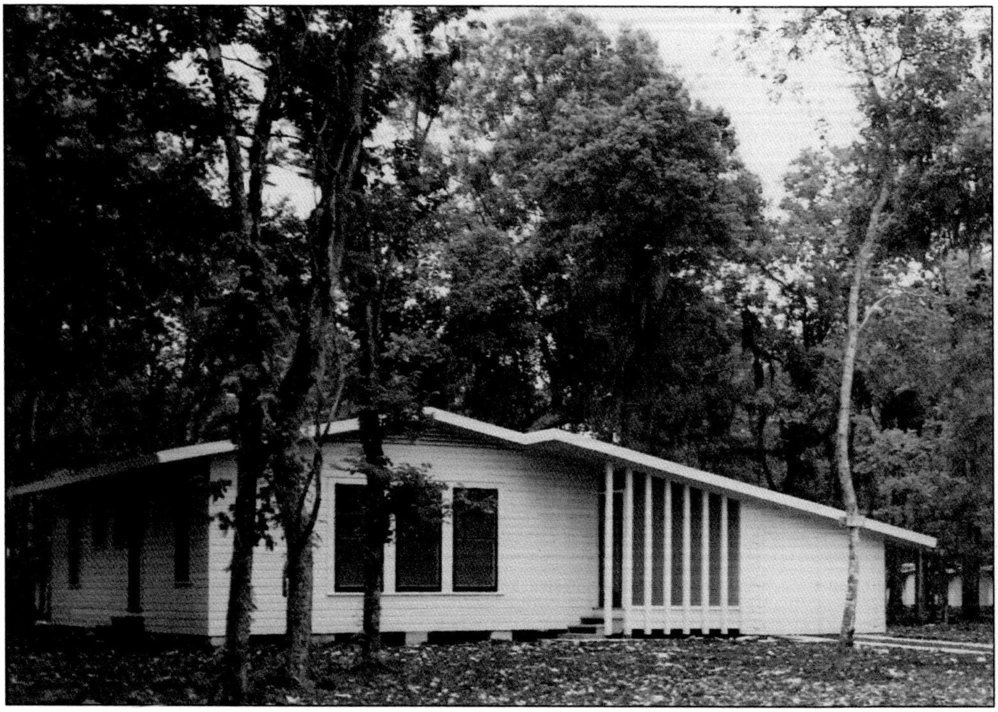

As pictured here, houses were built on blocks which caused cold floors in the winter. Baseballs also accumulated under the houses.

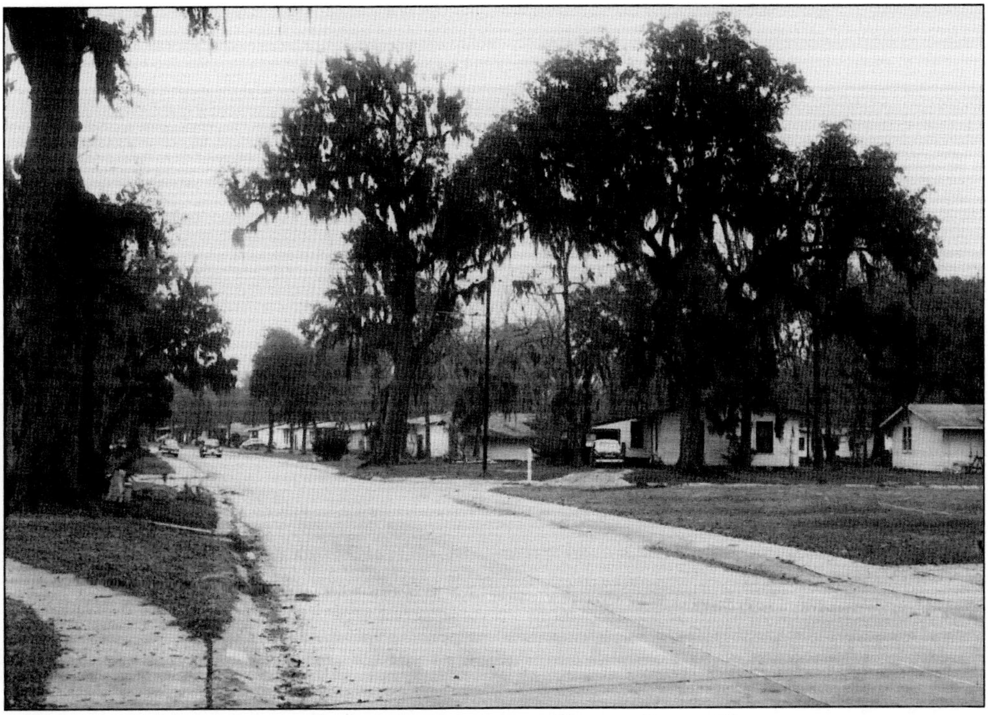

Beyond the duplexes were single-family residences on Yaupon Street. The streets were concrete, which improved the quality of life and minimized the expense of street repairs over the years.

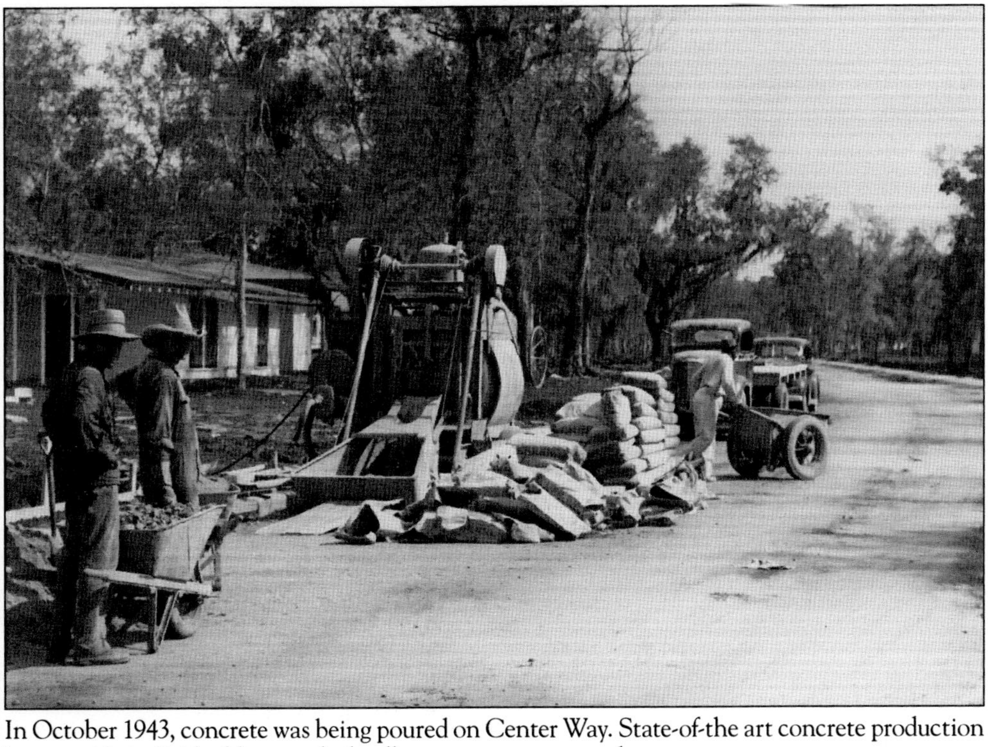

In October 1943, concrete was being poured on Center Way. State-of-the art concrete production began with individual bags and wheelbarrows to transport the wet cement.

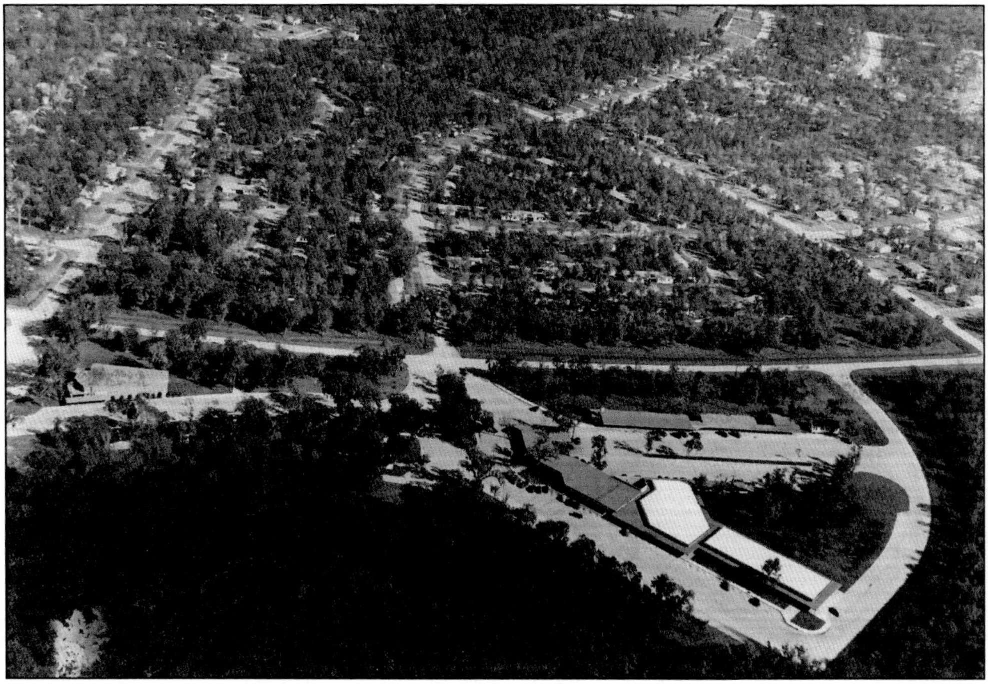

Facing east, this is an aerial view of early buildings in downtown Lake Jackson with the duplexes adjacent to the business district. The theater is on the left, and the center structure in the foreground is Lake Drug, Ben Franklin 5 &10, Stylemart Clothing, and the Piggly Wiggly grocery store.

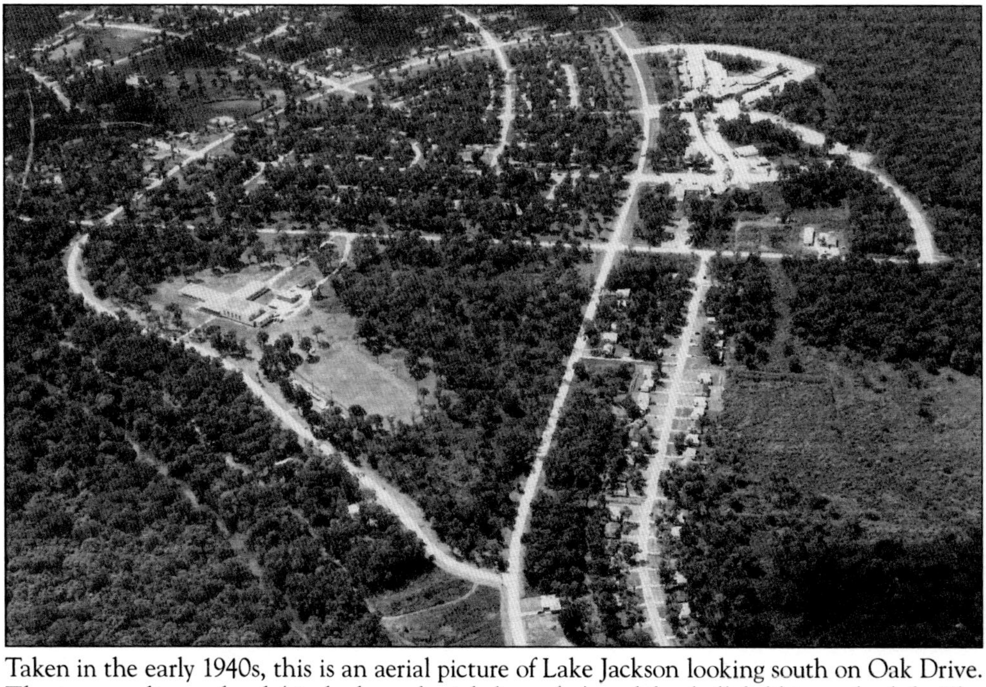

Taken in the early 1940s, this is an aerial picture of Lake Jackson looking south on Oak Drive. The intermediate school (sixth through eighth grades) and football field is to the left. The duplexes appear to have been fully constructed. There are two softball fields, which are still in use as of 2010.

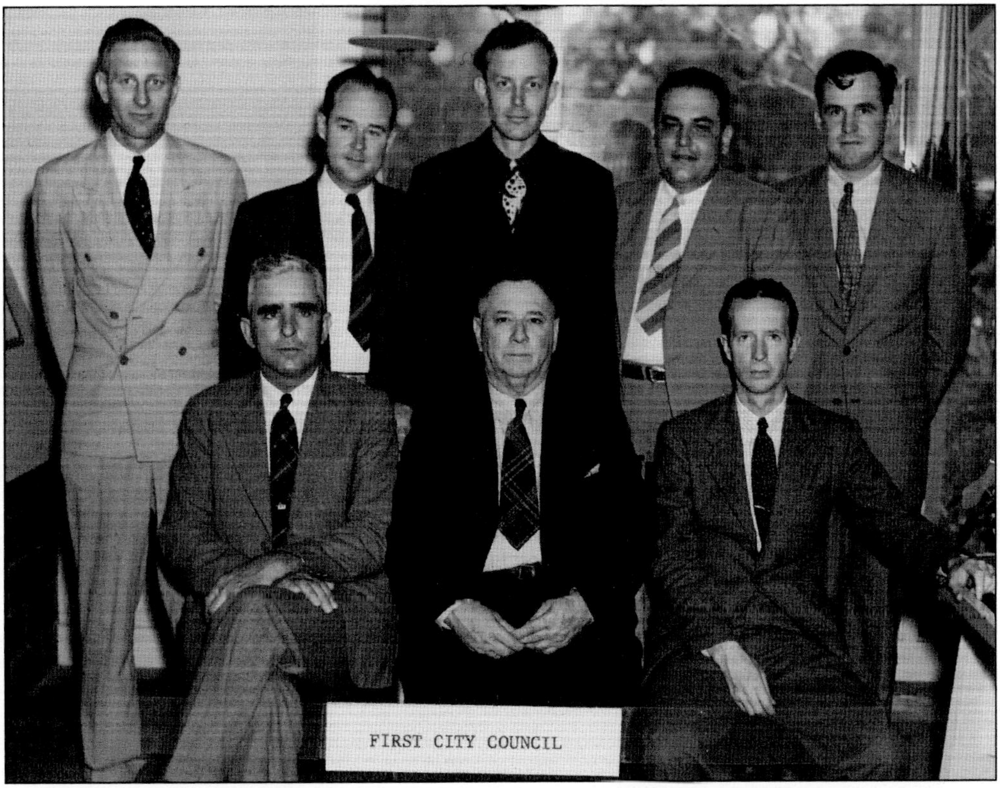

The first Lake Jackson City Council was elected on April 18, 1944. They are, from left to right, (first row) city marshal John S. Brown, mayor J.W. Leah, and treasurer T.J. Dunbar; (second row) councilman C.L. Lee, councilman H. Lee Harris, councilman Ray Laesby, councilman W. Palm, and councilman A.J. McCracklin. The picture was taken in Alden Dow's office, which was adjacent to city hall.

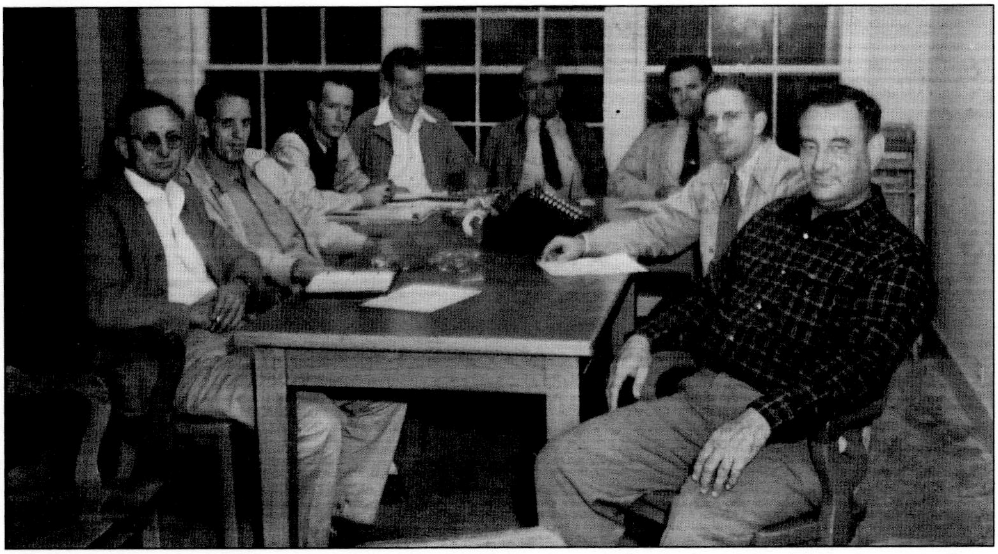

This meeting was held at city hall in Carriage Square in the early 1940s. The picture is from Robert Lindviet's images, published in his father's *Lake Jackson News*.

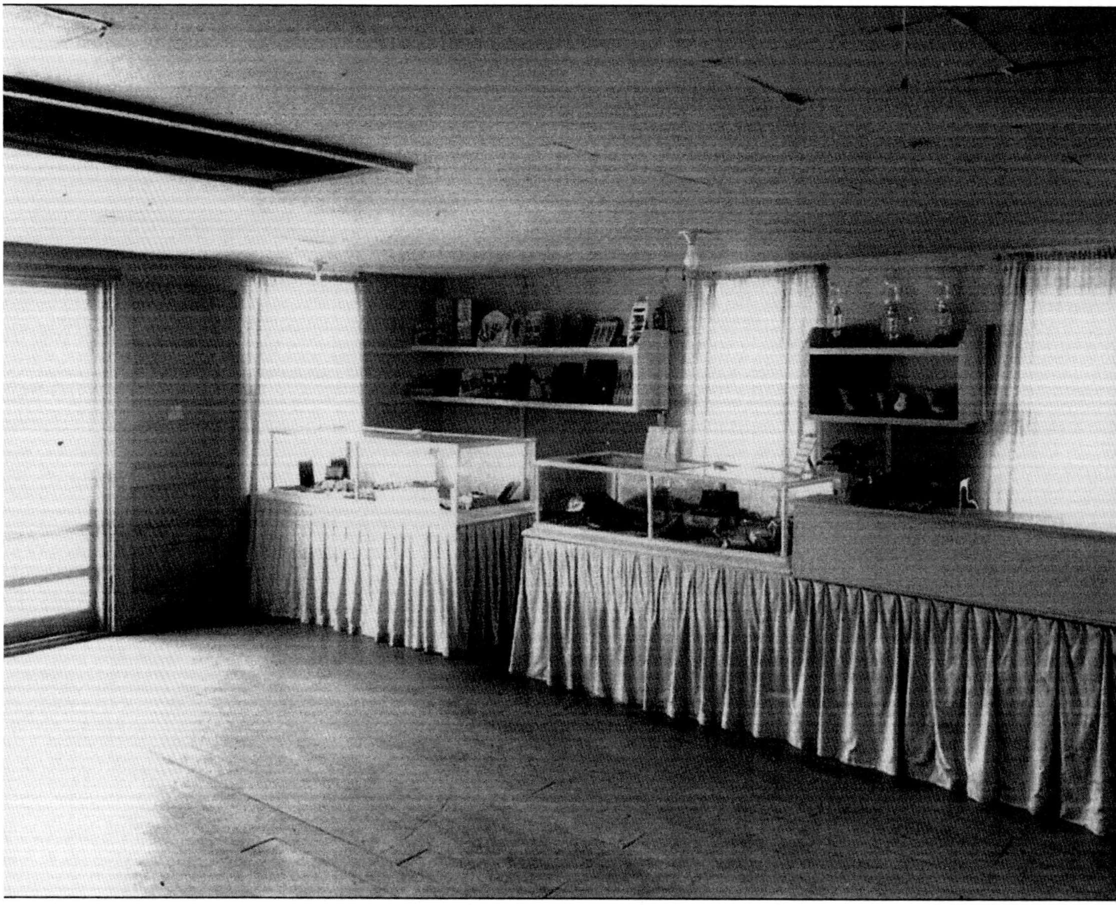

The inside of the Dowell Jewelry in downtown was rather stark and with low inventory. The store was cooled through a screen door.

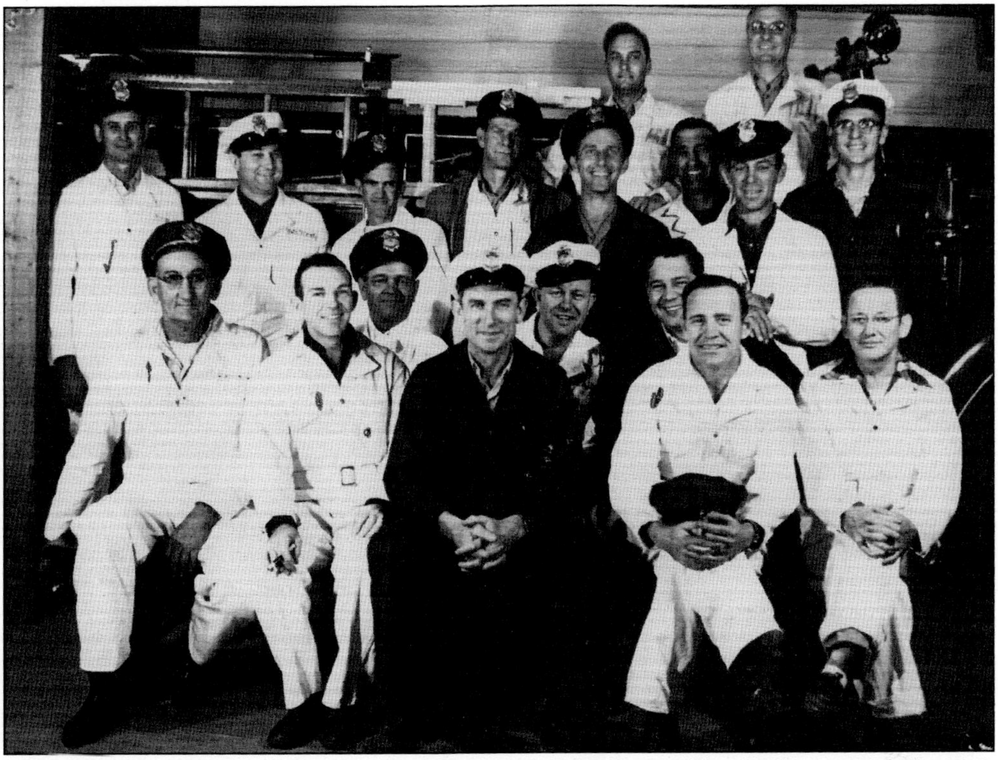

These are the volunteer firemen in 1950. The chief was Sam Strickland. The men are, from left to right, (first row, seated) Earl Barrow, unidentified, J. Pousson, Sam Strickland, Chick Green, Gene Morgan, unidentified, and John Alford; (second row, standing) four unidentified men, Joe Mitchell, Denny Riggins, unidentified, Bill Zimmerman, unidentified, and Fred Korenek.

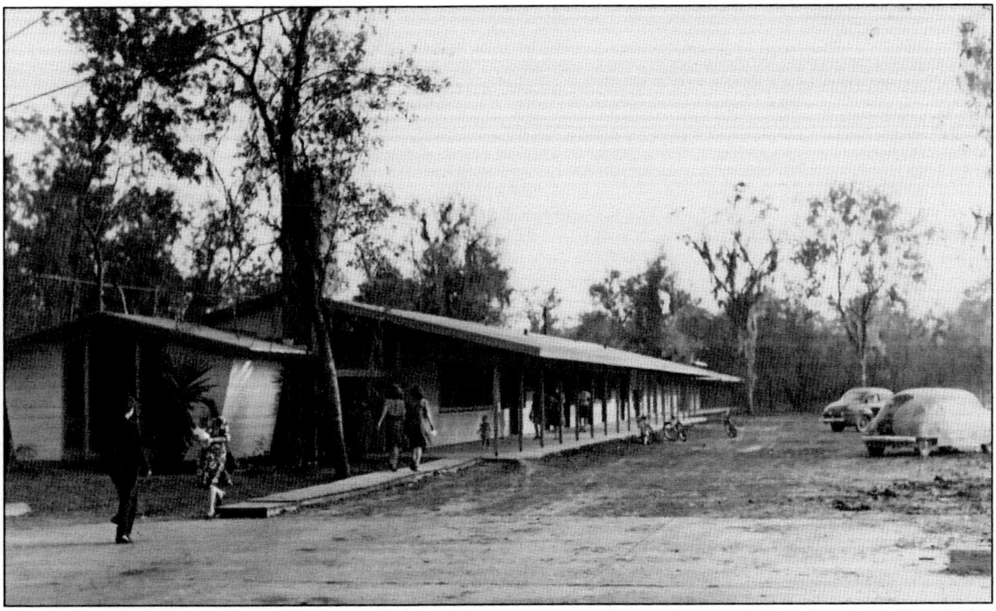

Alden Dow's office was next to city hall and was initially located in a field of mud. Alden Dow owned a Scarab car that was hand-built. It may be the car on the right.

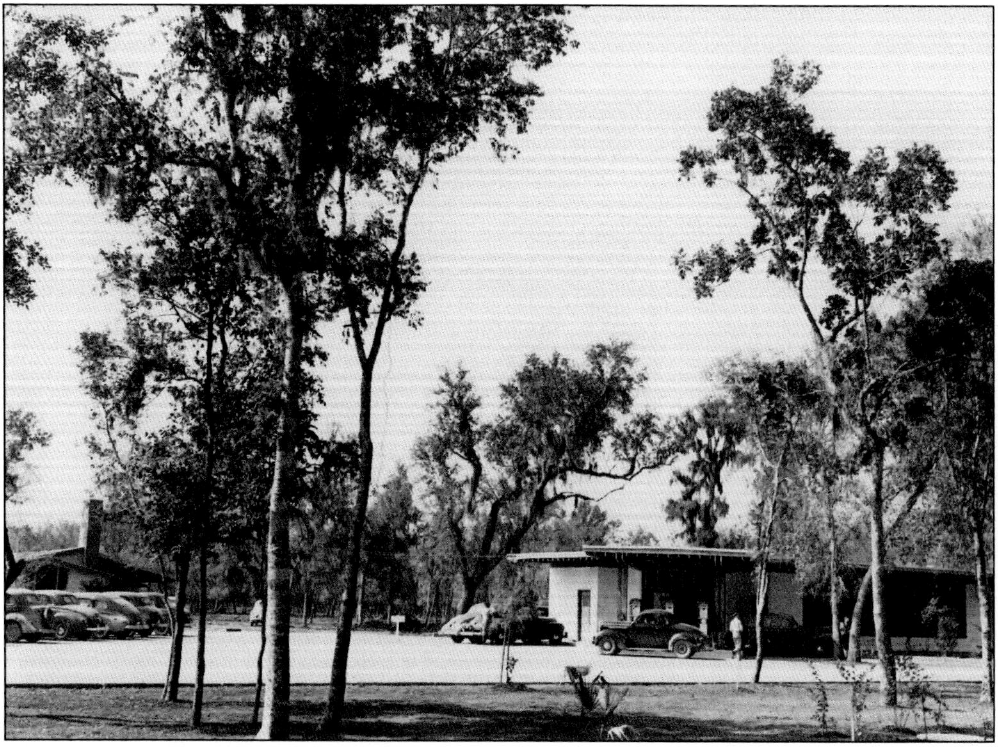

Schmidt's Service Station in the 1940s is seen from the median. Alden Dow's office is to the left. Lake Drug was on the right.

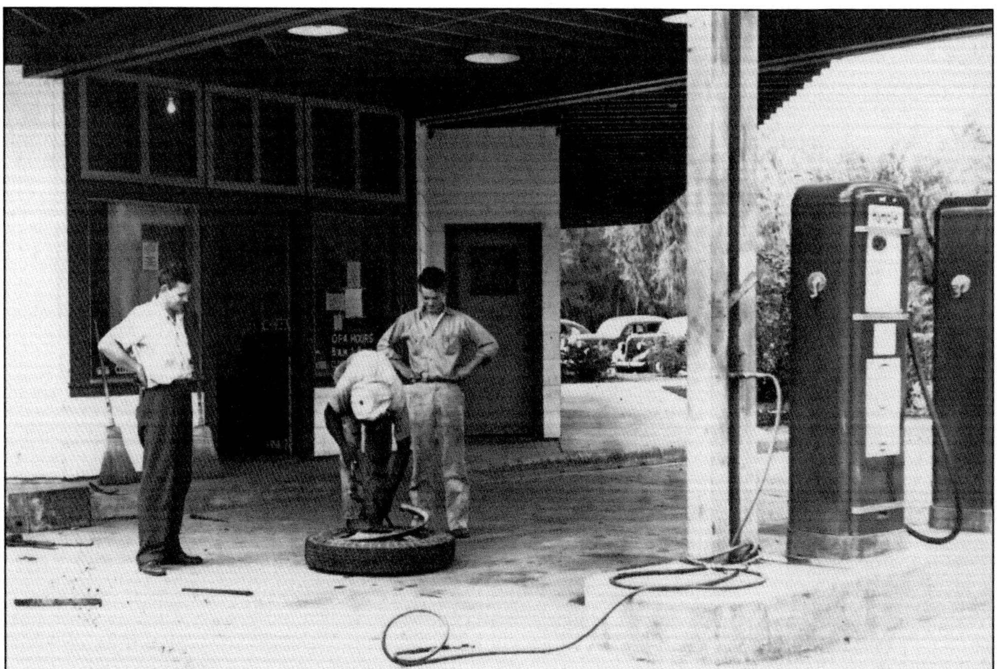

Burley Schmidts owned the service station downtown next to Lake Drug. It was a Humble station, and later became Exxon.

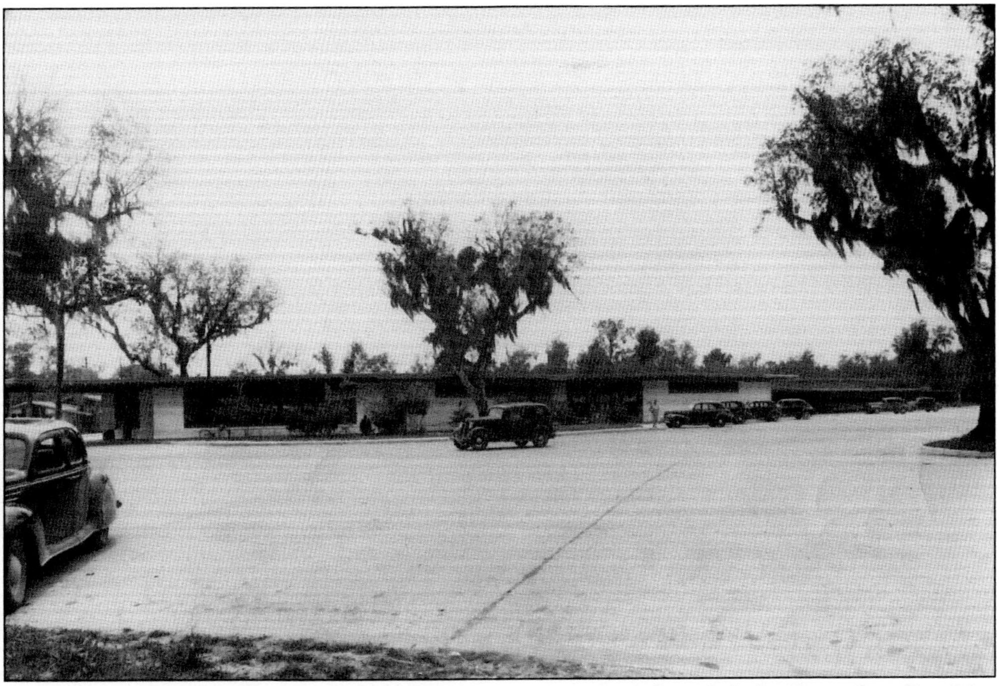

Some downtown businesses were Schmidt's Service on the left with Lake Drug, Ben Franklin 5 & 10, Stylemart Clothing, and the Piggly Wiggly Grocery Store. The building on the right eventually became the Museum of Natural Science.

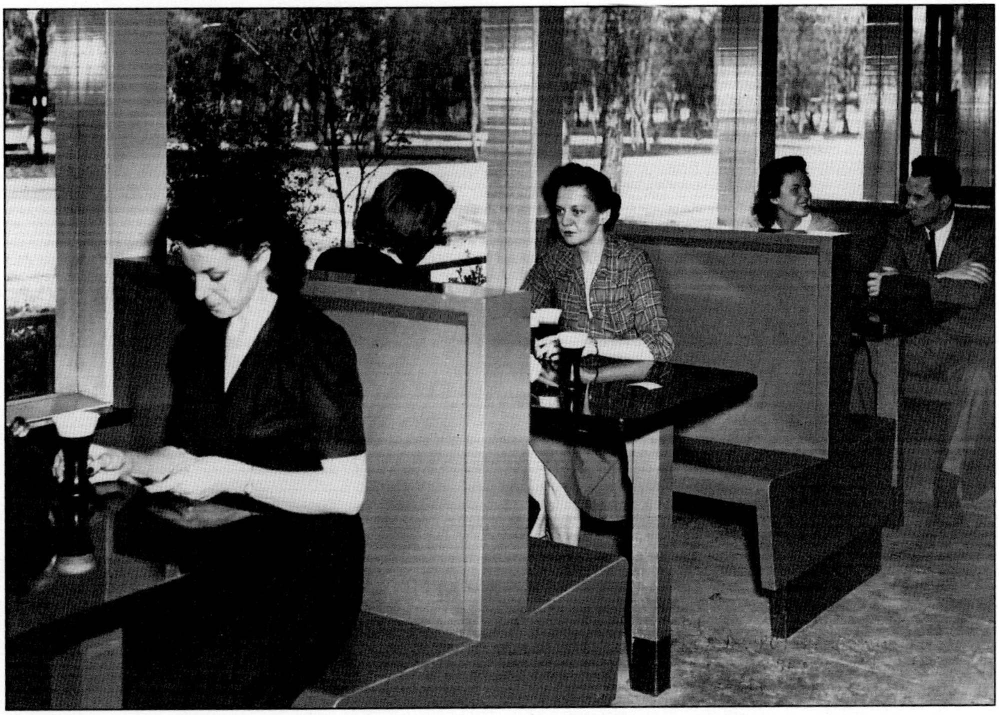

Lake Drug featured a fountain. The windows allowed plenty of light. Construction is very utilitarian. The plastic holders for paper cups had to be novel in the 1940s.

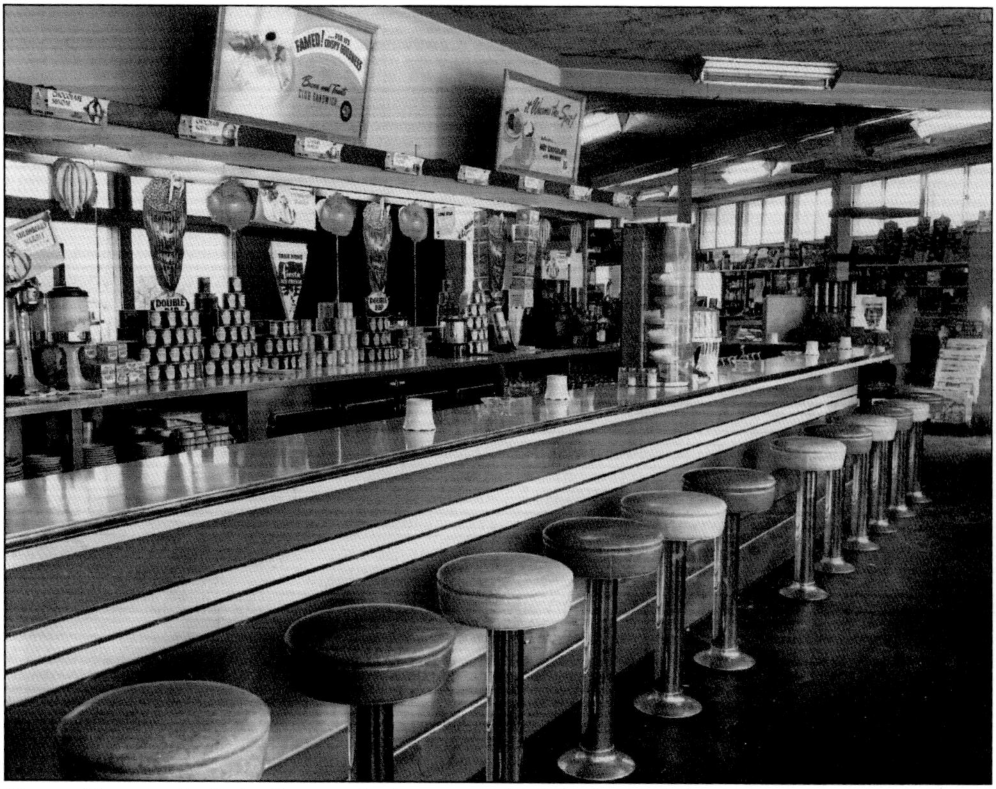

Pictured here is the Lake Drug soda fountain, which had 40¢ club sandwiches and Heinz soup cans at the ready.

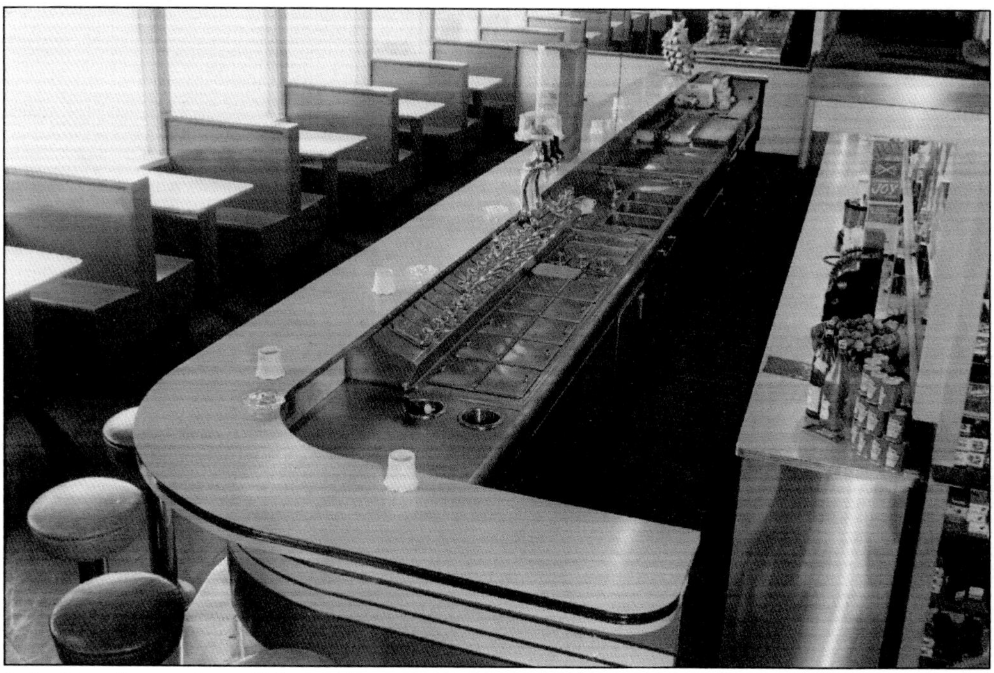

Lake Drug featured a well-fitted chrome service area.

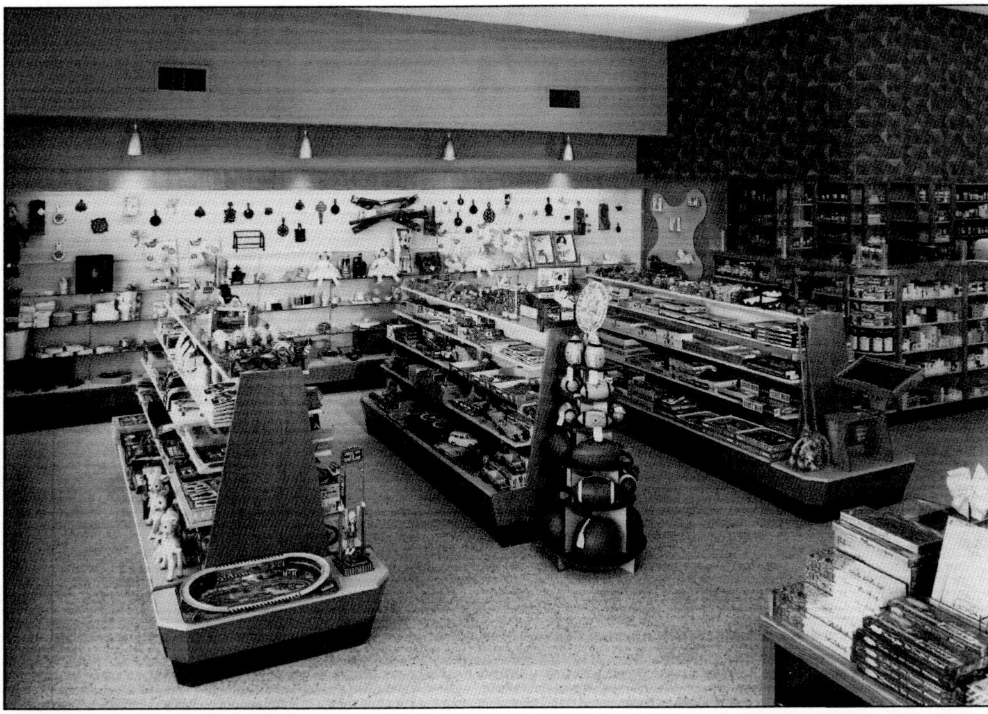

Lake Drug offered a variety of items for sale, such as candies, footballs, toys, BB guns, dolls, trivets, and more.

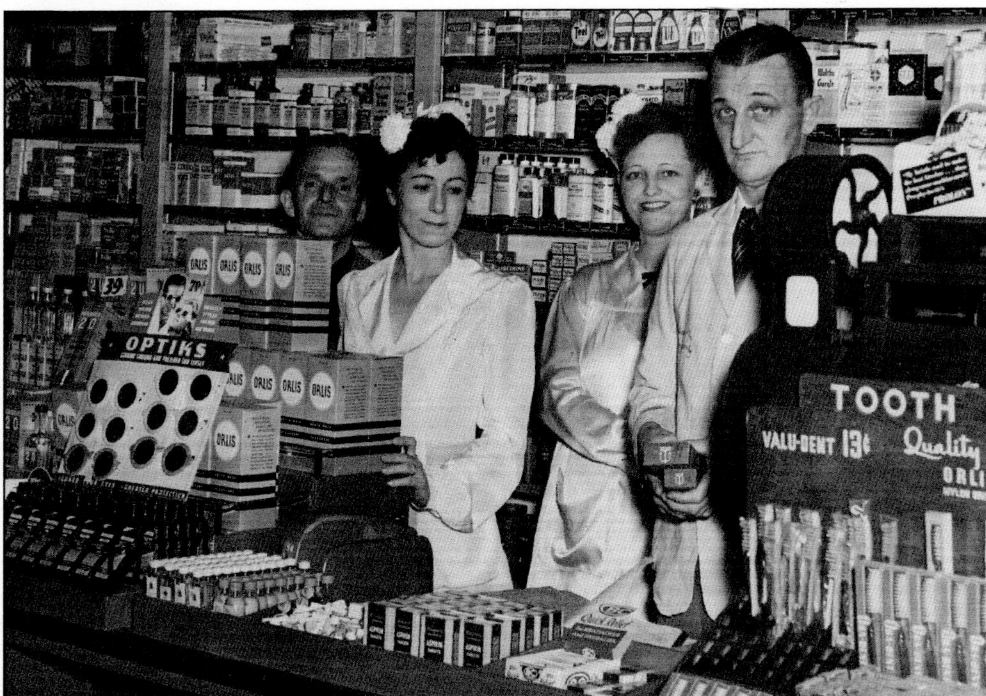

Pictured here is the Lake Drug staff. They are, from left to right, owners Art and Elizabeth Webb, and pharmacist Hartman and his wife. Note the utilitarian sunglasses on the left.

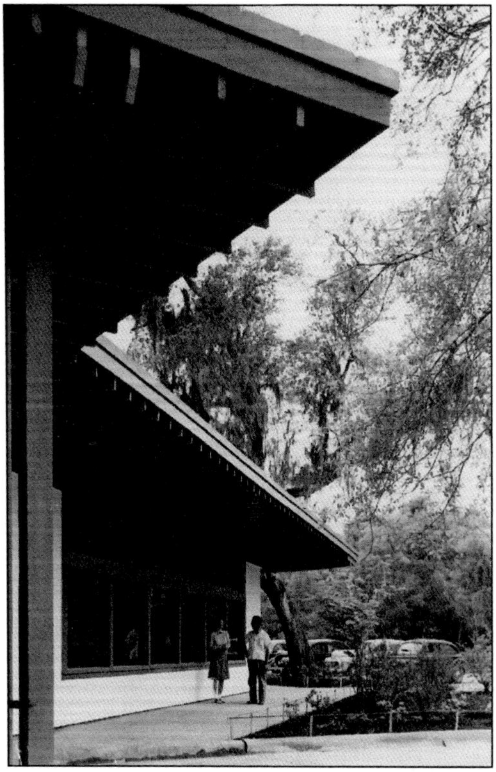

In front of Lake Drug, Merle Schultz, chief telephone operator, visits with Carl Schredner, a master carpenter who made building models for Alden Dow.

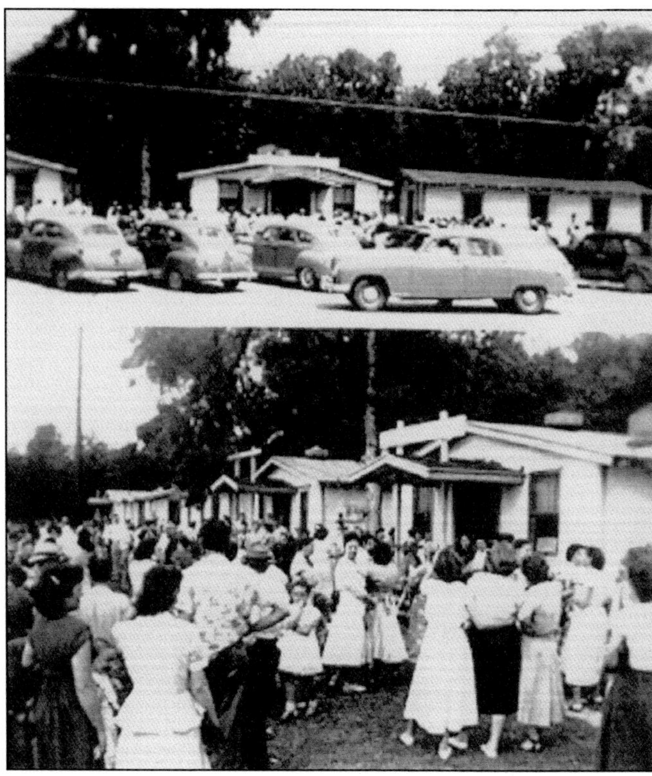

Additional barracks were moved in adjacent to Dowell Jewelry by 1947. One of the additional stores was LaVelle, a lady's clothing store, owned by Julia May.

The Lake Hardware and Lumber Co. is pictured here with owner Rube and Mildred Tracy in 1948. Their first three boys are with them, Ade, John, and Mike.

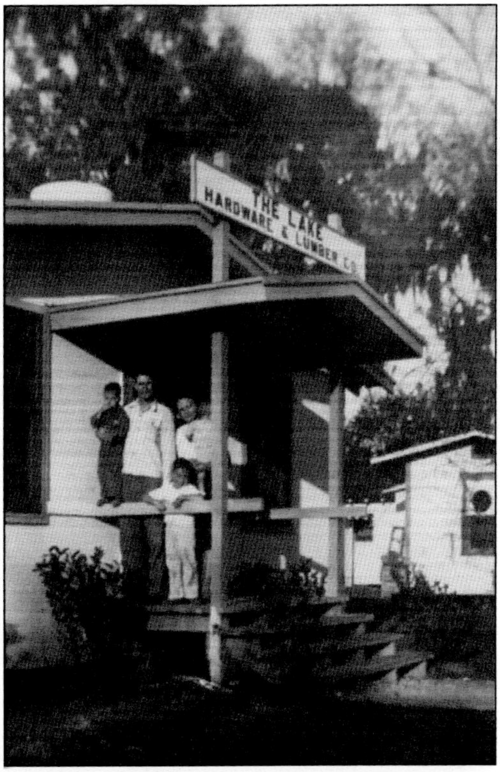

Rube Tracy (in back with a tie) is pictured inside his second Lake Hardware and Lumber location. This store was located across from Lake Drug in a triangular building that was later the laundromat and is currently Domino's Pizza.

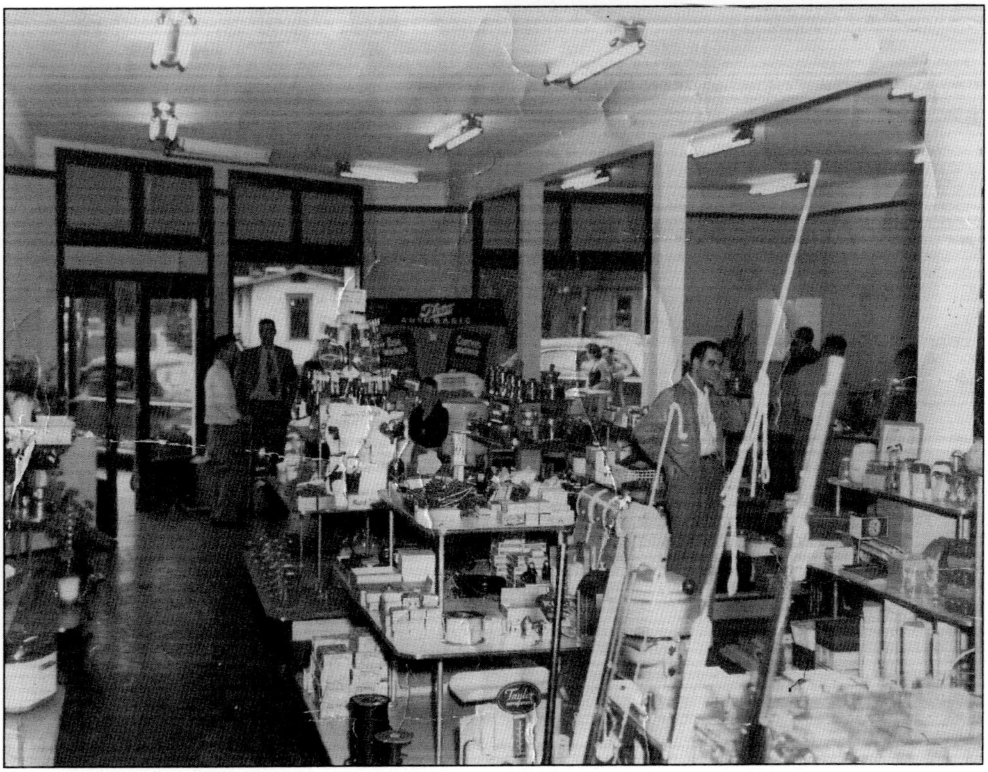

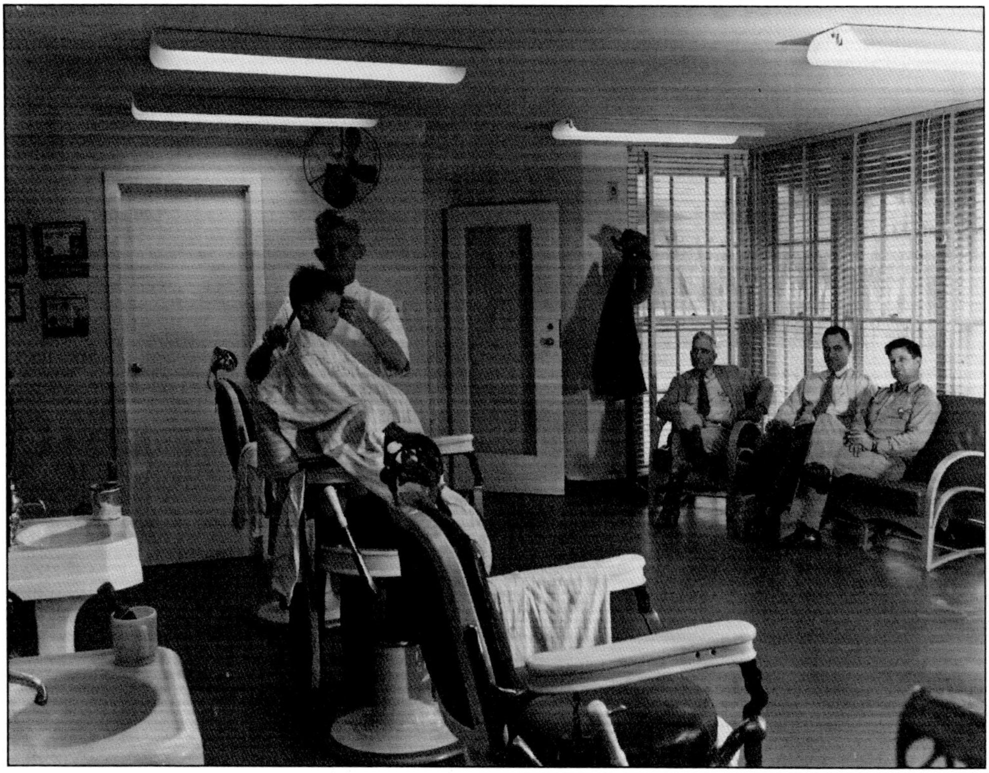

The first barber in the city was Tom Vaughn. Dickie Frerking is receiving a cut while Captain Brown, Ivan Greer, and M.D. Frerking wait their turn. Four chairs indicate an expectation of city growth.

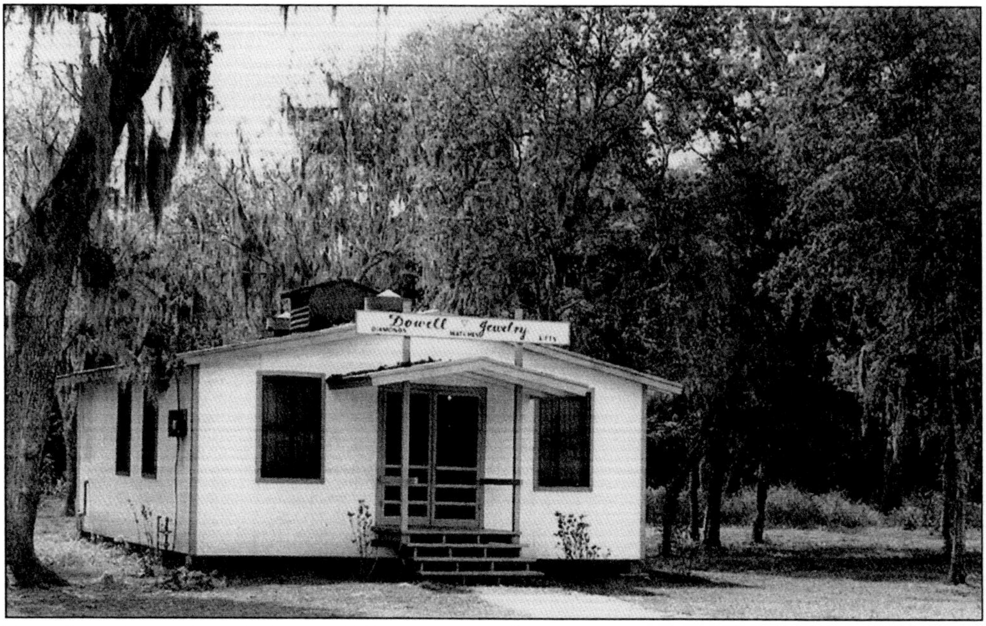

Dowell Jewelry on North Parking Way was opened in April 1945. It was located in this temporary building provided by Dow Chemical. The rent was a percentage of sales.

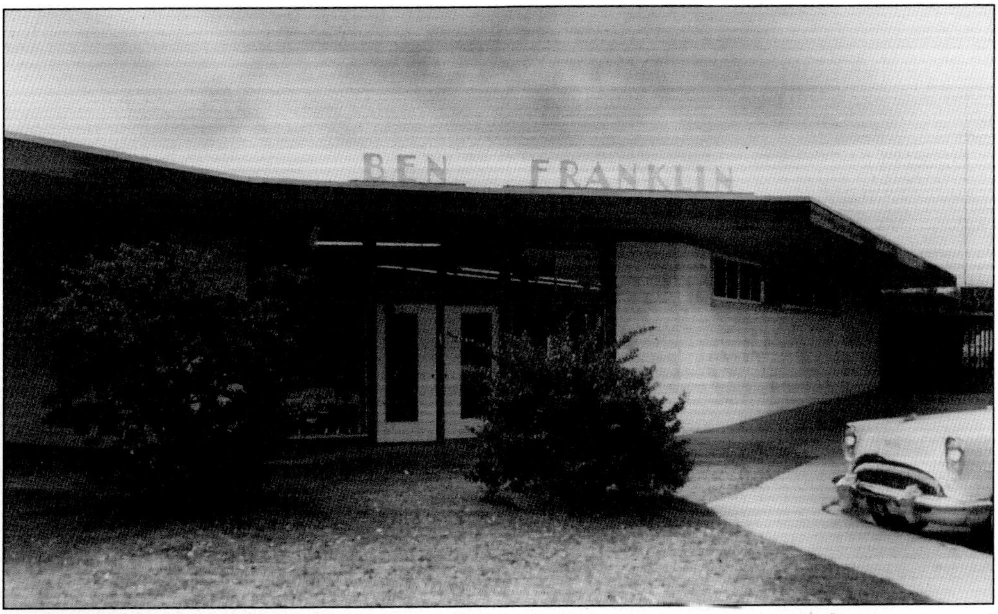

Ben Franklin was a local variety store owned by Ernie Rea, an entrepreneur, philanthropist, and mayor from 1954 to 1958. The store was adjacent to Lake Drug.

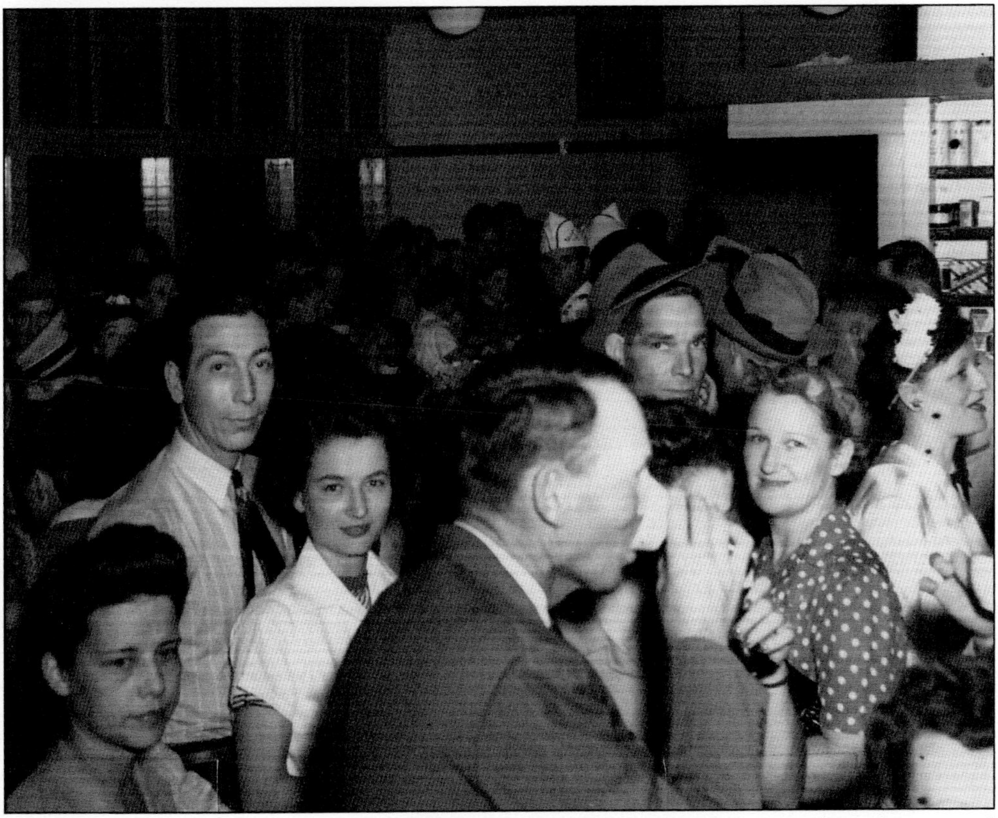

Lake Drug was the site of a very crowded celebration on October 22, 1943. It has been commented that few people in Lake Jackson were old enough to have gray hair.

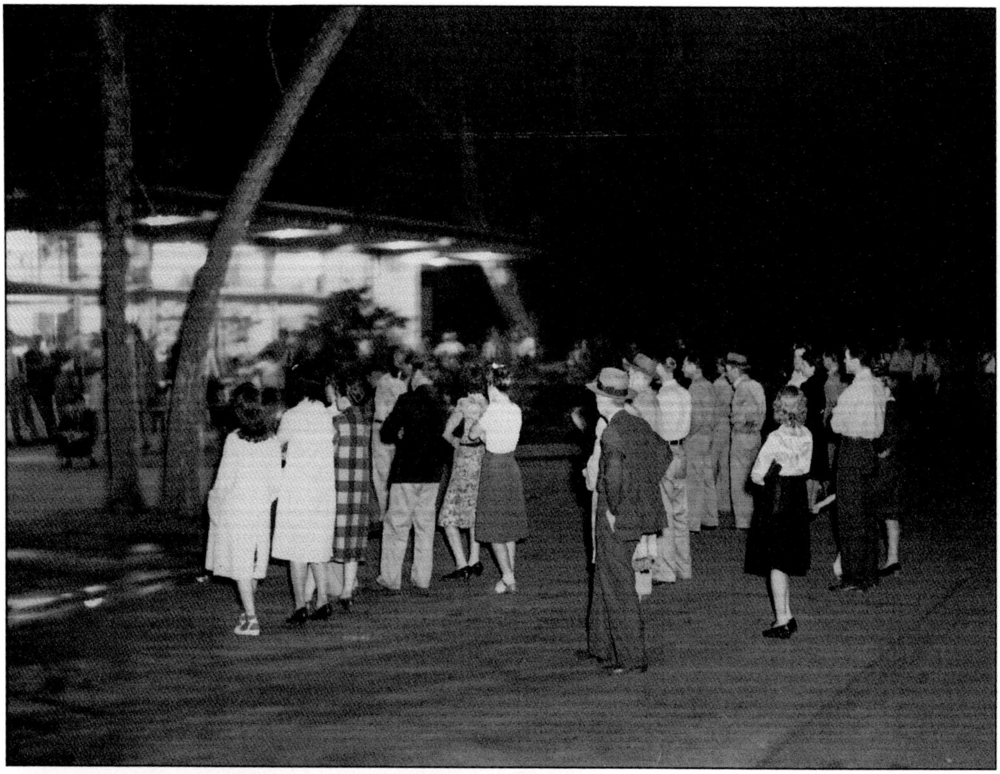

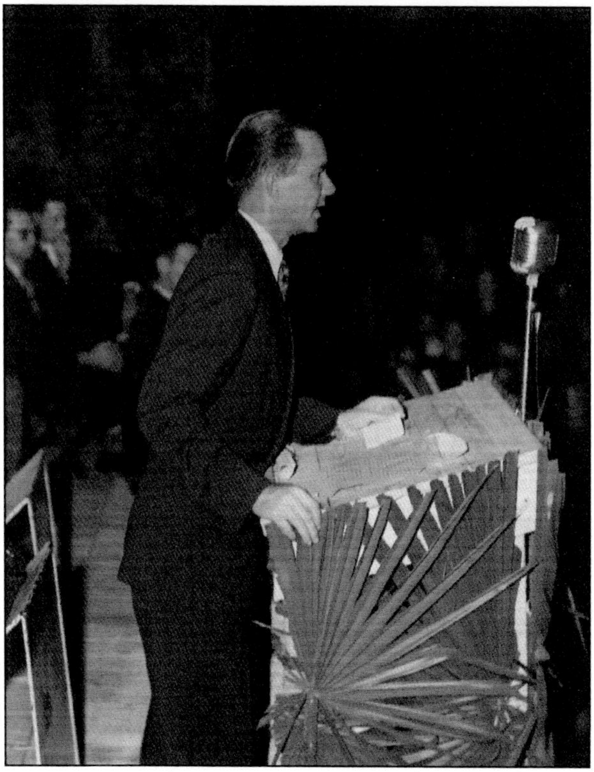

The first city election featured campaign speeches in the street at Schmidt's Gas Station.

This political speech was brief, based on the notes.

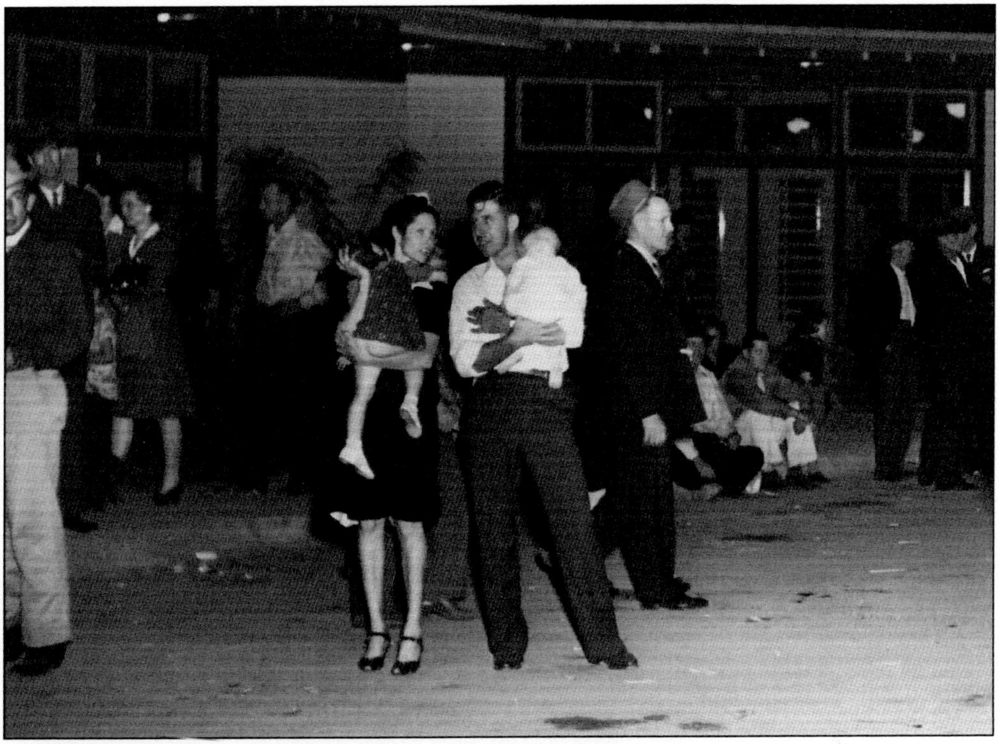

This October campaign night brought out the whole family.

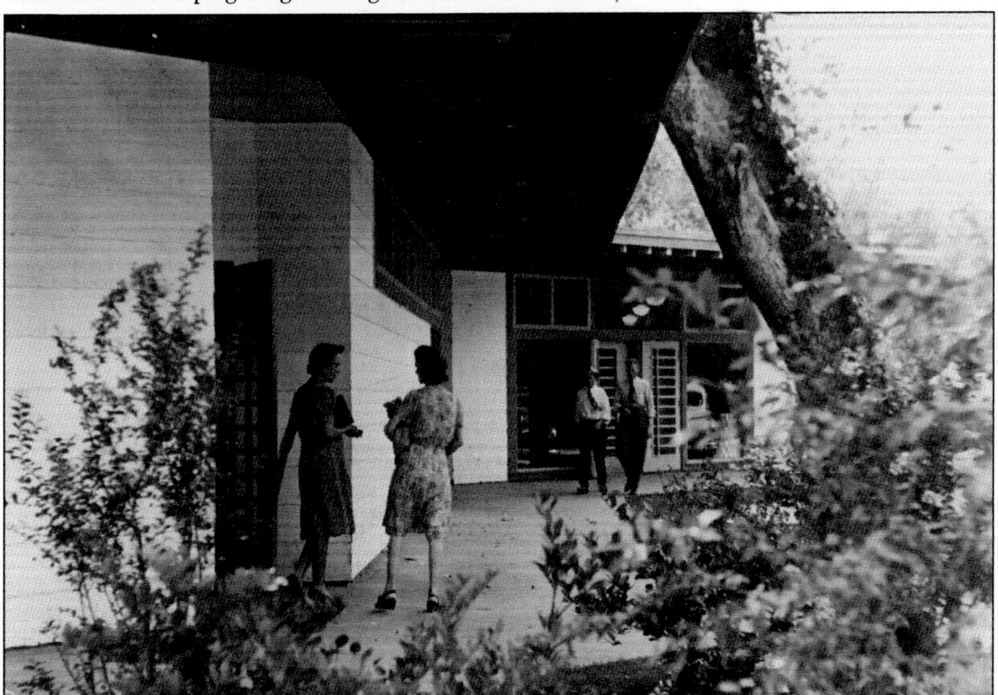

The grocery store downtown was in a modern-designed structure which minimized square corners. The tree passed through the eave.

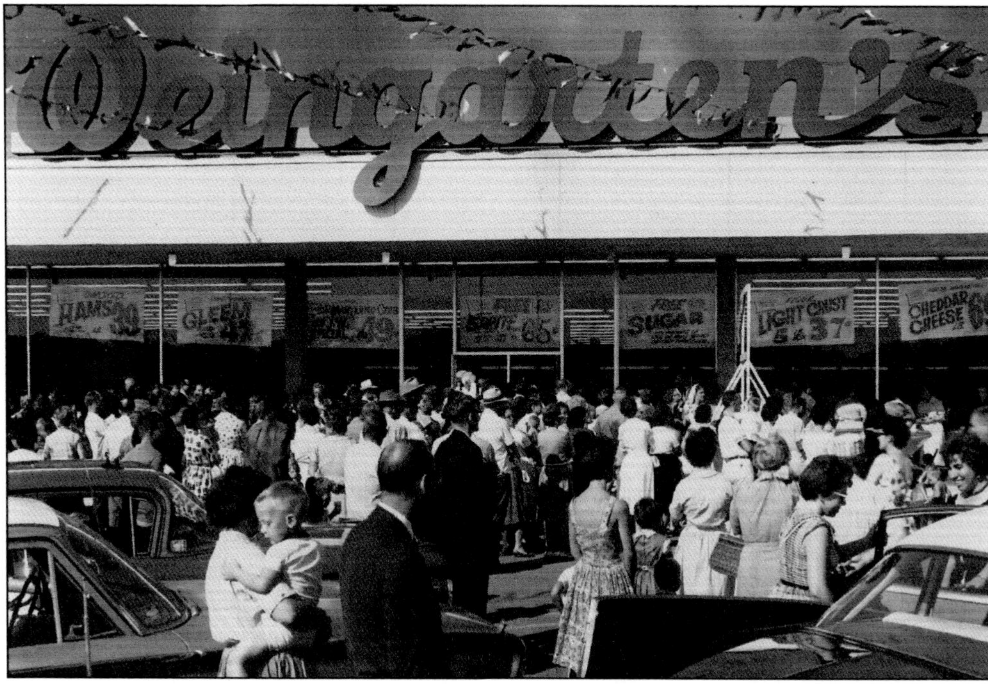

Weingarten's, a regional grocery store, opened in a new shopping area adjacent to Clute in 1962. This marked the beginning of a secondary shopping area in the city. New businesses were always well received. The prices of groceries for that era provide an interesting view of the past.

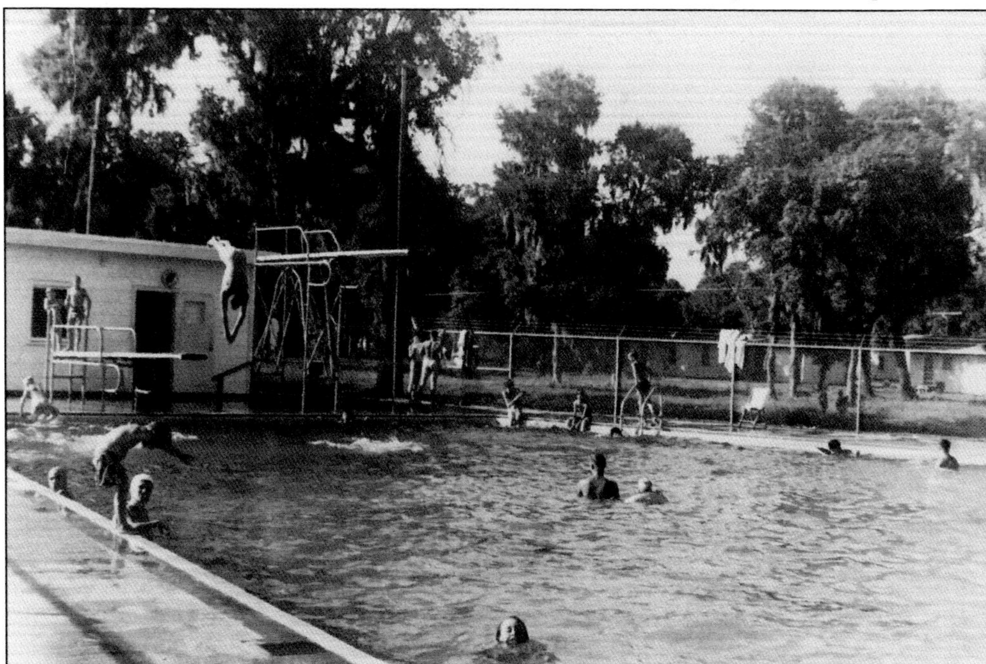

Lake Jackson provided the first pool in Brazoria County. It was referred to as "the Colegrove Pond," also known as the mayor's name, or Oakdale Plunge. Before the pool was replaced, it was stocked one winter with catfish for children's fishing.

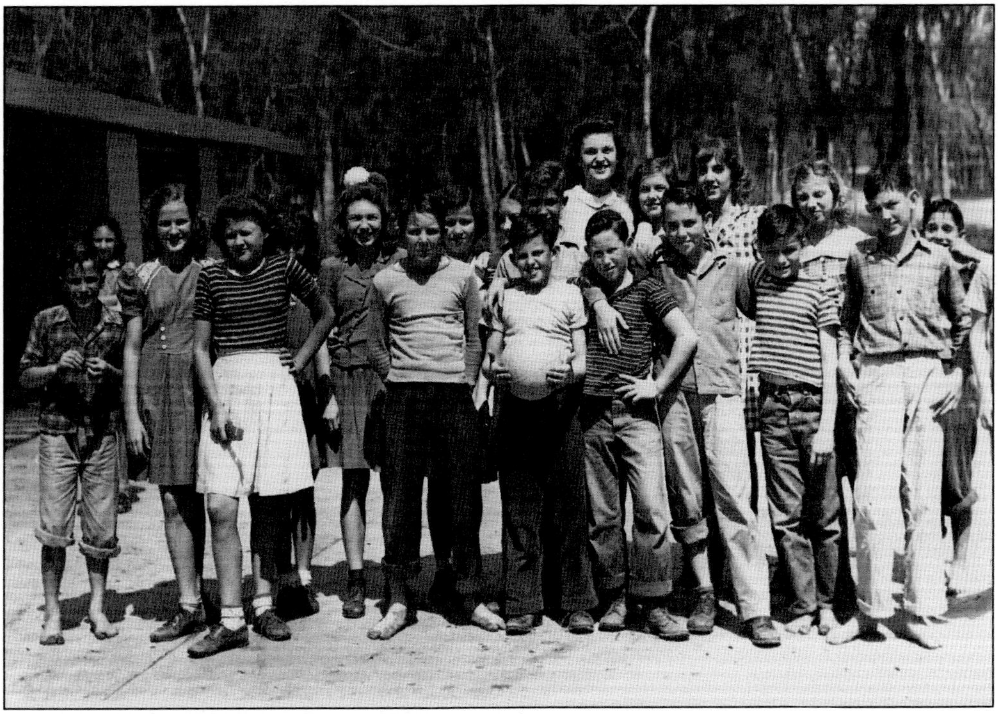

These adolescent students are not identified except for Addison Johnson at the far left, but their clothes and shoes speak to an era long ago.

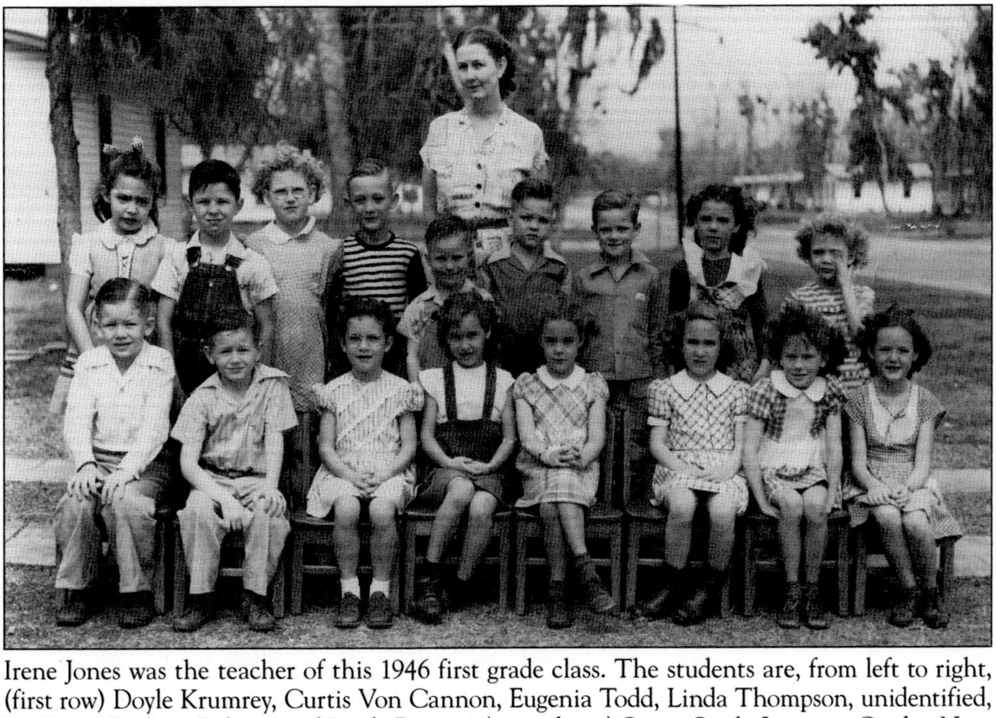

Irene Jones was the teacher of this 1946 first grade class. The students are, from left to right, (first row) Doyle Krumrey, Curtis Von Cannon, Eugenia Todd, Linda Thompson, unidentified, Pat Ryan, Barbara Rehms, and Linda Riggan; (second row) Susan Stark, Jennings Gerdes, Nata Lea Hood, Graham Bridges, and four unidentified students.

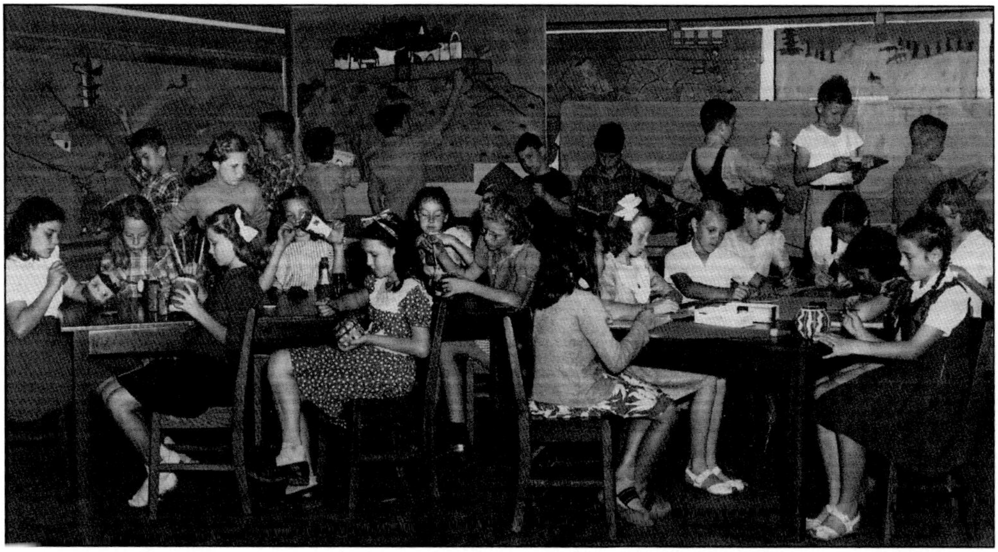

An elementary art class is working very intensely. William "Peewee" Roye is standing second from the right.

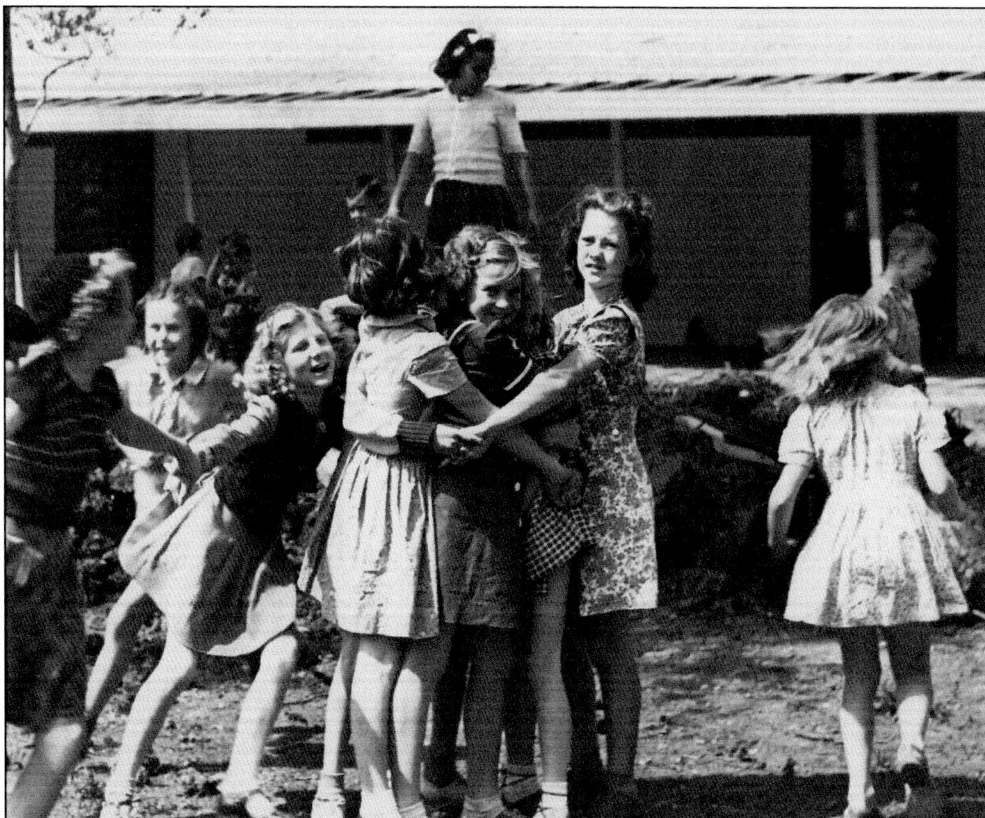

The elementary school, which became Elisabet Ney Elementary School, was in use before the grounds had been cleared after the construction. Dresses and curls characterize these children. These buildings were located on Yaupon.

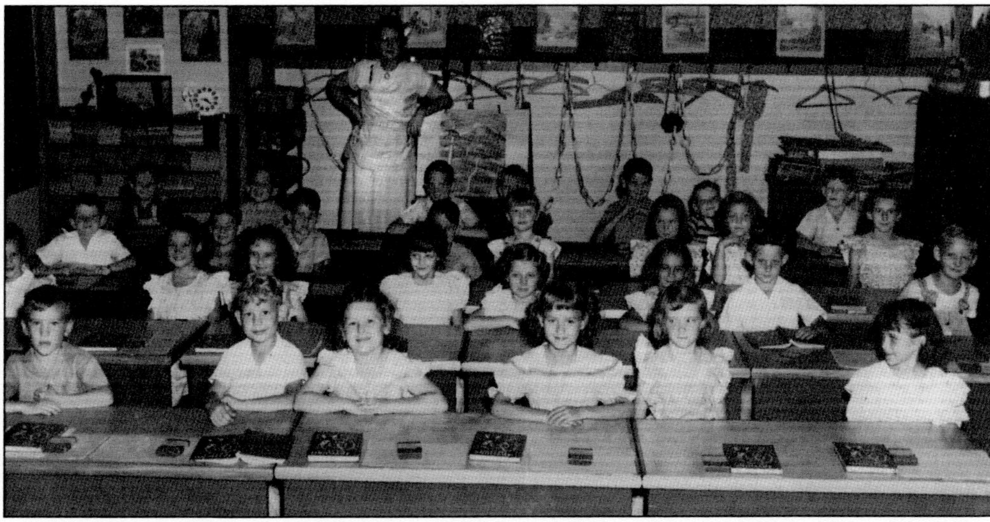

In 1949, Mrs. Vaughn's first grade class is pictured at the elementary school. The students are, from left to right, (first row) unidentified, Bobby Monical, Virginia Carlson, Annanella Schultz, Ernestine Lee, and Dorothy Andrews; (second row) Judy Dean, Sharon Suggs, Pamela McNair, Claudine Kirk, Delores Hess, Alice Joy, Ronnie Yates, and Kenneth Bear; (third row) Jerry Roye, Leon Johnson, Lonnie Garner, Jonnie Garner, Sherry Roland, Sus Gage, Becky Hudgins, and Mary Louise Barrington; (fourth row) Robert White, Terry Speed, J.E. Brooks, Jimmy Neece, Jerry Young, Jim Hiner, Paul Nichols. The building was relatively new, but storage was already a problem as can be seen. Lots of art is displayed on the walls and it does not appear to be first grade work.

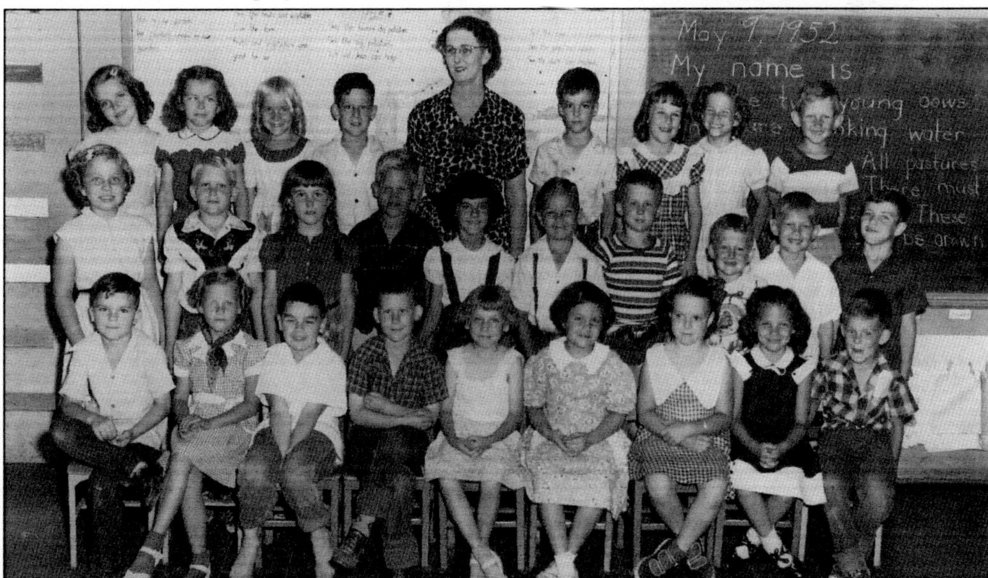

Pictured is Irene Jones, Elisabet Ney Elementary's first grade teacher in 1952. The students are, from left to right, (first row) three unidentified students, Vic Grandjean, unidentified, ? Graves, unidentified, ? Greenberg, and Jimmy Baggett; (second row) Opal Evensole, Royce Wood, unidentified, Bill Holmberg, unidentified, Bill Elliott, Jim Lane, ? Perry, Freddy Haish, and unidentified; (third row) Carol Peace, Judy Hiner, unidentified, Ron Langenkamp, Irene Jones, ? Stewart, and three unidentified students.

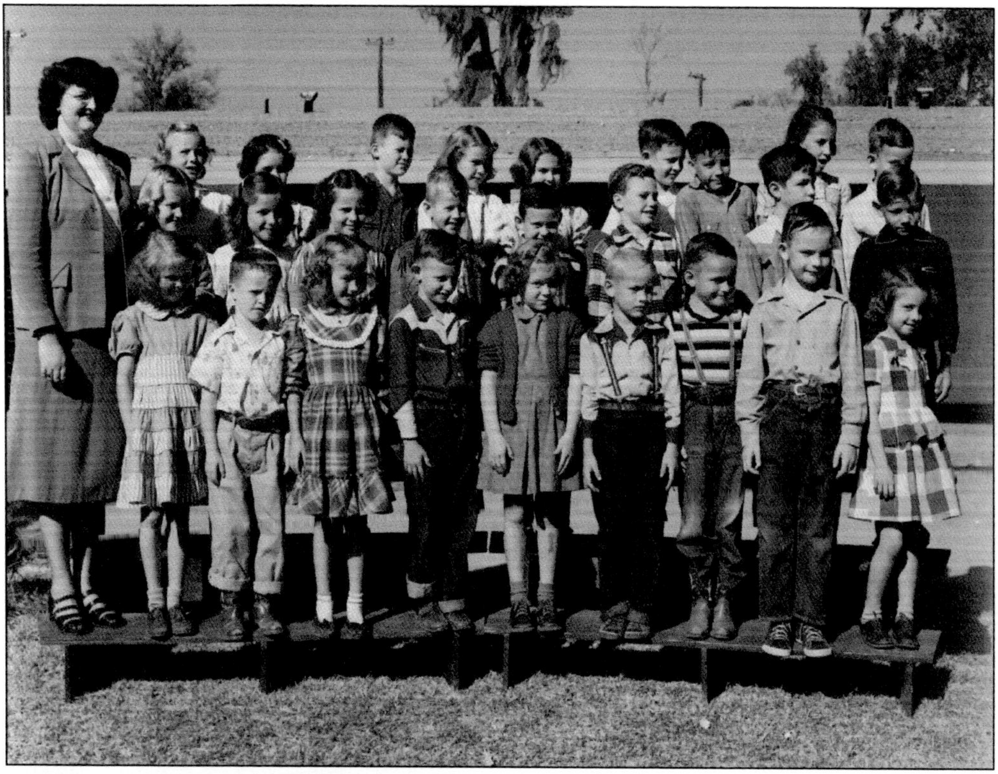

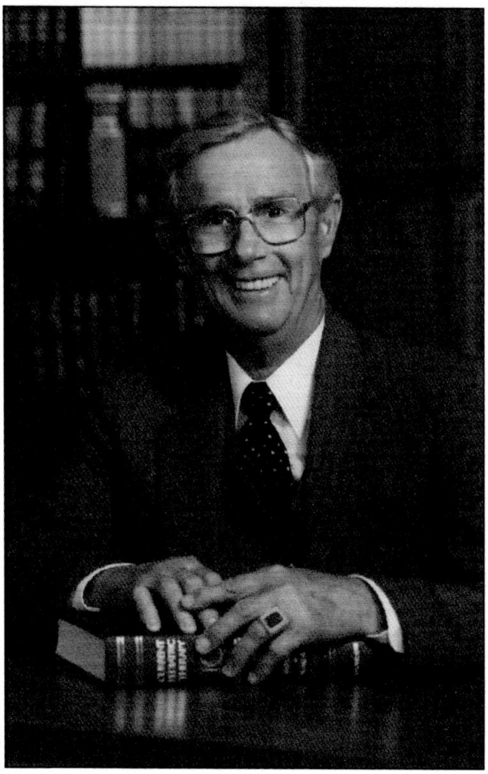

Mrs. Whitehead taught the second grade in 1950. The students are, from left to right, (first row) Portia Fipps, Marshall Bethel, Annanelle Schultz, Ronnie Yates, Becky Hudgins, Charles Kindle, Russell Jasek, Terry Forbes, and Sue Gage; (second row) Carol Jane Marrison, Betty White, Beverly King, Larry Voncannon, Terry Speed, Freddie Hart, James Little, and Edward Reinhart; (third row) Jo Carol Geren, Carolyn Ahlrich, Richard Linnartz, Lyn Boundy, Sharon Suggs, Hollis Meadows, Mac Hester, Mary Louise Barrington, and Bruce Breeding.

Dr. Oscar Johnson was the first pediatrician in Brazoria County. He began his practice with his car as his office on a house call–only basis in 1953. He had just completed his residency. He chose Lake Jackson due to the great number of children and lack of a children's doctor. He practiced until shortly before his death at the age of 63. Johnson was recognized for his leadership for the single most successful immunization campaign in the nation against polio. (Courtesy of the Oscar Johnson Family.)

Four

How Do Creative People Entertain Themselves?

Lake Jackson has always been a collection of highly educated and driven people. Recreational and societal stimulation was a natural outgrowth of such a group. Churches began to form after members initially met in homes and the community house, which was the office for the duplexes and unofficial post office.

Horseback riding was an early recreation. Trails were formed at the lake, which also became a park with a pavilion and barbecue pits. Fishing, picnicking, and feeding ducks became great memories for the many children in town.

Dow Chemical Company formed a community band for both the benefit of the musicians and the local residents. It was known as the Dow Styrene Band initially. The name was eventually changed to the Dow Community Band. Membership was not restricted to employees and local band directors participated.

A garden club formed, and the long growing season promoted beautiful yards. The club also featured arrangements, bringing the exciting floral features inside.

The Jaycees (Junior Chamber of Commerce) was formed in 1943 for young men to teach leadership, provide service, and provide a social setting for the members and their wives. One of the early roles was sorting mail. The Jaycees were a sponsor for the first Boy Scout troop in the area, troop No. 25. For the duration of the local group's life, the Scouts were recognized nationally for their many projects.

The Gators, a very successful semiprofessional softball team, were formed with the assistance of selective hiring by Dow Chemical Company. State and national finals were an indication of the caliber of the team.

An air-conditioned movie theater was designed by Alden Dow and opened in 1945. It provided the only cool location and became a gathering place of many youth. John Heubel purchased the theater in 1948 and operated it until his retirement.

The Masons began meeting in the Brazoria Lodge in 1948 and moved into their own lodge in Lake Jackson in 1953.

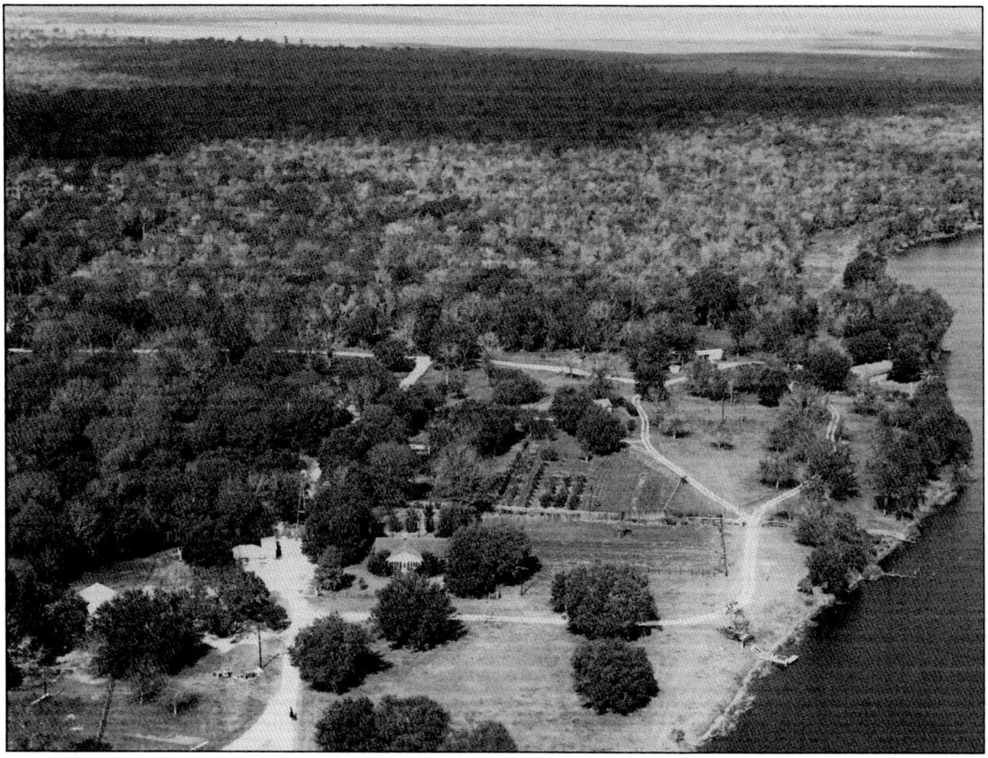

A.P. Beutel, Dow Chemical Company's site manager, had a modest home on Lake Jackson with a large garden and a dock.

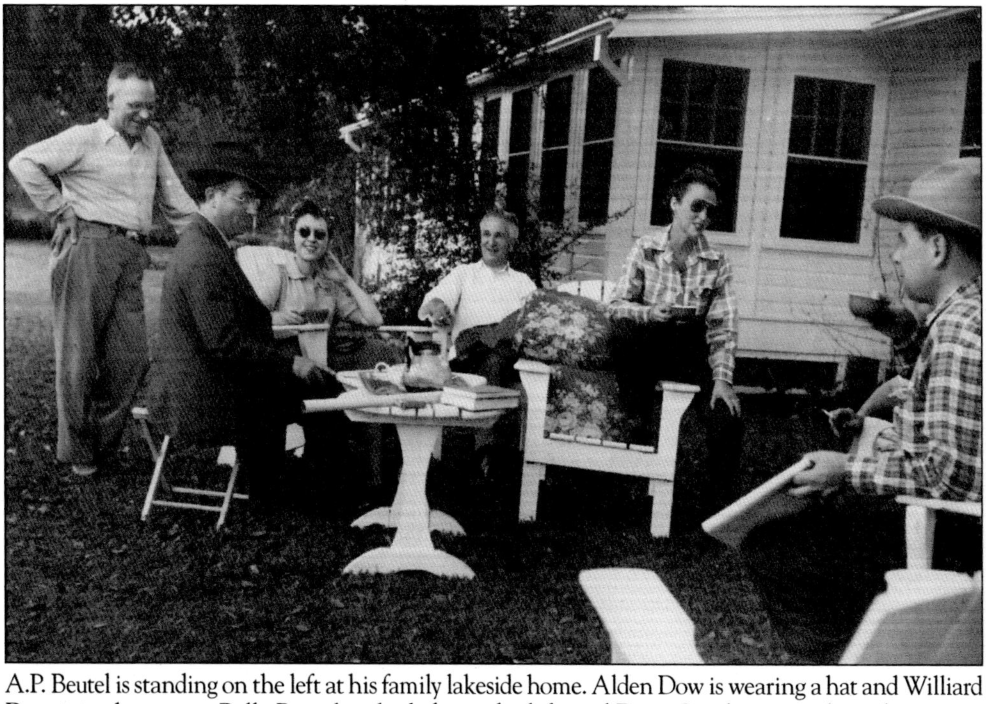

A.P. Beutel is standing on the left at his family lakeside home. Alden Dow is wearing a hat and Williard Dow is in the center. Belle Beutel is the lady on the left, and Davy Crocket is on the right.

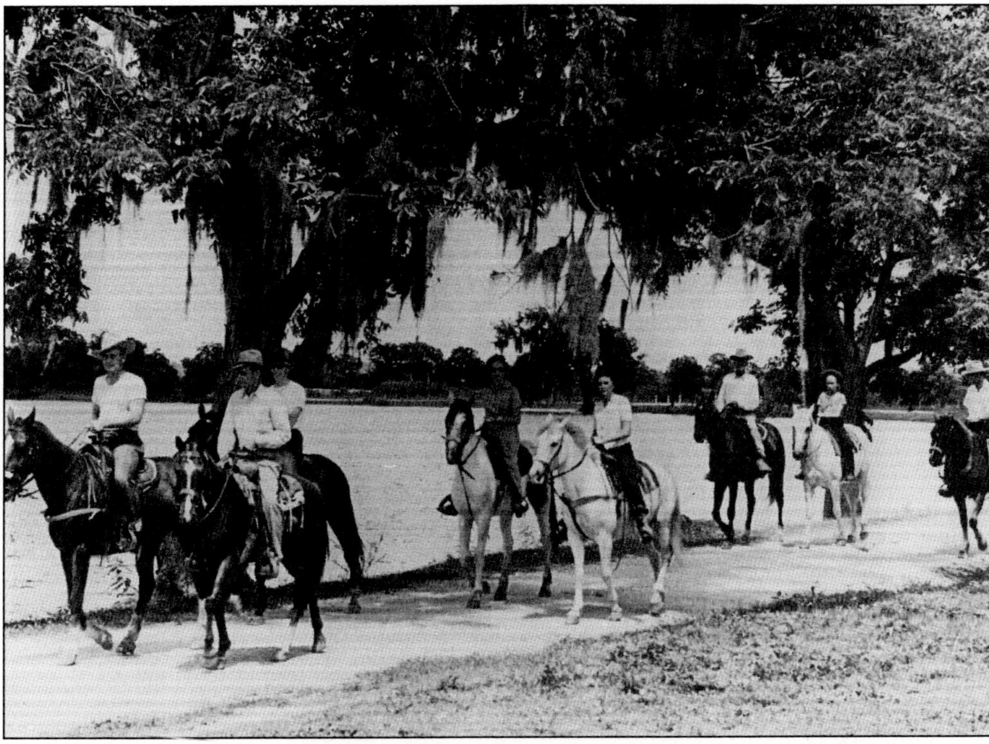

In 1943, recreation included riding at the lakeside on well-developed trails such as this.

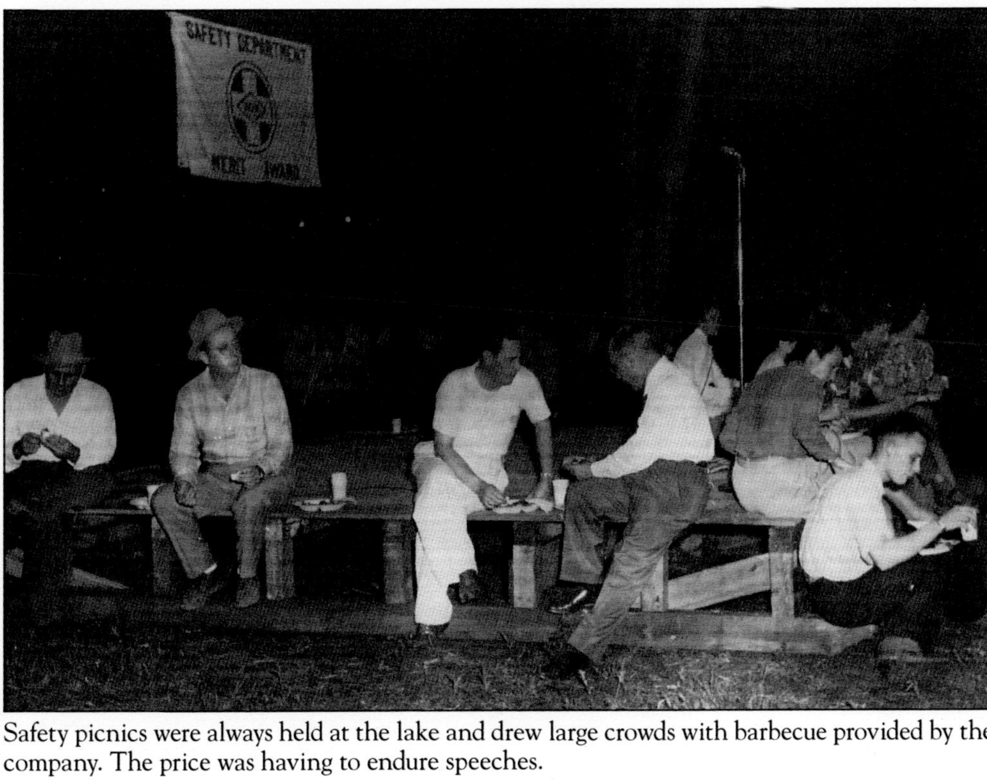

Safety picnics were always held at the lake and drew large crowds with barbecue provided by the company. The price was having to endure speeches.

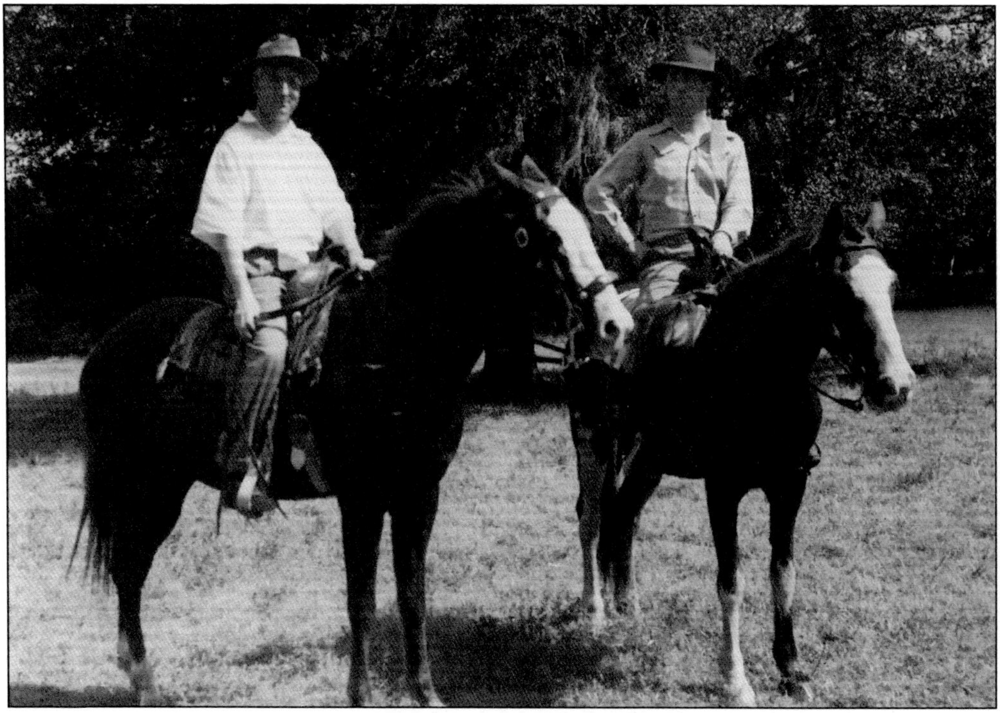

Brothers Willard Dow, left, and Alden Dow enjoy a day of horseback riding. The horse on the right was featured in the movie *Gone with the Wind* as Ashley's steed.

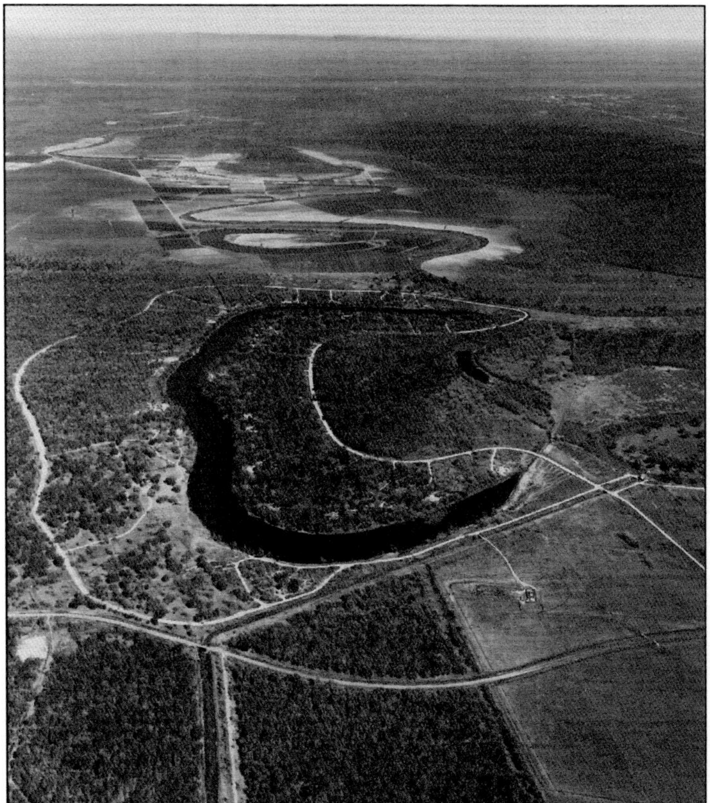

A 1952 aerial view of Lake Jackson shows the Dow Park with access roads through the Lake Jackson Plantation ruins. The old creosote bridge leads across the fresh water canal to a horse barn. Trails can be seen along the lake in the foreground and forgotten riding paths are near the sugar mill. The view is to the northwest. Oyster Creek snakes from the top through the Retrieve Prison Farm.

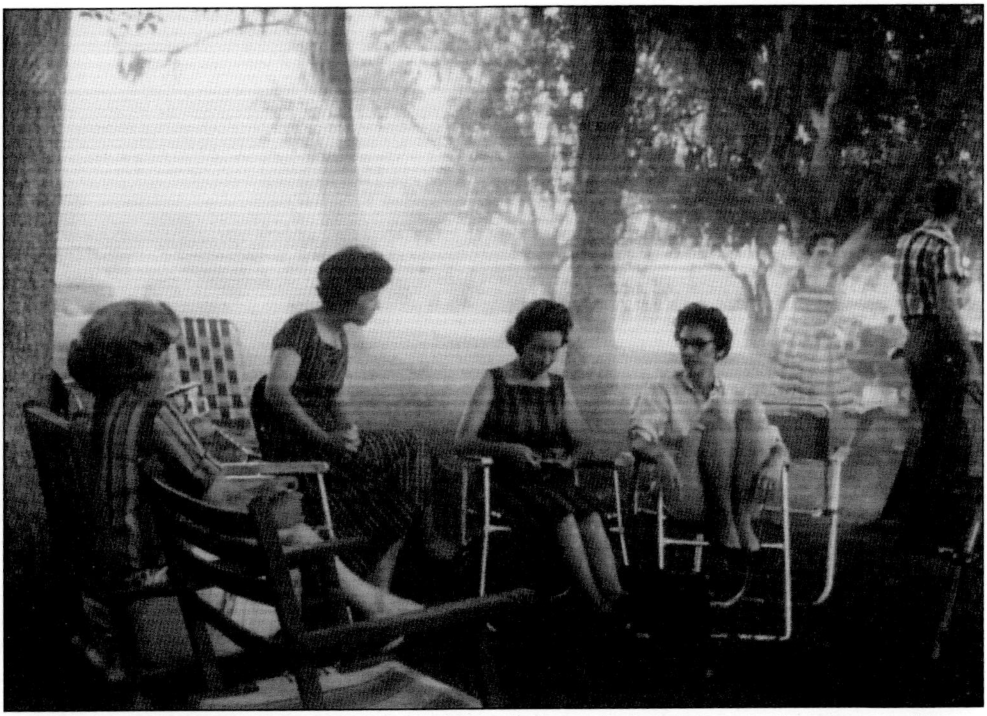

Enjoying a picnic in the 1950s at the lake are, from left to right, Mary Graves, Imo Sansom, Marcia Watzke, and Mickey Rea. Catherine Powell and D.W. Mays are in the background.

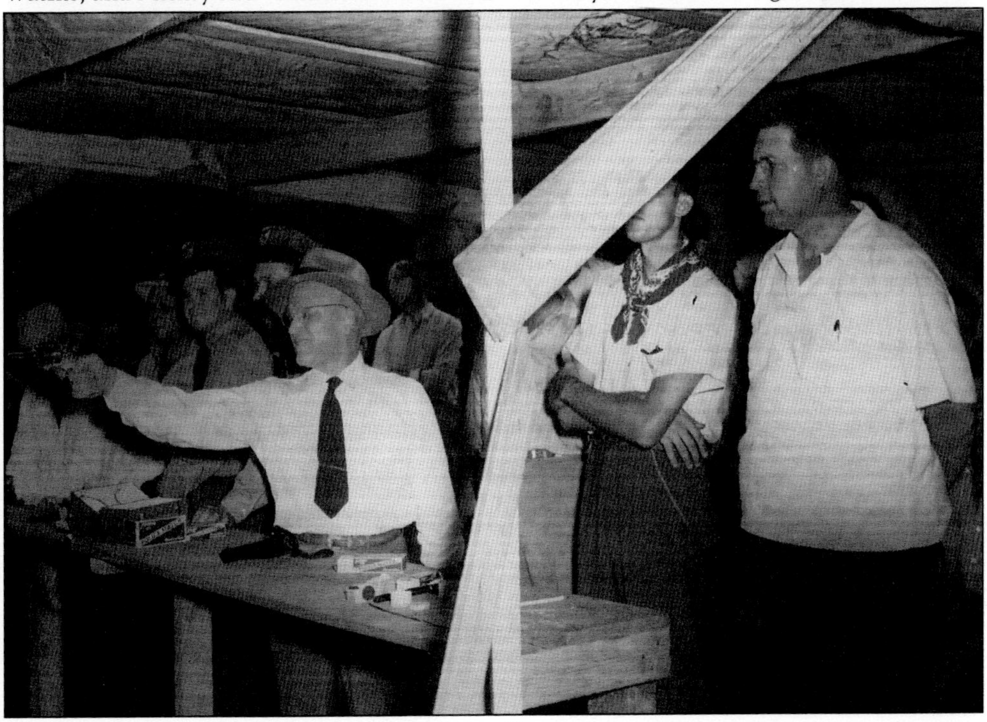

A.P. Beutel, the first site manager for the Dow Chemical Company, was the center of interest with recreational target shooting at a company safety picnic in the 1940s.

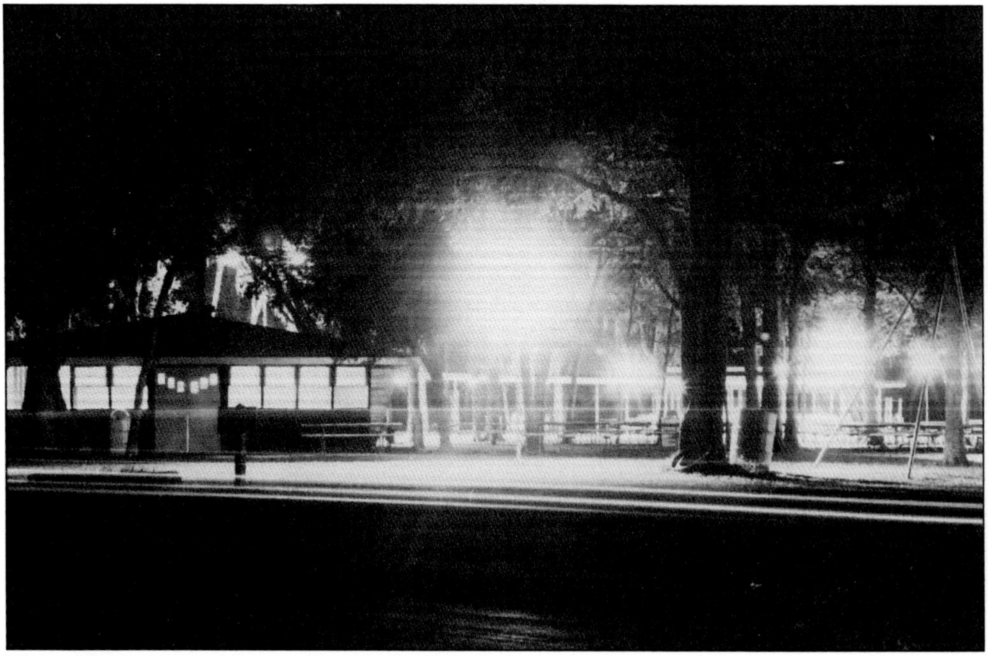

This night picture of the pavilion at the lake was the destination for many of the town's youth on weekends. It was a hike of one to two miles. The barbecue pits were on the right, which were used for Dow Chemical Company safety barbecues, church fundraisers, and the original site of the Brazosport Rotary Shrimp Boil and Auction.

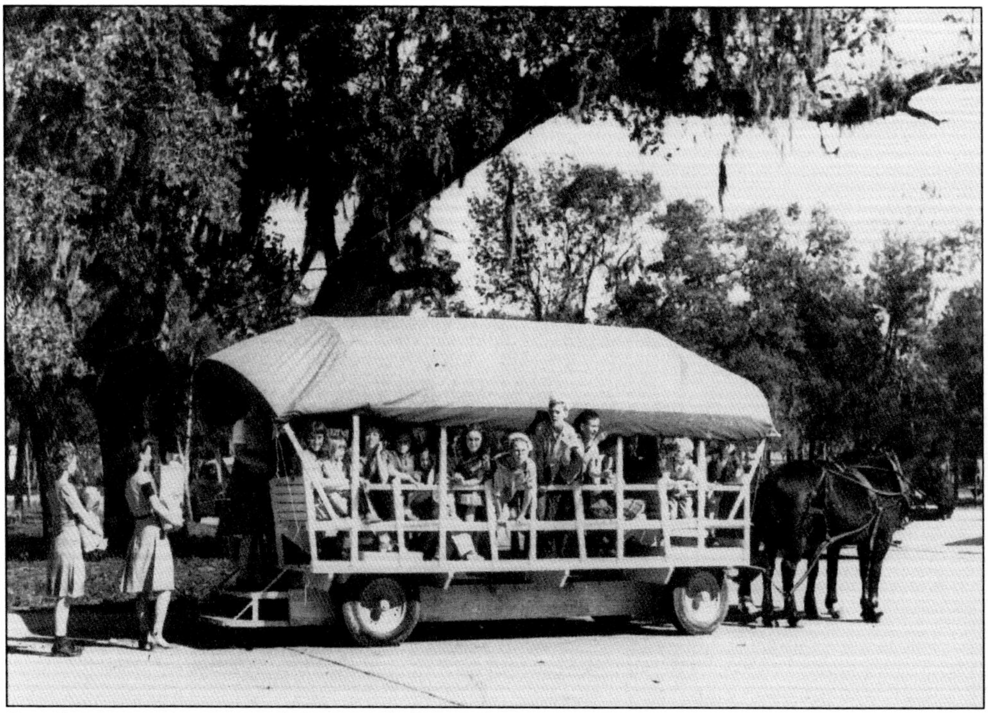

Gasoline rationing required the use of a horse-drawn wagon made of lumber and car axles. There are lots of kids pictured here, but this may be only for the photograph.

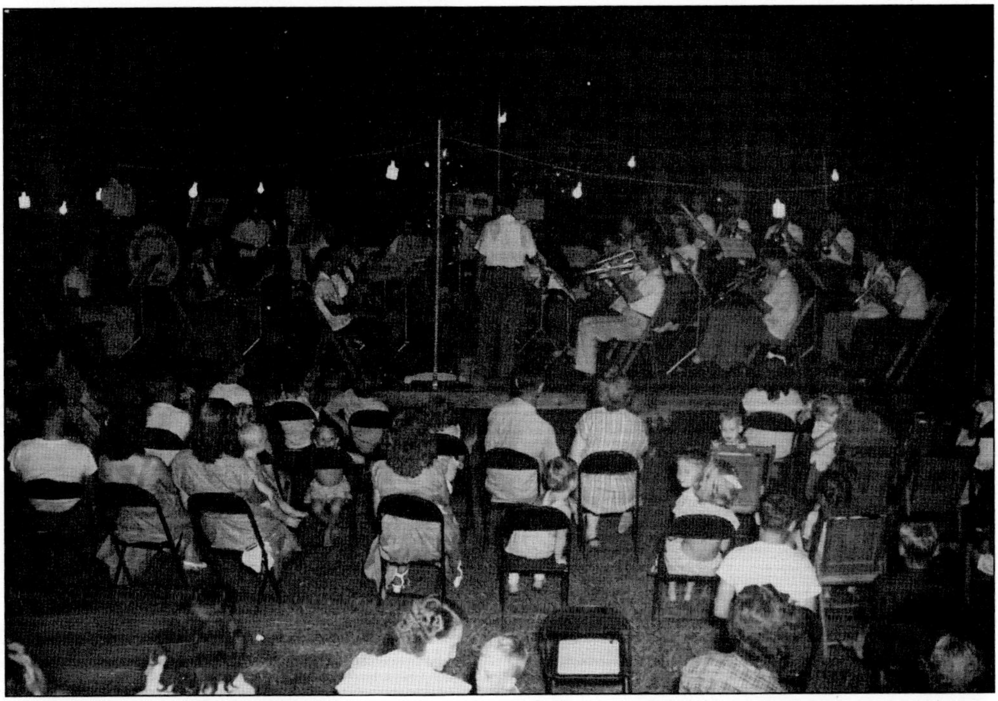

The Dow Concert Band offered an evening's entertainment in 1949. The baby boom had obviously occurred in the city also.

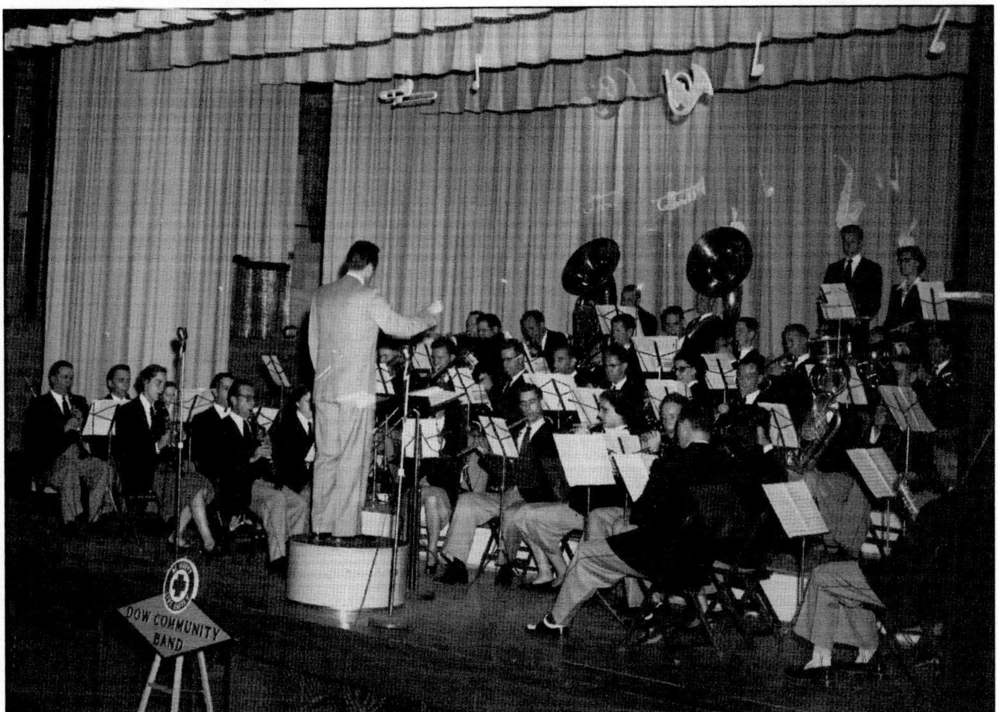

Dow Community Band included school band directors as well as employees. This group was disbanded in 1955.

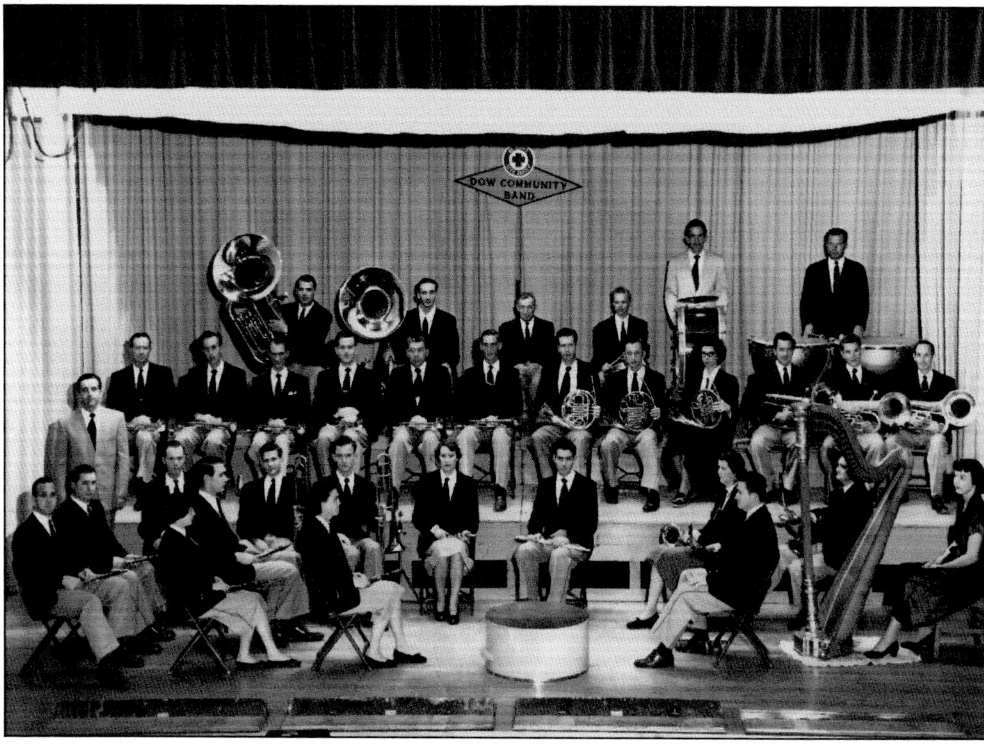

The Dow Community Band offered entertainment from the early 1940s to 1955.

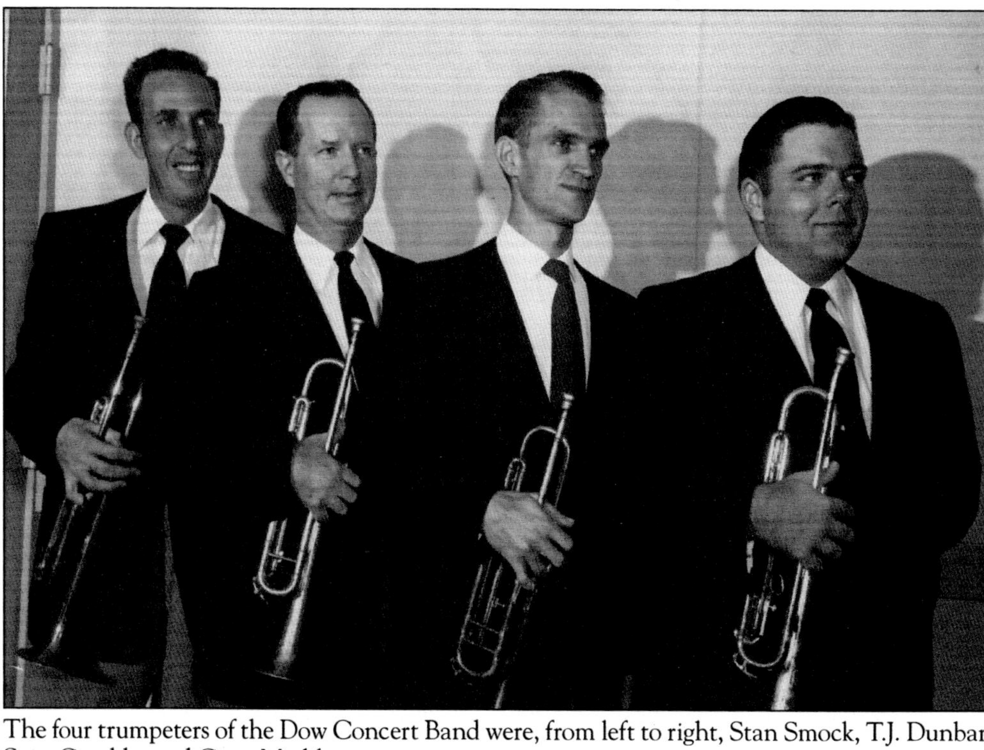

The four trumpeters of the Dow Concert Band were, from left to right, Stan Smock, T.J. Dunbar, Stan Gamble, and Gene Markley.

Virginia Robbins presented a harp solo in 1952 while the band took a break.

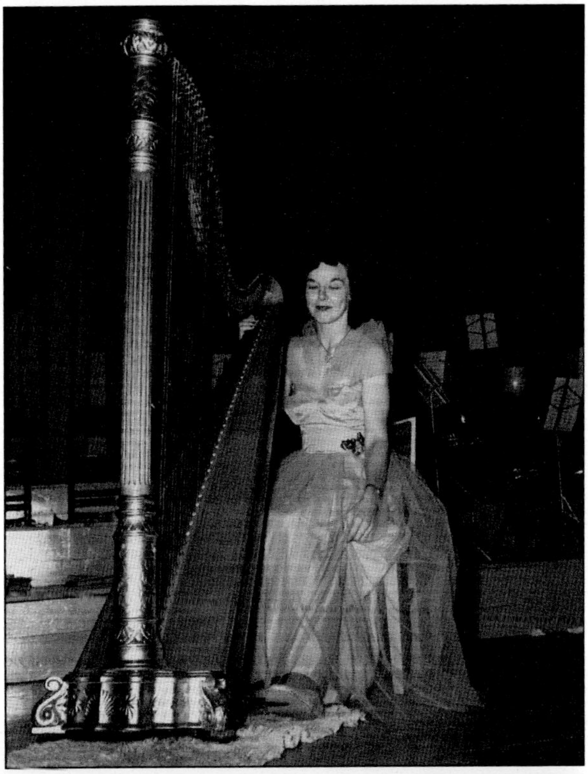

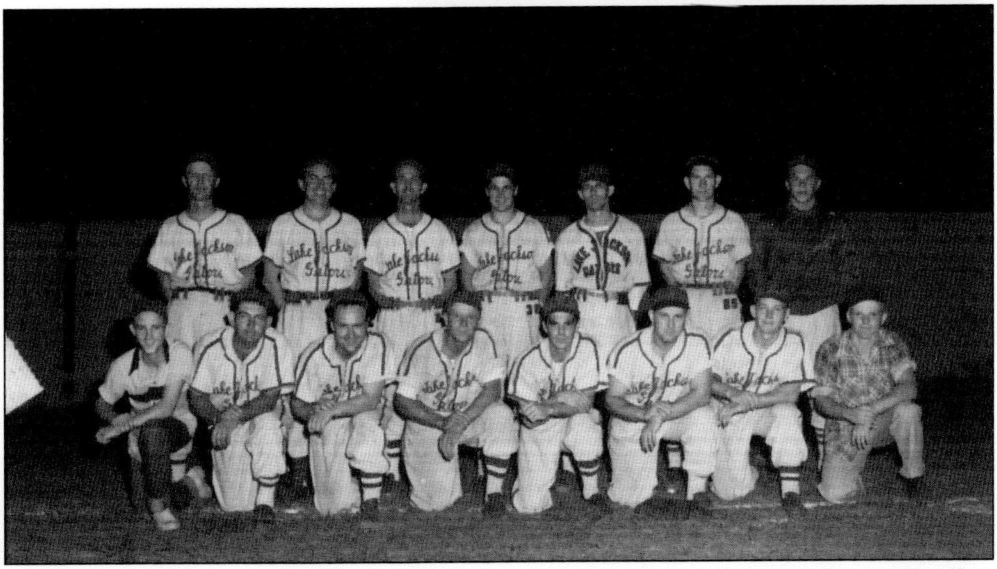

Pictured is the champion softball team Lake Jackson Gators. Members are, from left to right, (first row) Lynne D. Monical, unidentified, Les Tolbirt, Rusty Koenig, Bobby Reed, two unidentified members, and Darwin Schmidt; (second row) Ed Pisklak, Speedy Bullard, Soapy Lee, Billy Moore, Gene Faull, Clayton Dugger, and Kyo Koym. They were sponsored by the Lake Jackson Business Men's Association and formed in 1946. They were the state champions in 1946, 1950, 1951, 1953, 1955, and 1956. In 1953 and 1956, they also won the Southwest Regional Tournament. They went to nationals in Miami in 1953 and Sacramento in 1956. They disbanded in 1963.

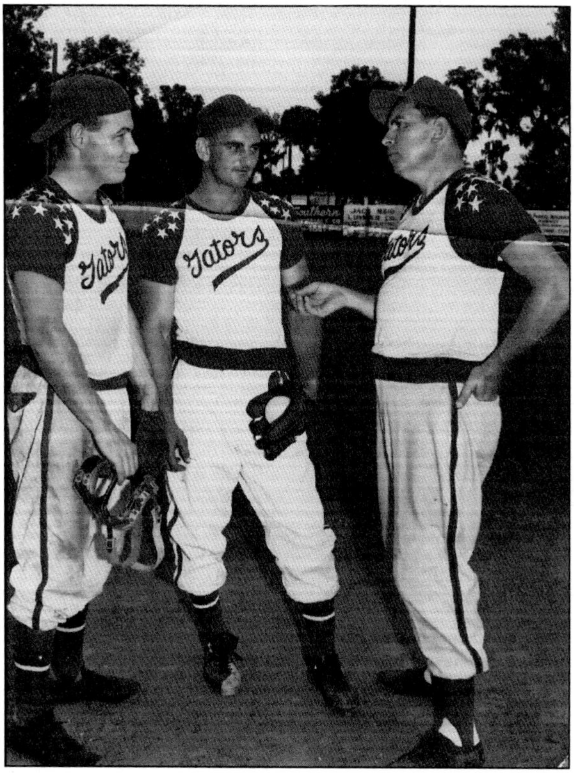

In 1952, three of the Gators were featured in the *Brazorian News*. They are, from left to right, Larry McGowan, Wilbur McGill, and Speedy Bullard.

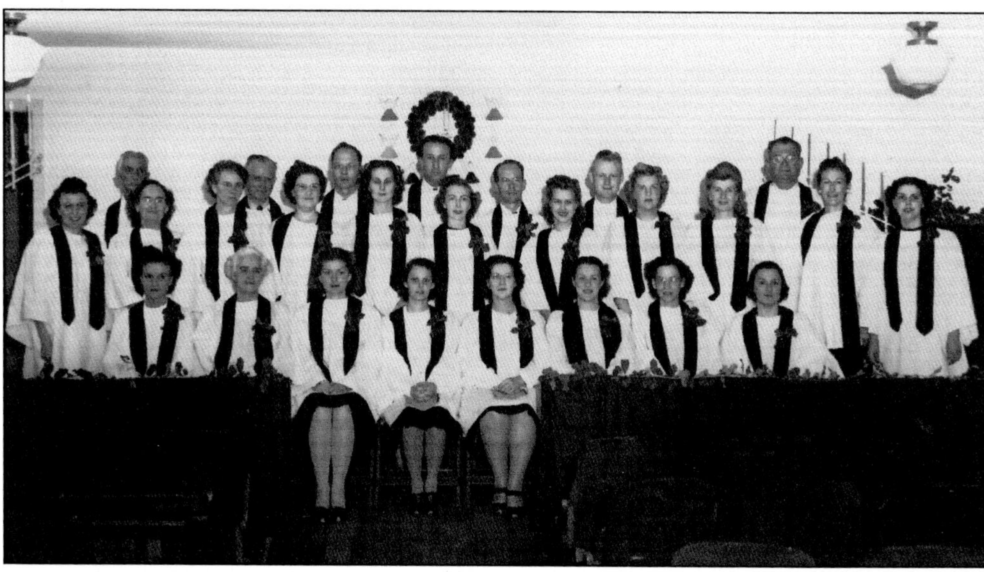

The Methodist Church was organized in 1943. It met in the community center in the duplexes. The members are, from left to right, (first row) Ethelyn Raney, unidentified, Virginia (Brown) Mays, Virginia Murrell, director Gail Douglas, unidentified, Bernice Gibbs, and Marie Bridges; Margaret Israel, Kitty Waller, Edna Skeete, unidentified, Ruth Epps, ? Bagg, Madalyn Reichenbach, Sena Colegrove, unidentified, Alada Callerain, and Iris Durham; (third row) three unidentified, Lawrence Epps, Troy Israel, unidentified, and "Major" Bridges. (Courtesy of the First United Methodist Church.)

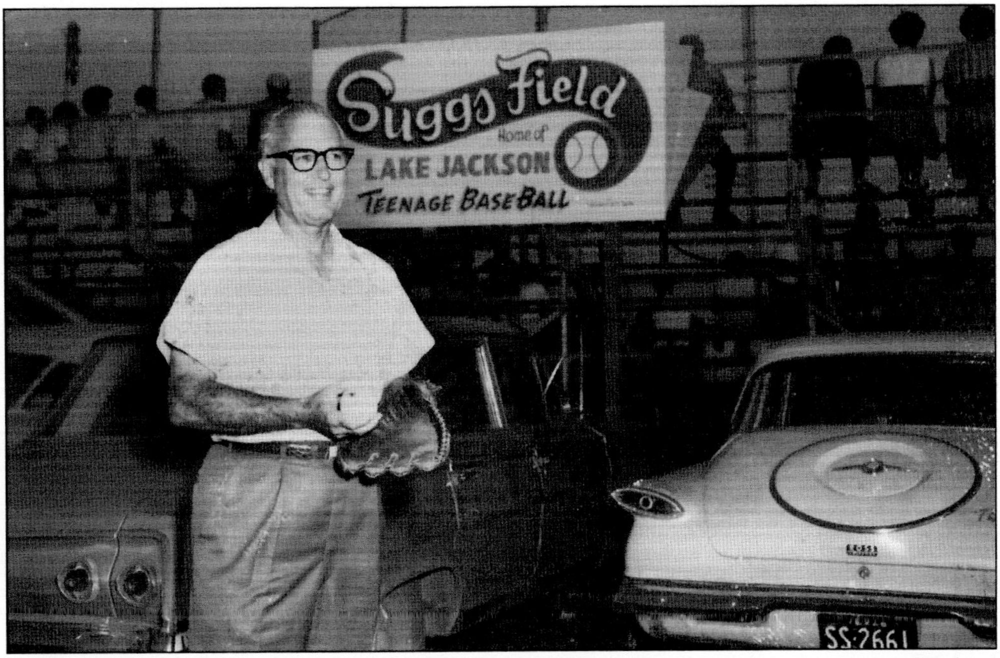

Johnny Suggs was a young engineer for Dow Chemical Company in the 1940s. He was involved in the selection of the location of Lake Jackson. His personal claim to fame was the shapes of the curbs in the city; they did not require being cut for residential driveways. He became a business owner and philanthropist. He contributed the land that provided several baseball fields for Lake Jackson's youth. The fields were named in his honor.

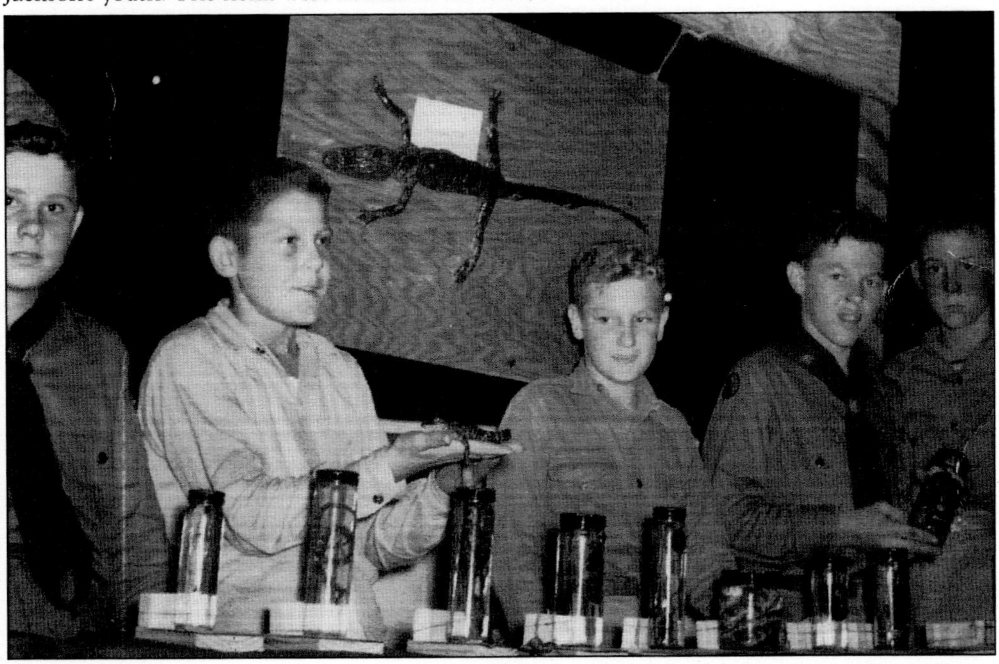

These Lake Jackson Scouts show their reptile collections. Concerned citizens, according to Scout records, sponsored the first troop—troop No. 25. The next sponsor was the Jaycees until about 1958 when the First Methodist Church assumed responsibility.

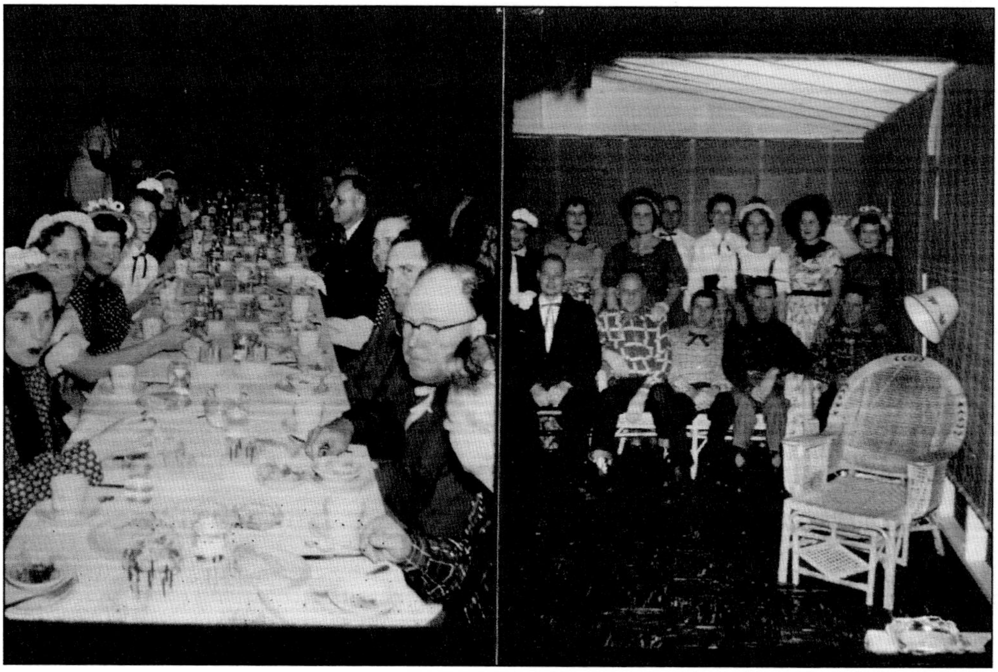

People gathered to celebrate the 10th anniversary of the city in 1953. At the table on the left side, from front to back, are Dickey Nowlin, Shirley DiPucio, Edna Walters, Lorraine Sullivan, and Lucille Floyd. On the right side, from front to back, are two unidentified people, Charlie DiPucio, Joe Walters, and Clayton Leak. In the picture on the right, from left to right, are (first row) Clayton, Finus Floyd, Acie Sullivan, Charlie DiPucio, and Roy Harper; (second row) Vera Leak, Beth Harper Morris, Lucille Floyd, Joe Walters, Dottie Mitchell, Shirley DiPucio, Nadine Harper, and Edna Walters.

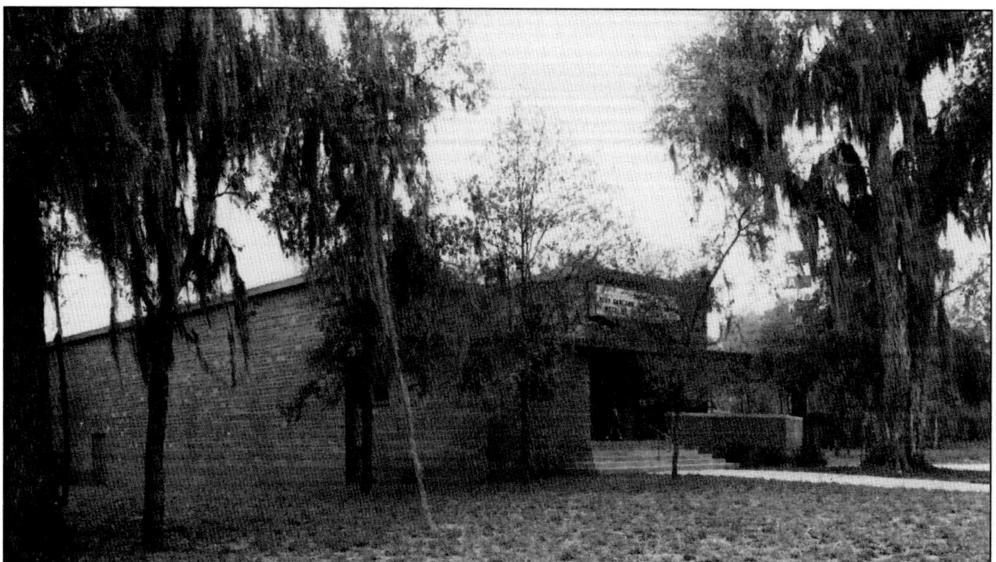

The Lake Theater was the only air-conditioned building in town in the late 1940s. John Heubel was the owner and he knew all the children in town who came to the movies frequently. Everyone had in their homes a schedule of all the upcoming movies for the month.

A 1951 city event honored Gene Franklin with a "This is Your Life" program. Educator Grady Rasco, on the left, acted as the master of ceremonies. Gene's husband, Bob, is on the right.

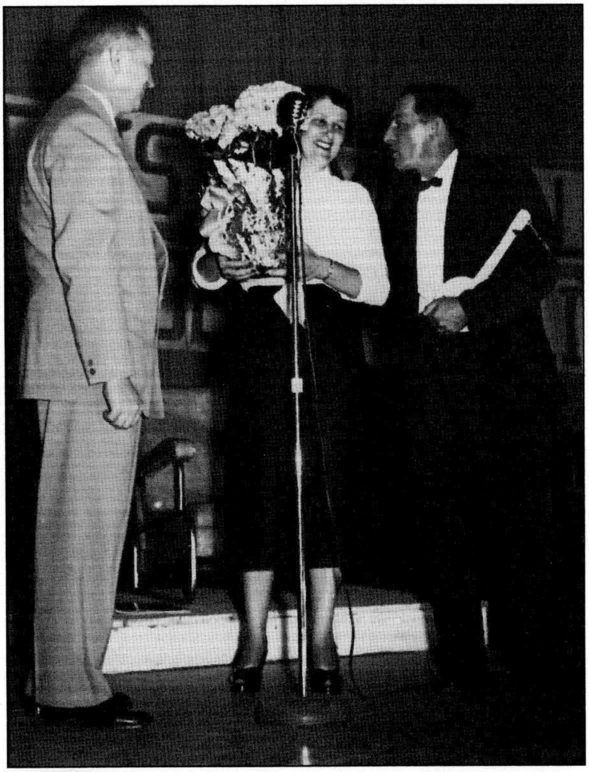

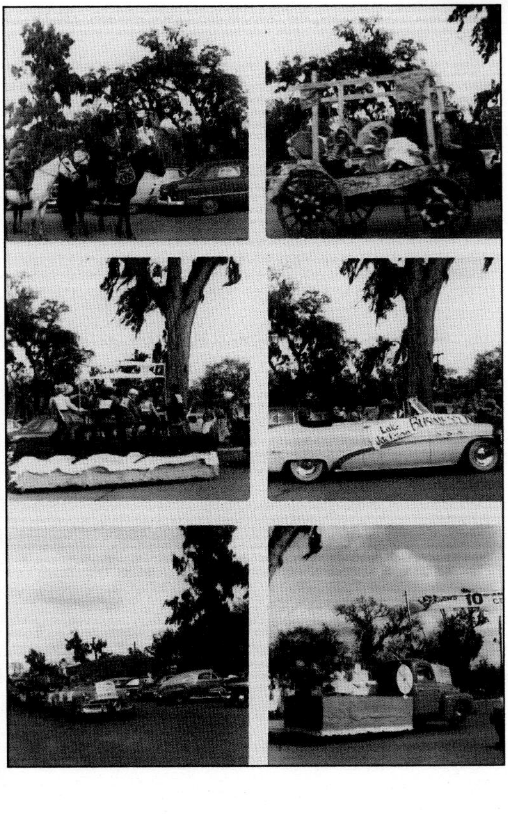

The 10th anniversary of the city was celebrated with a parade in 1953.

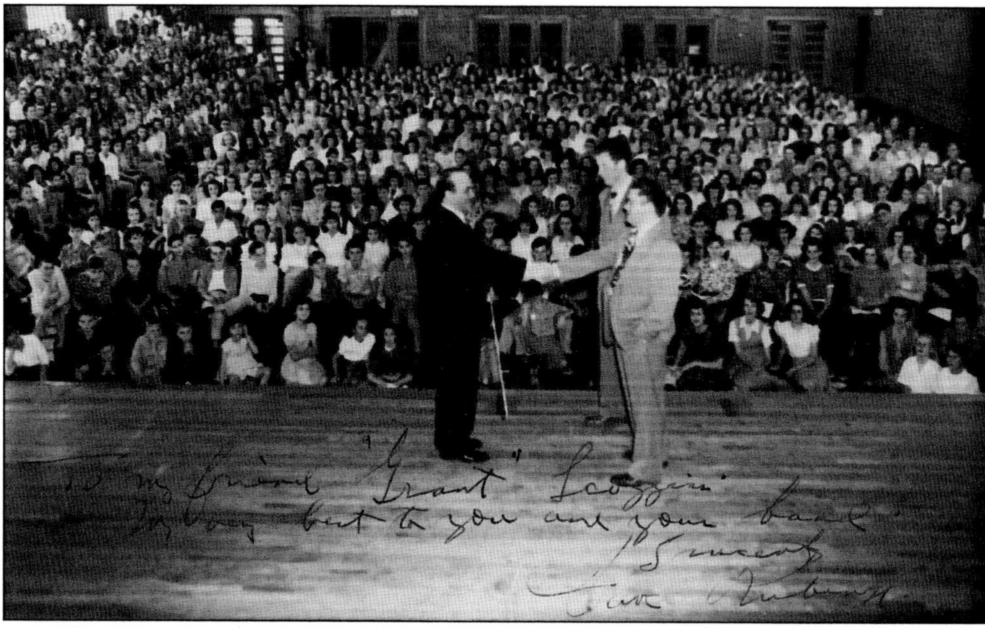

Grant Scoggins, the junior high band director (taller man on the right), welcomes a dignitary in the school auditorium and basketball gym. He received this autographed picture signed by Dave Rubinoff, and his magic violin, whose fame has faded since this day in 1949. The third person is a local sponsor, such as a member of the Jaycees who had funded the celebrity visit.

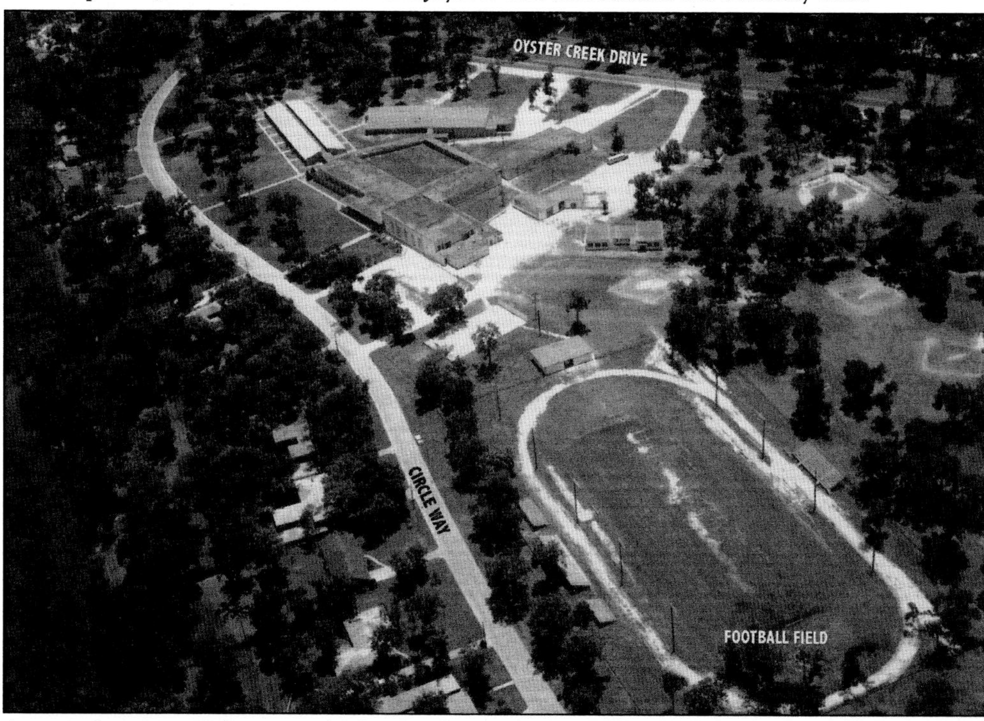

An aerial picture of the junior high school in 1960 shows the evolution of a football field with lights, seats, and a rudimentary track. A baseball field is present with several practice fields. There is a bus in one of the lots.

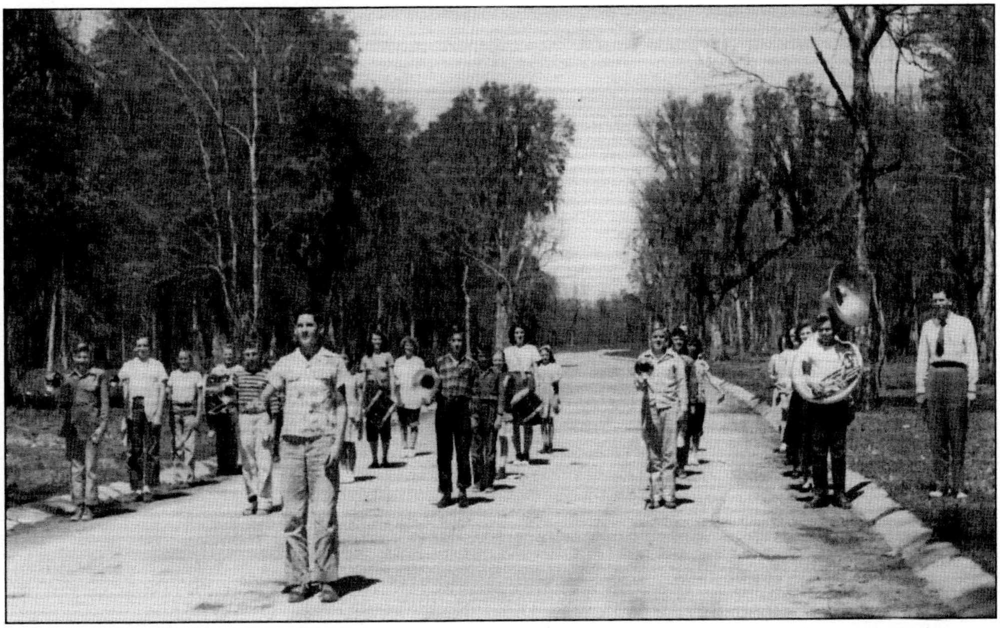

Grant Scoggins was the first band director for the junior high, serving from 1947 to 1956. This was the 1947–1948 A band. Members are, from left to right, Travis Wilkes, Kenneth Muckelroy, J.E. Coburn, Darwin Schmidt (bass drum) Charles Seibert, and Dayton Grover (drum major). Inez Cobb is behind the snare drummer. Wade Jones and Carlton Hall are in the middle column, and Travis Bundy leads the fourth column from the left. Scoggins is to the right of the group.

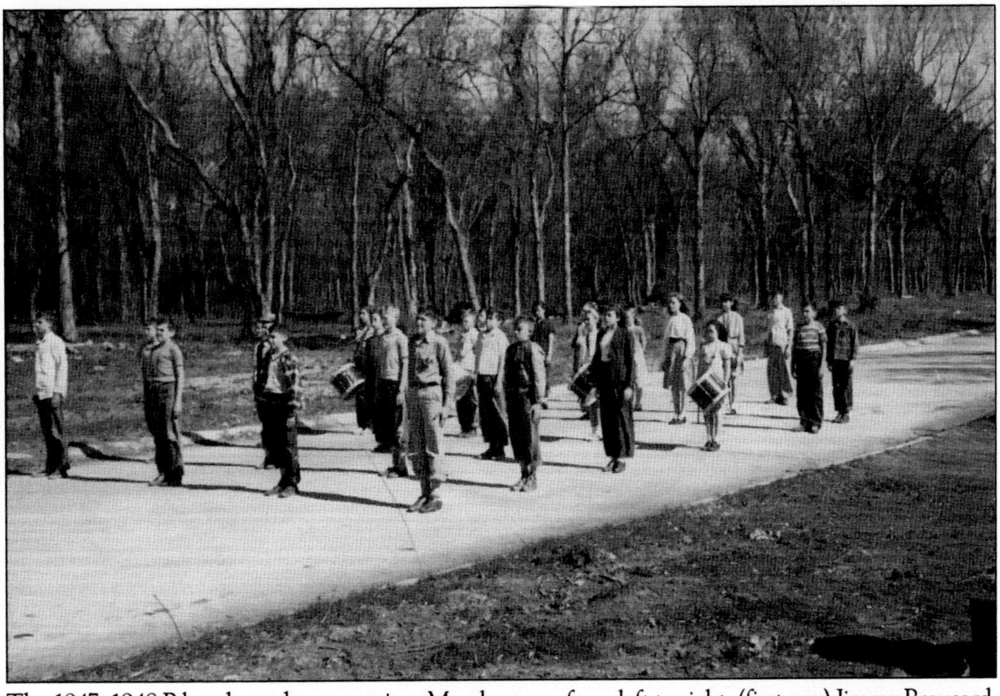

The 1947–1948 B band stands at attention. Members are, from left to right, (first row) Jimmy Brousard, John Alvinzene, Alton Sanders, and Leroy Cast with Randall Terry behind Alton. Behind Leroy are Harold Earl Monical, Doris Riggan, Jackie Bonnet, Jerry Pouson, and Tommy Suggs.

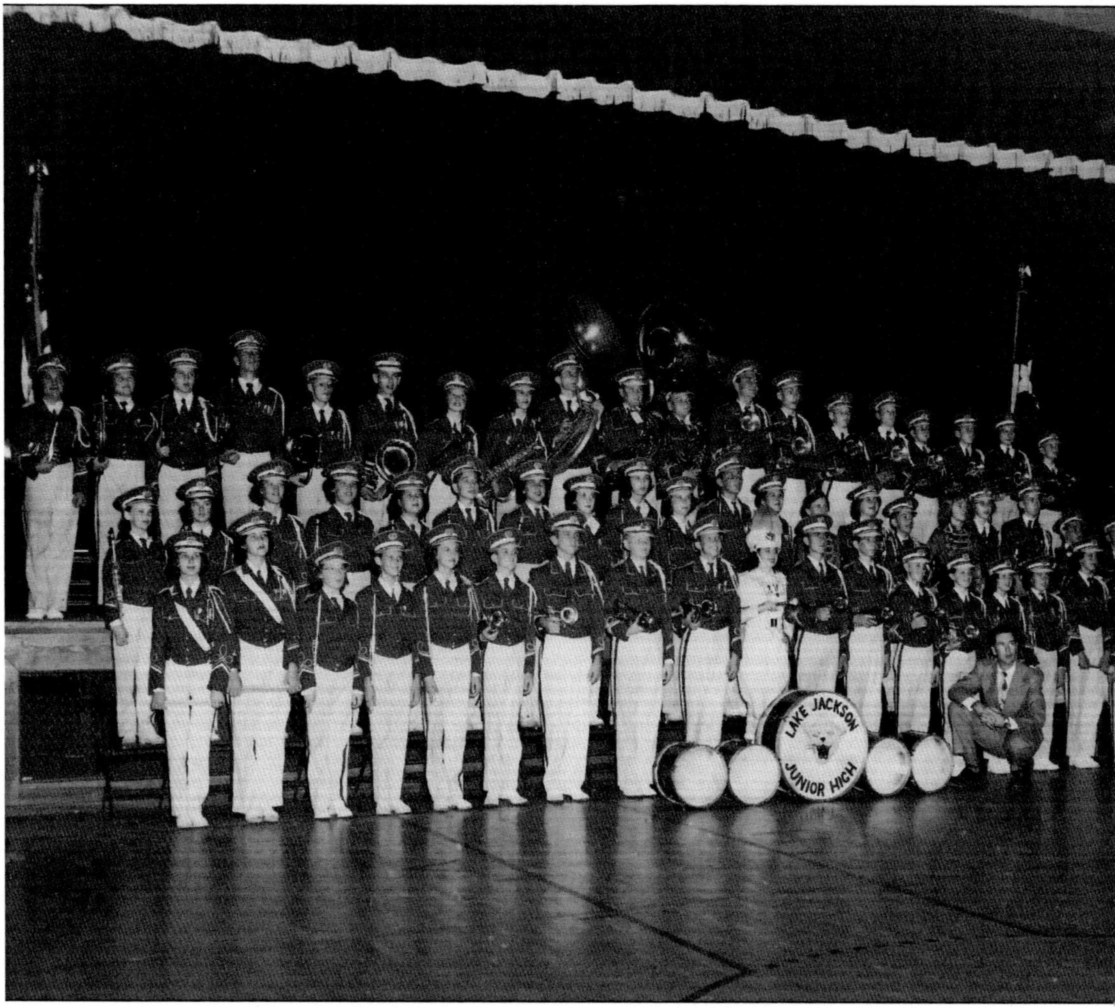

Grant Scroggins is with the 1950–1951 junior high band. The band had uniforms at this time but that practice was discontinued within 10 years. Students included Faralou Alford, Neoma Antilli, L.B. Barnett, Jackie Bennett, Burnie Blackburn, Claydell Blackburn, Jewel Bradshaw, Carolyn Brewer, Harvey Browning, Peggy Browning, Carliene Carpenter, Gene Caskey, Leroy Cast, Johnny Cooke, Rovert Coyner, Ruth Crowely, Jack Cutshall, James Elbert, Carol Ann Floyd, Don Floyd, Eugene Foster, Bill Frizzell, Joan Garrett, Killian Gibbs, Jerry Hoobler, Gaylen Jones, Marilyn Jordan, Jerry Jordon, Kay Kirk, Kenneth Kyle, Leonard Kyle, Ervilene La Gasse, Sherry Leak, Fain Lindveit, Linda Looper, Ruth Lorton, Reber Mann, Joan Malone, Harold Monical, Mary Helen Muckelroy, Mary Nelson, Marilyn Newson, Beverly Newton, Karline Perkins, Edward Pate, Ronald Perryman, Dana Prather, Phyllis Pratt, Shirley Pruitt, Jerry Pousson, Kathrine Ramey, Loyd Reinhart, Curtis Richards, Doris Riggan, Raymond Ripple, Frank Ripson, George Sander, and Wanda San.

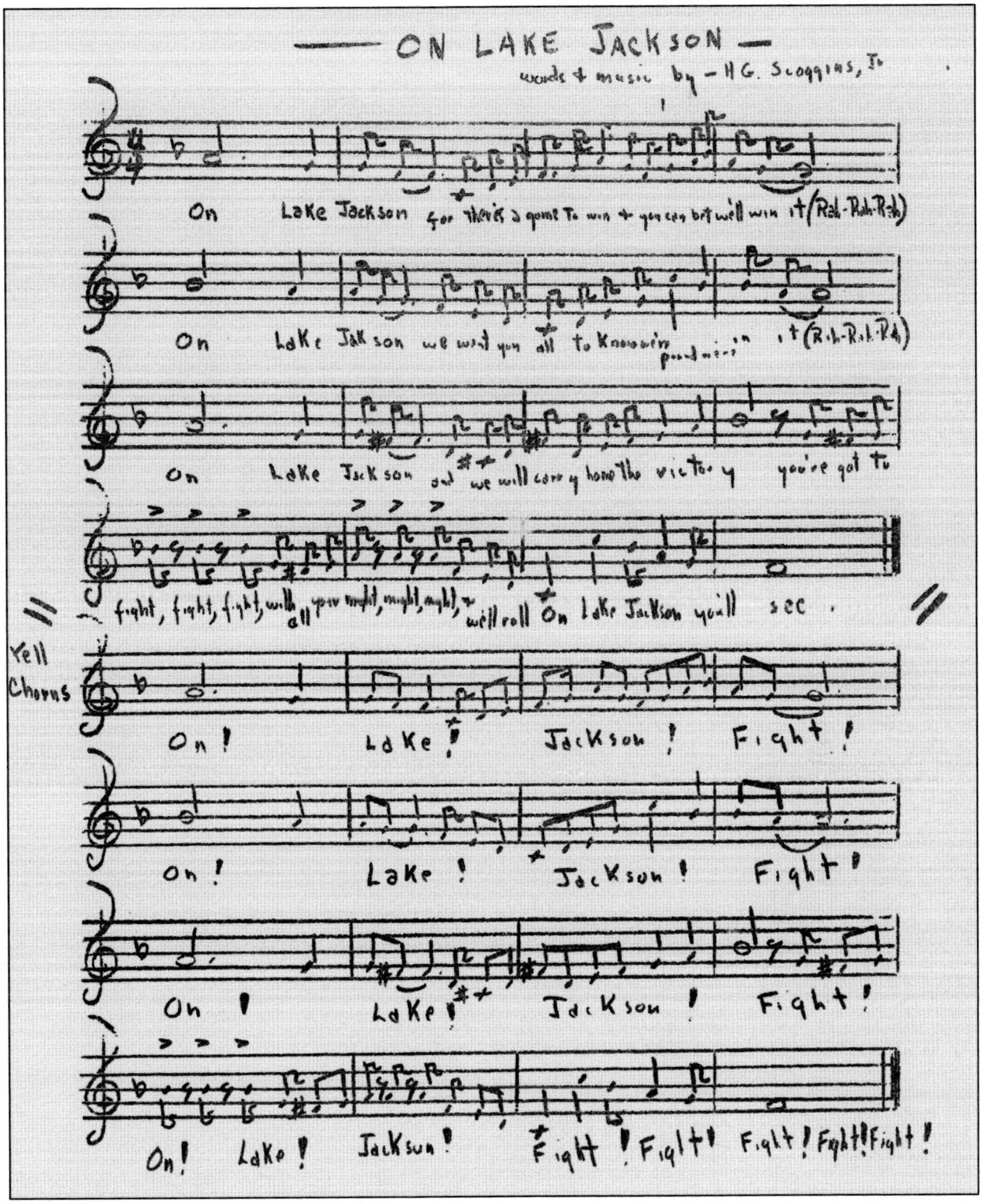

Grant Scoggins wrote "On Lake Jackson" for the new school in 1947. The handwritten music was reproduced by mimeograph.

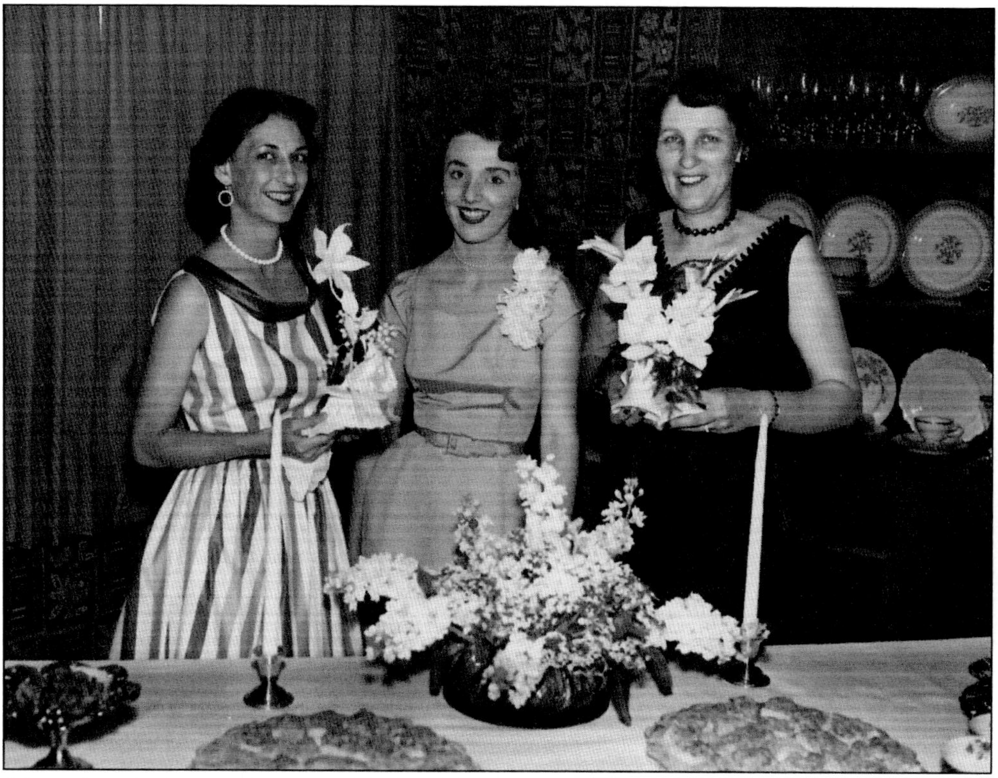

These three ladies were hosting a 1945 wedding reception. They are, from left to right, Margaret Scoggins, Sandra Wilcox, and Gene Franklin.

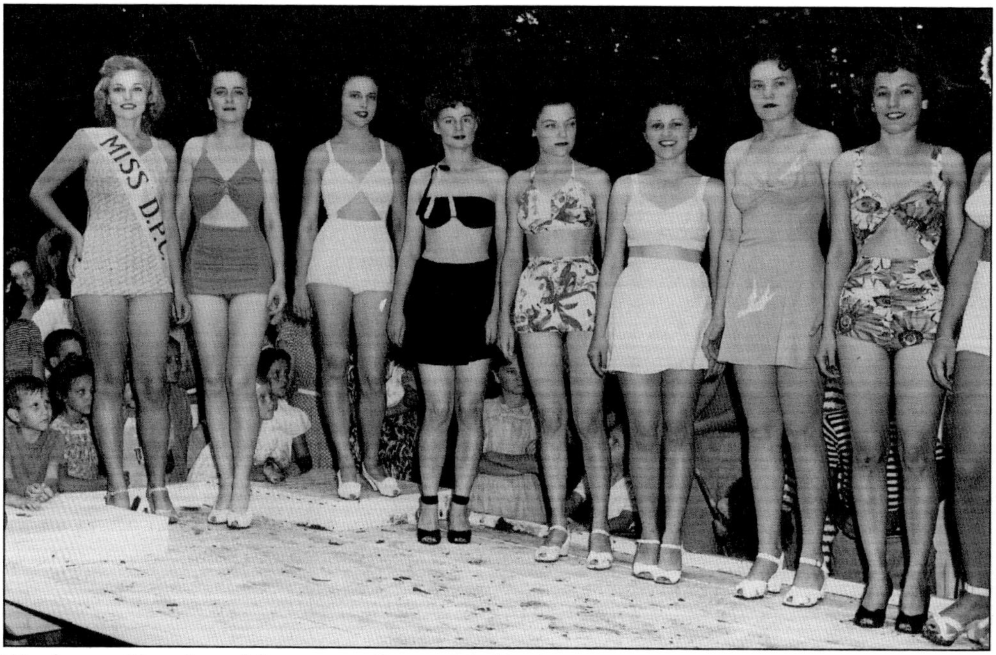

The Junior Chamber of Commerce (Jaycees) held a beauty contest in 1945. The first woman on the left is June Weidie (Epps), second is Betty Ansley, and fourth from left is Miss Wilkes.

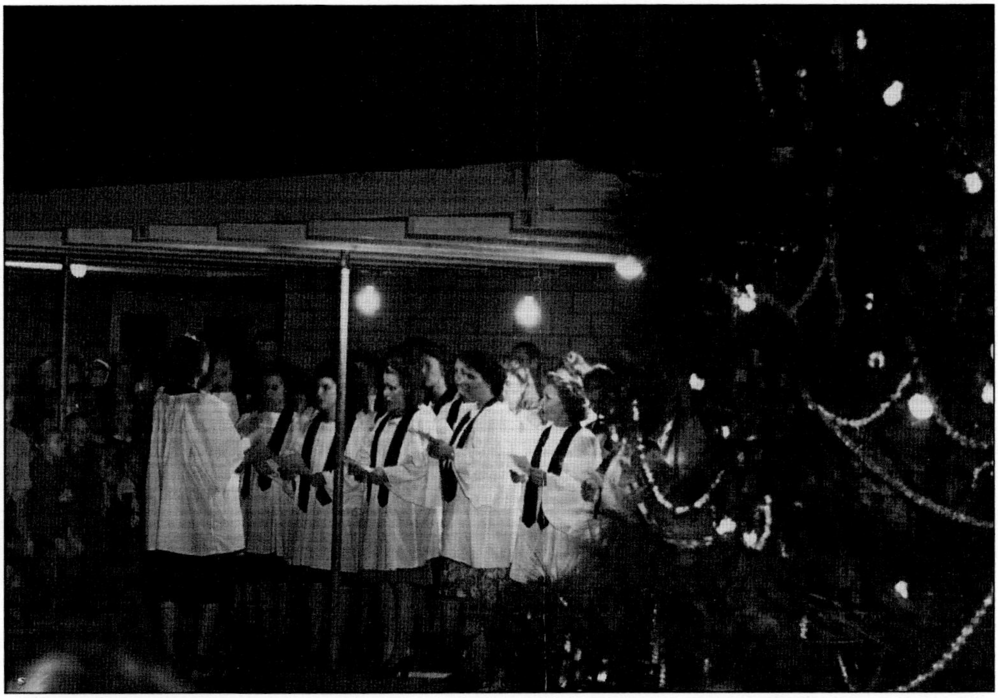

The choirs of the First Baptist and Methodist Churches combine to sing at the Jaycees Christmas party in 1944. (Courtesy of First United Methodist Church.)

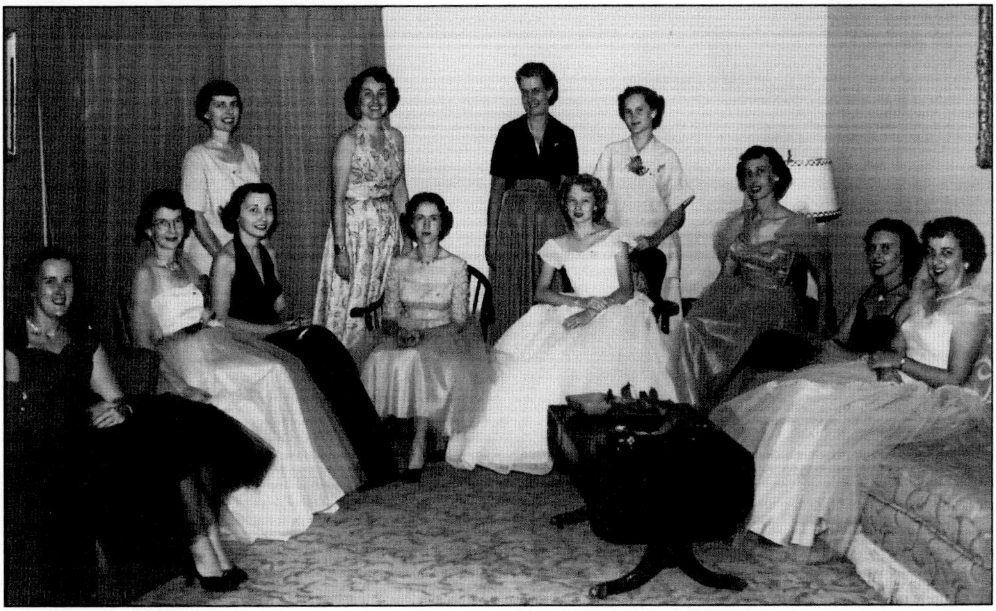

Beta Sigma Phi-Nu Mu Chapter, a social and cultural sorority, was established in Lake Jackson in 1953. Several of the ladies transferred from Freeport and other Texas cities. This picture of an early meeting shows how formal the attire was. The members are, from left to right, (first row) Beverly Clarke, Betty Hausman, Joyce Carman, Elaine Oelfke, Flora Alice Hamilton, Margie Grisham, Myrtle Turner, and Frances Romer; (second row) Joyce Mitchell, Mary Alice Egleson, Frances Lindveit (sponsor), and Myrtie Logsdon. Hausman is still active as of 2010.

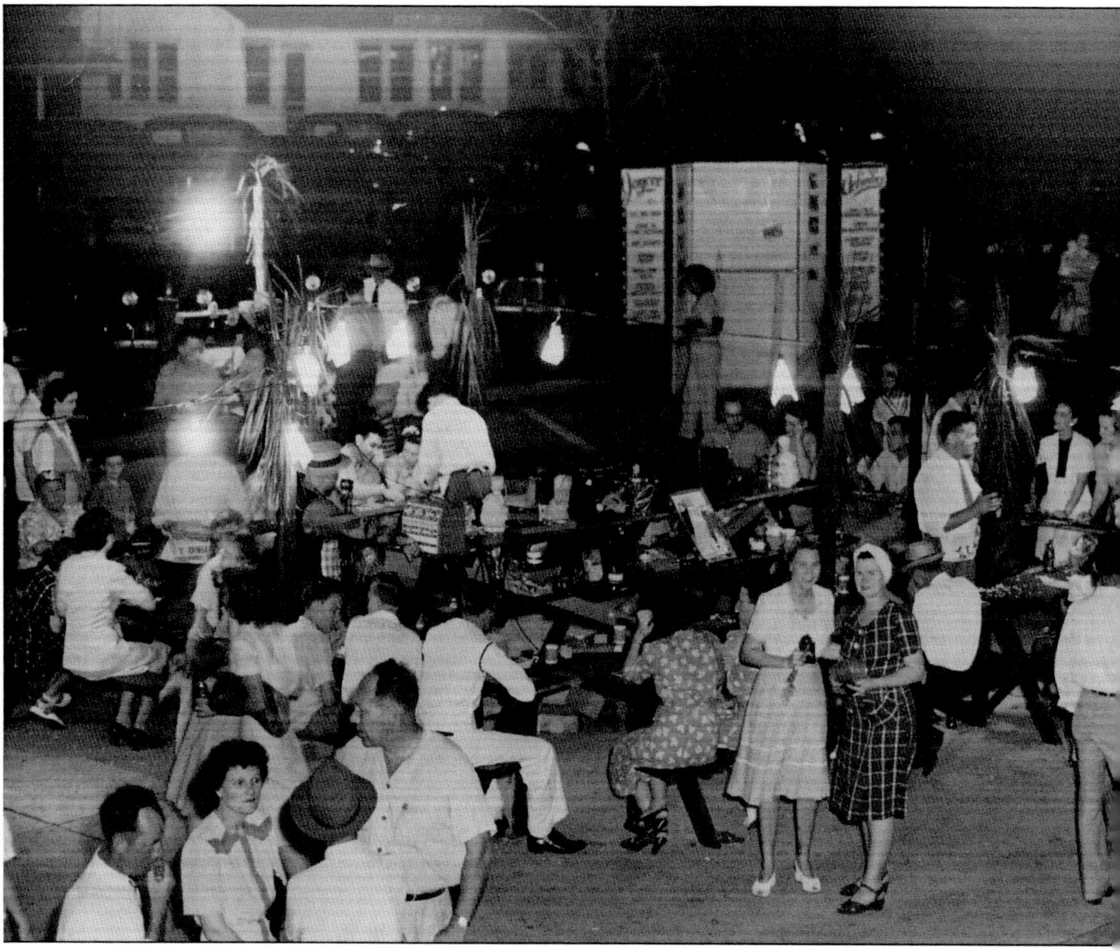

The Jaycees, a young men's service group, had a fundraiser in the 1940s. The organization was both service and social. Members sorted mail for the city, sponsored the Boy Scouts, organized the Fourth of July celebration, and much more. Glen Lateer is identified fifth from left on the bottom. Peggy Kirtley is in a white blouse in the foreground.

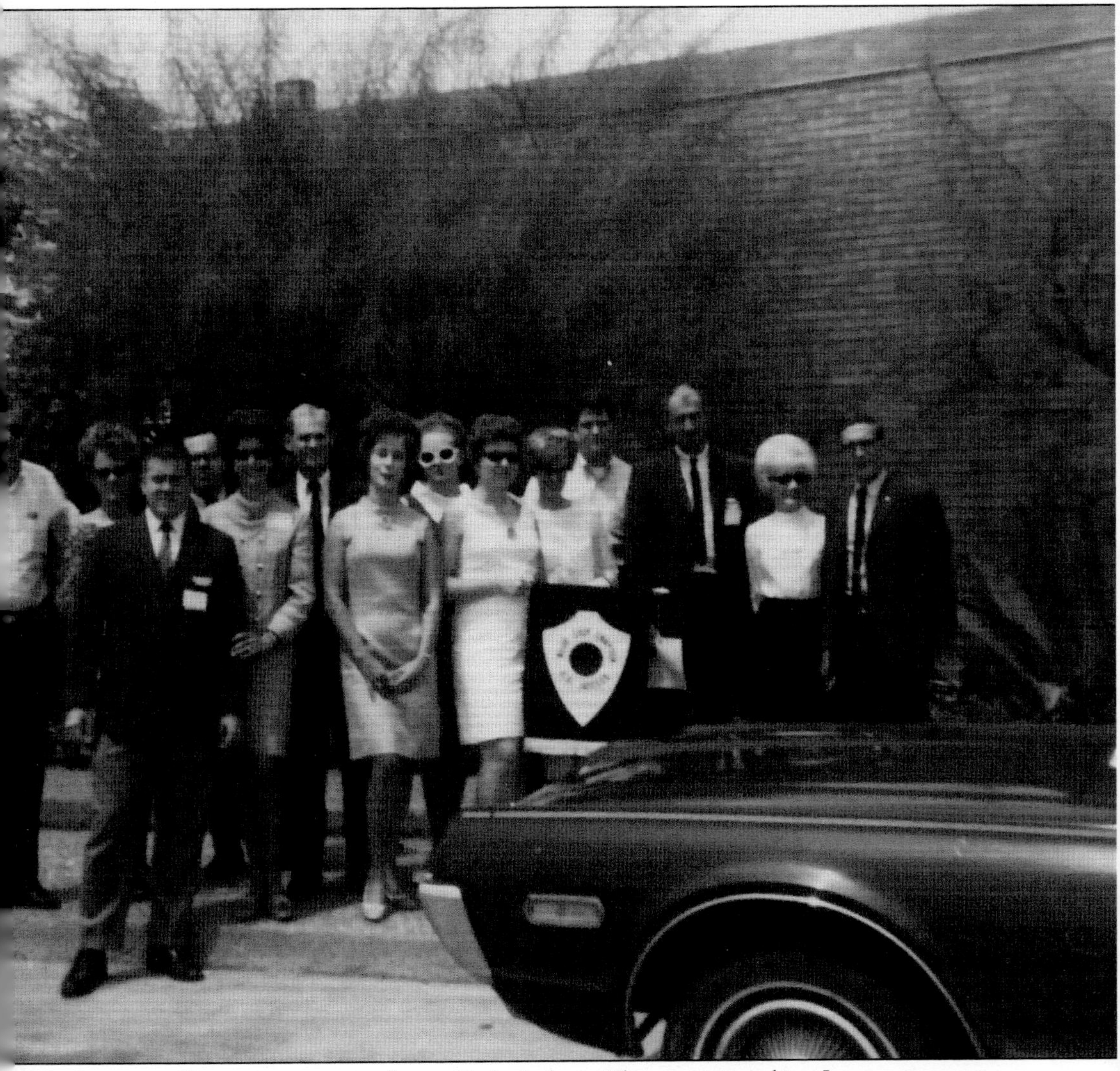

The Jaycees and Jaycettes were active beyond Lake Jackson. They participated in a Jaycees convention in Port Arthur in August 1968. Pictured here are, from left to right, Buddy Hargan; unidentified; Russell Burnett in the street next to wife, Suzanne; unidentified, Floyd and Diane Johnson; Fran Hargar; Cecil June; Susie Hugar; Jim Hugar; Franz June; Terri Webb; and Paul Webb.

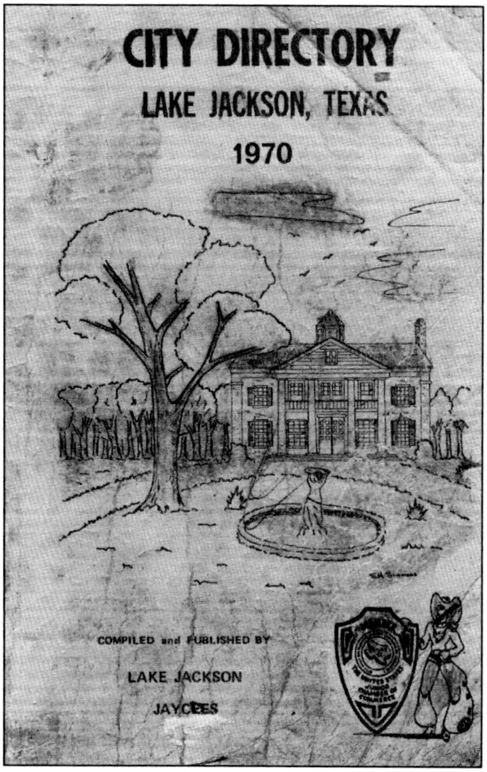

The Jaycees directories were very well used. The largest entry was all the residential phone numbers, which also provided all the family members' names, the occupation of the head of the family, their address, and phone number. Next was a section listing the family names by street addresses. The following section was all the phone numbers listed sequentially with family names. A section of church information was listed, followed by all the businesses, which advertised in the directory with their phone and location of their ad in the book.

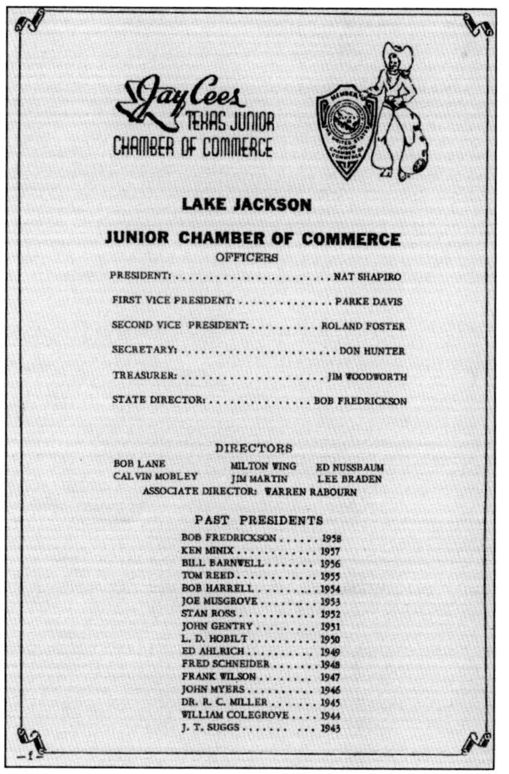

JayCees TEXAS JUNIOR CHAMBER OF COMMERCE

LAKE JACKSON

JUNIOR CHAMBER OF COMMERCE

OFFICERS

PRESIDENT: .... NAT SHAPIRO
FIRST VICE PRESIDENT: .... PARKE DAVIS
SECOND VICE PRESIDENT: .... ROLAND FOSTER
SECRETARY: .... DON HUNTER
TREASURER: .... JIM WOODWORTH
STATE DIRECTOR: .... BOB FREDRICKSON

DIRECTORS

BOB LANE — MILTON WING — ED NUSSBAUM
CALVIN MOBLEY — JIM MARTIN — LEE BRADEN
ASSOCIATE DIRECTOR: WARREN RABOURN

PAST PRESIDENTS

BOB FREDRICKSON 1958
KEN MINIX 1957
BILL BARNWELL 1956
TOM REED 1955
BOB HARRELL 1954
JOE MUSGROVE 1953
STAN ROSS 1952
JOHN GENTRY 1951
L. D. HOBILT 1950
ED AHLRICH 1949
FRED SCHNEIDER 1948
FRANK WILSON 1947
JOHN MYERS 1946
DR. R. C. MILLER 1945
WILLIAM COLEGROVE 1944
J. T. SUGGS 1943

-1-

The Jaycees produced a city directory each year. The officers of 1959 and all previous presidents are listed on this cover page. The Jaycees spanned from 1943 to 1987, with young men learning leadership skills and servicing the community through helping with Boy Scouts events, Fourth of July celebrations—which included free fireworks, watermelons, and hot dogs—city parks, and many other projects.

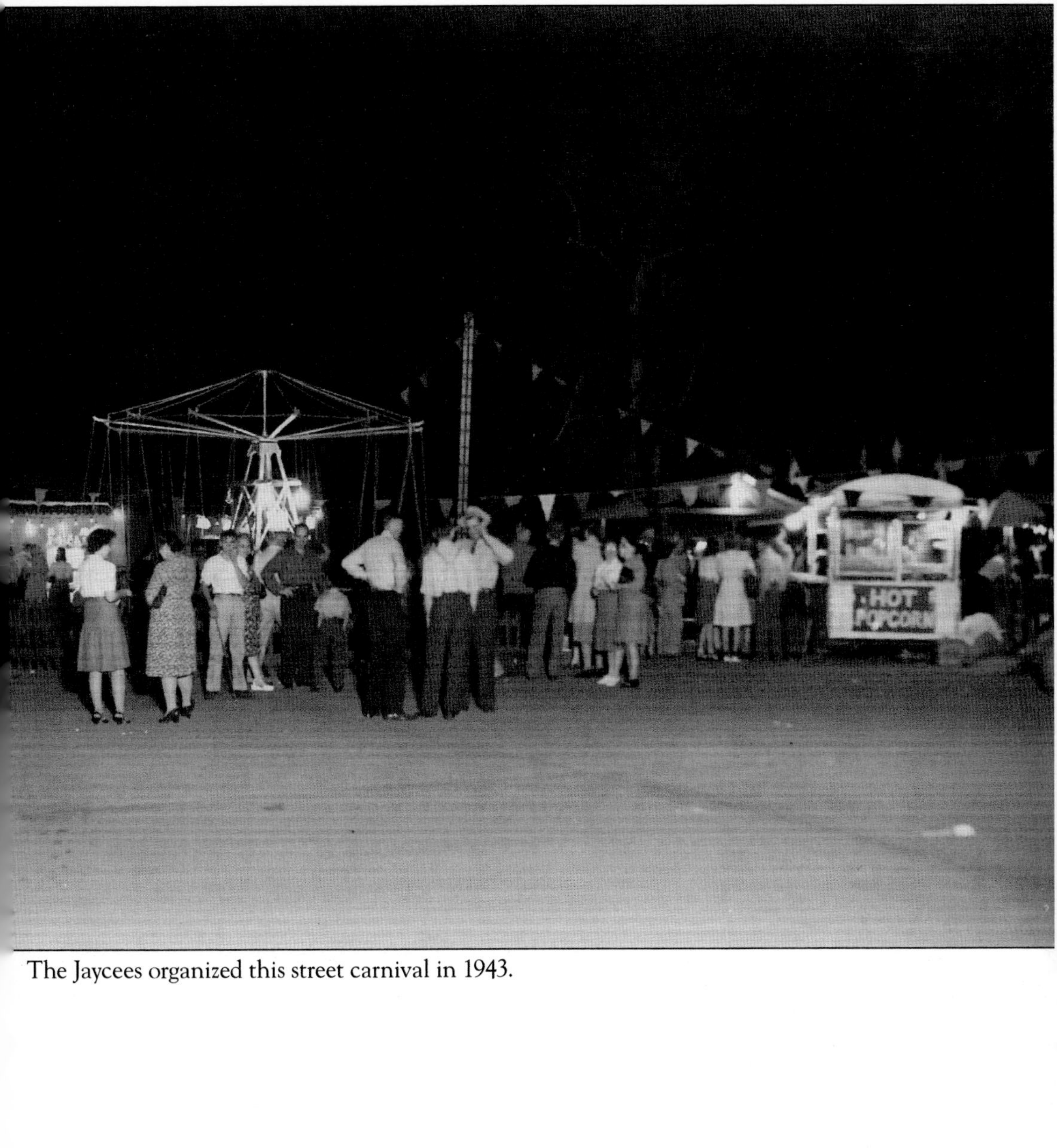

The Jaycees organized this street carnival in 1943.

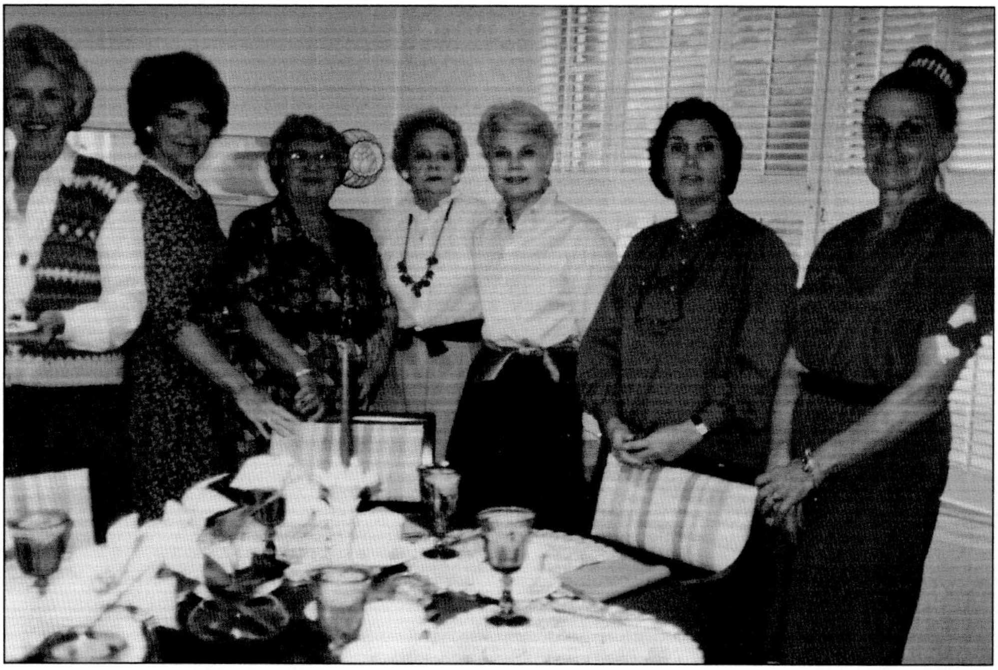

The November Lake Jackson Garden Club meeting was held at the home of Jean Engibous, seen at the far left. Next to her are, from left to right, Genearle Hughes, Mary Cutshall, Margaret Sharp, Millie Leever, Eileen Levine, and June Harris.

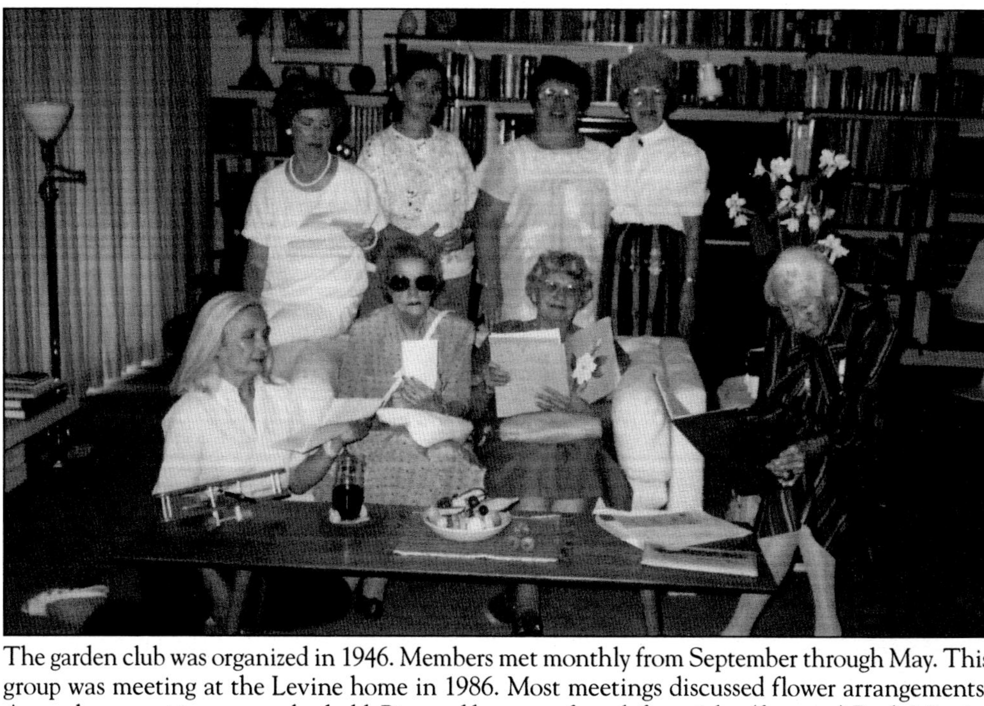

The garden club was organized in 1946. Members met monthly from September through May. This group was meeting at the Levine home in 1986. Most meetings discussed flower arrangements. Annual competitions were also held. Pictured here are, from left to right, (first row) Ruth Martin, Margaret Sharp, Vivian Sharp, and Lillian McPeak; (second row) Genearle Hughes, Eileen Levine, Grace Smith, and Anna Diether.

A major addition to the Brazosport Museum of Natural Science's shell collection was the purchase of the personal shell collection of Freeport resident W.C. DeWitt in 1967. Alvie Merrill, pictured second from left, provided the transportation to the museum. The $5,000 purchase price was considerably below market value but was accepted to keep the collection in the area. Jim Nabors, newspaper publisher and local activist, led the campaign to get donations for the purchase, and N.D. Criswold was a major donor.

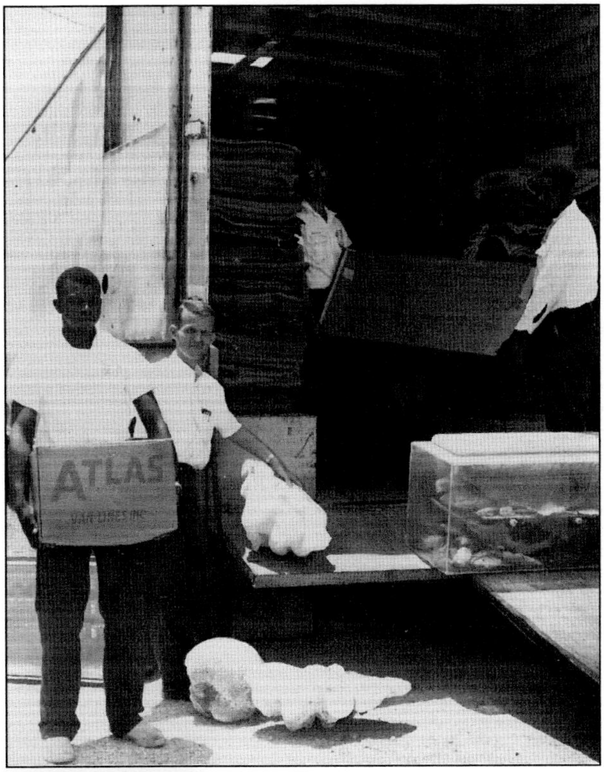

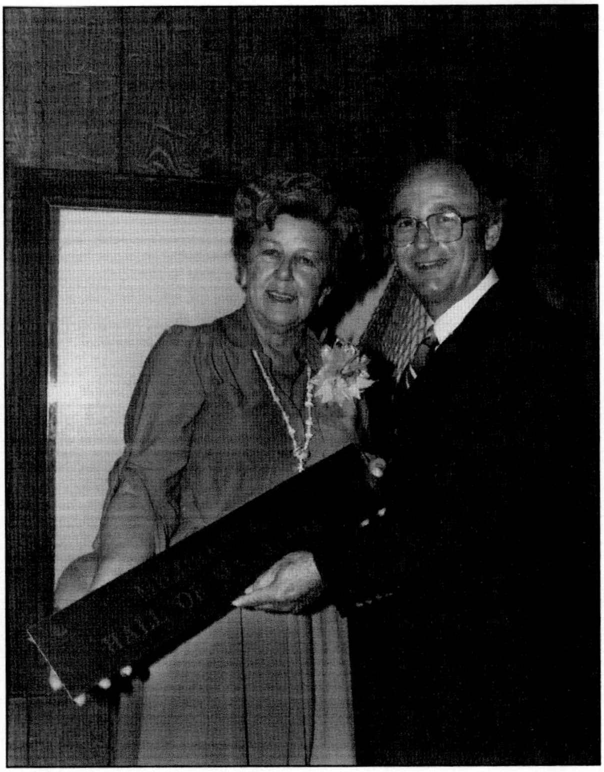

Mildred Tate, founder of the Brazosport Museum of Natural Science, is shown being recognized by James Nabors, the *Facts* publisher and member of the Texas Historical Commission. Tate moved to Lake Jackson with her husband in the early 1940s and developed a passion for the shells of the Gulf Coast. She formed the first shell club in 1960. She established the shell exhibit for the county fair. She also was a charter member of the Archeology Club and the Ecology Club. The Mildred Tate Hall of Malacology was established in 1978. She campaigned for the lightning whelk, a local shell, to become the official state shell, which was signed into law April 22, 1987.

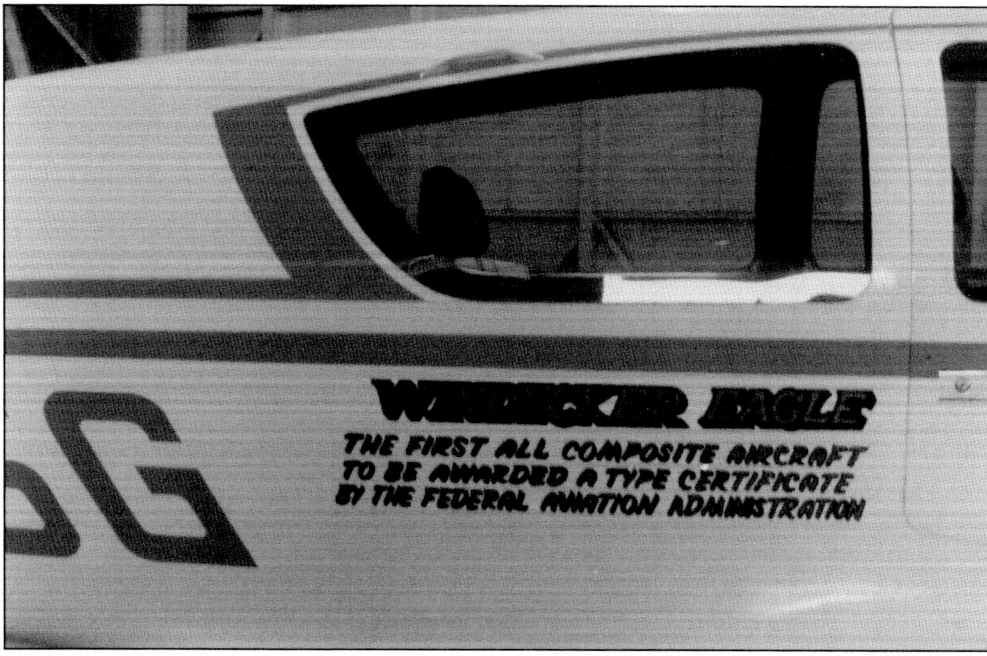

The Windecker Eagle was certified by the Federal Aviation Administration as the first all-composite aircraft. It was first flown on October 7, 1967. This was a joint project with Dr. Leo Windecker, his wife, Dr. Fairfax Windecker, and the Dow Chemical Company. Leo's personal plane is featured in the Lake Jackson Museum.

The Windeckers donated their Windecker Eagle N4197G (S/N 006) to the National Air and Space Museum in 1985. Lab director Dr. Tom Harriston of Dow Chemical Company is kneeling. The Windeckers are behind him and Mac Pruett, of Dow Chemical Company, is fifth from the right.

Five

HOW DOES A COMMUNITY DEVELOP A CULTURE?

The population reached 2,897 in 1950 and had grown to 11,090 by 1958. In 1954, residents voted to become a home rule city with a council-manager form of government. A.A. MacLean, an extremely fiscally conservative city manager, ran the city from 1956 to 1991. He developed a fiscally sound organization that was continued by his protégé Bill Yenne.

In 1969, the school district opened a second high school which serves Clute and Lake Jackson. Brazoswood High School provides a fine education for the youth of these cities. It has been recognized for its achievements in academics, fine arts, and athletics.

In 1976, a regional shopping mall opened in the city that ultimately provided a sales tax base for the city, which exceeded the city's population. This resulted in a city with lower property taxes.

The Little Theater organization began in Velasco in a converted residence. An Art League was formed in 1955 for the area. A museum of natural science was developed in Lake Jackson in 1964. These groups were consolidated in the Brazosport Center for the Arts and Sciences in 1976. The building is located in Clute adjacent to Lake Jackson and serves the Brazosport area. The center was funded by a trust fund of a Dow Chemical Company president, the Dow Chemical Company, and local contributors. A music theater, symphony, and planetarium completed the family of organizations in the center.

In 1968, Brazosport College was established in Freeport in some school district facilities. A new campus in Lake Jackson was developed immediately. The college provides vocational training as well as associate degrees. A baccalaureate degree program was added in 2003 by the Texas Legislature.

Two individuals who saw a need for researching sudden infant death syndrome (SIDS) created the Southwest Research Institute. It opened its clinic in the new hospital in 1984 and has contributed greatly to the knowledge and avoidance of this syndrome on a national scale.

The Brazosport Rotary formed in 1953 and the Junior Service League began in 1970. Both have been a force in the community to join young talent in philanthropic projects.

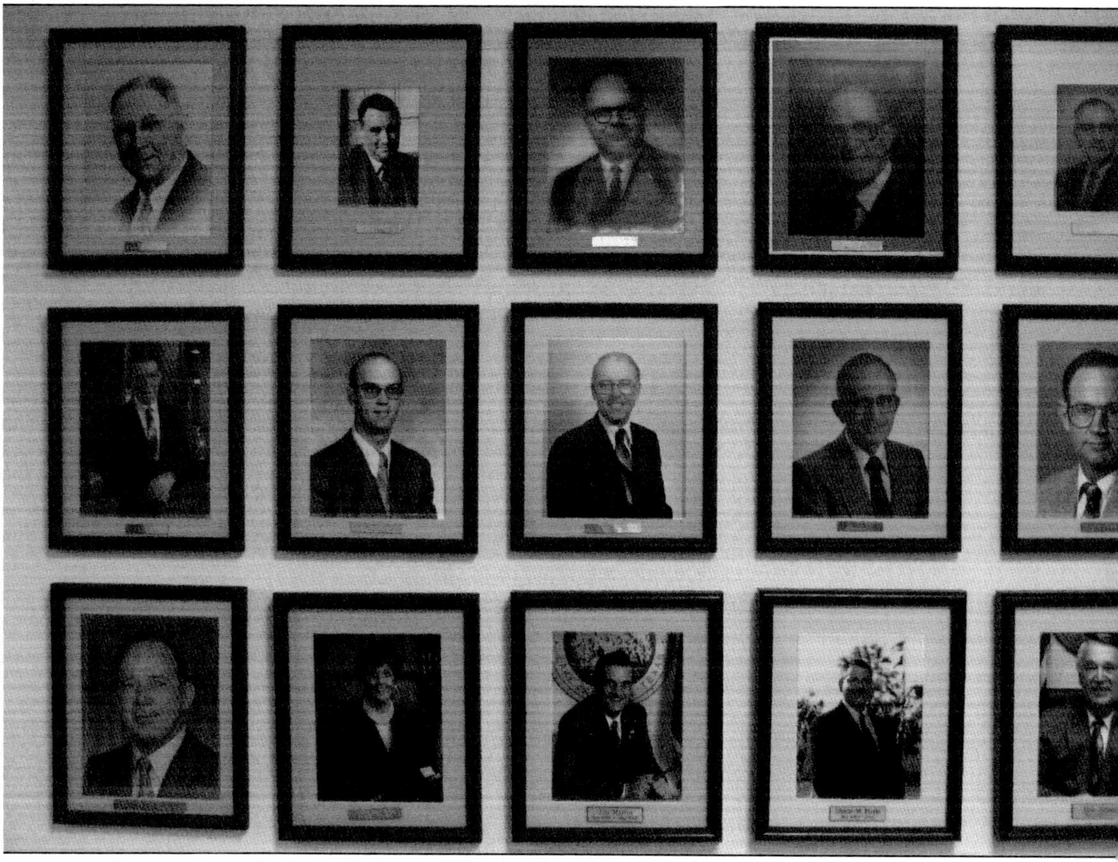

Pictured are the Lake Jackson mayors. They are, from left to right, (top row) J.W. Leak, April to October 1944; J.H. Greer, 1944–1948; Bill Colegrove, 1948–1954; Ernie Rea, 1954–1958; and K.L. Cooper, 1958–1968; (second row) Jack Reid, 1968–1972; Roy Vining, 1972–1974; Bill Frizell, 1974–1976; Bill Rollwage, 1978–1979; and Dick Birdwell, 1979–1980; (third row) Vic Vickers, 1976–1978 and 1980–1988; Doris Williams, 1988–1996; Jim Martin, 1996–2000; Shane Pirtle, 2000–2006; and Bob Sipple, 2006 to beyond publication date.

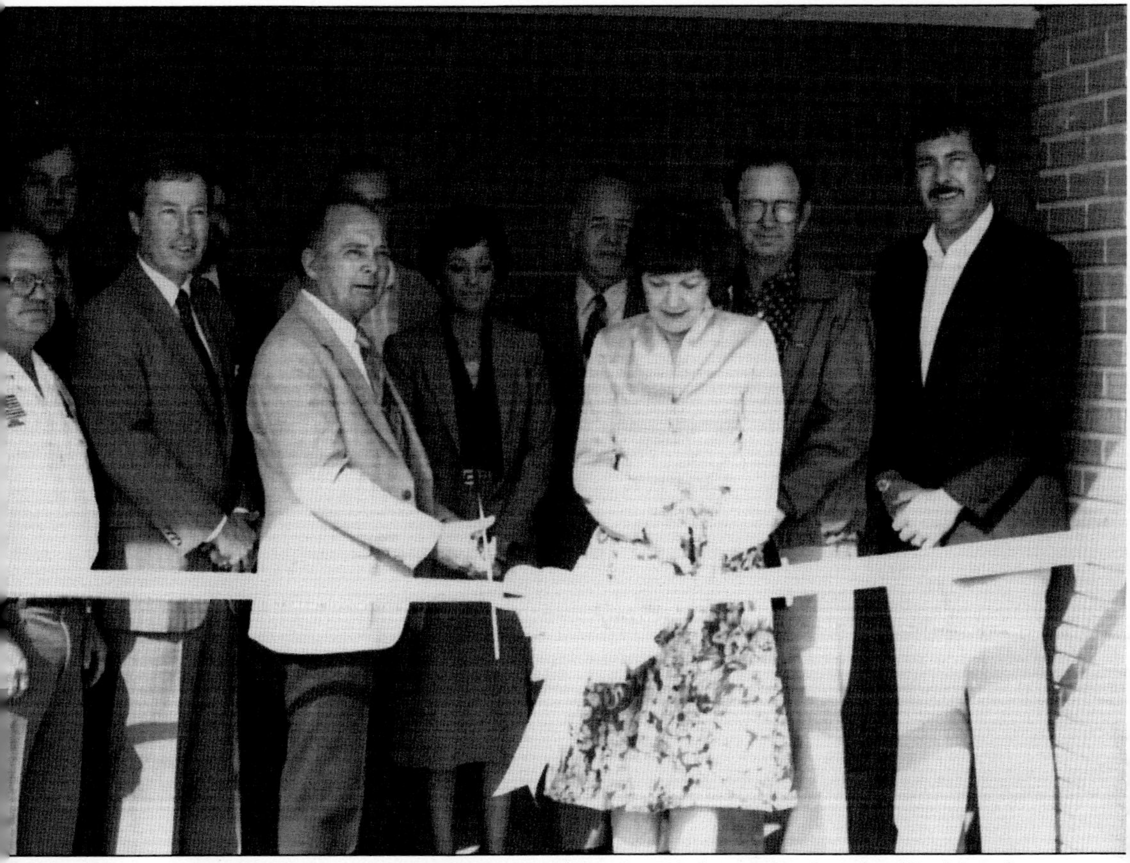

The new city hall addition opened in 1988. Pictured are, from left to right, fire chief Paul Israel; councilman Chuck Hogan; Sen. Buster Brown; police chief Jim Hinton; Mayor Vic Vickers; councilman Charlie Golden; councilwoman Doris Williams; city manager A.A. MacLean; unidentified; past mayor Dick Birdwell; and councilman Ron Dripprey.

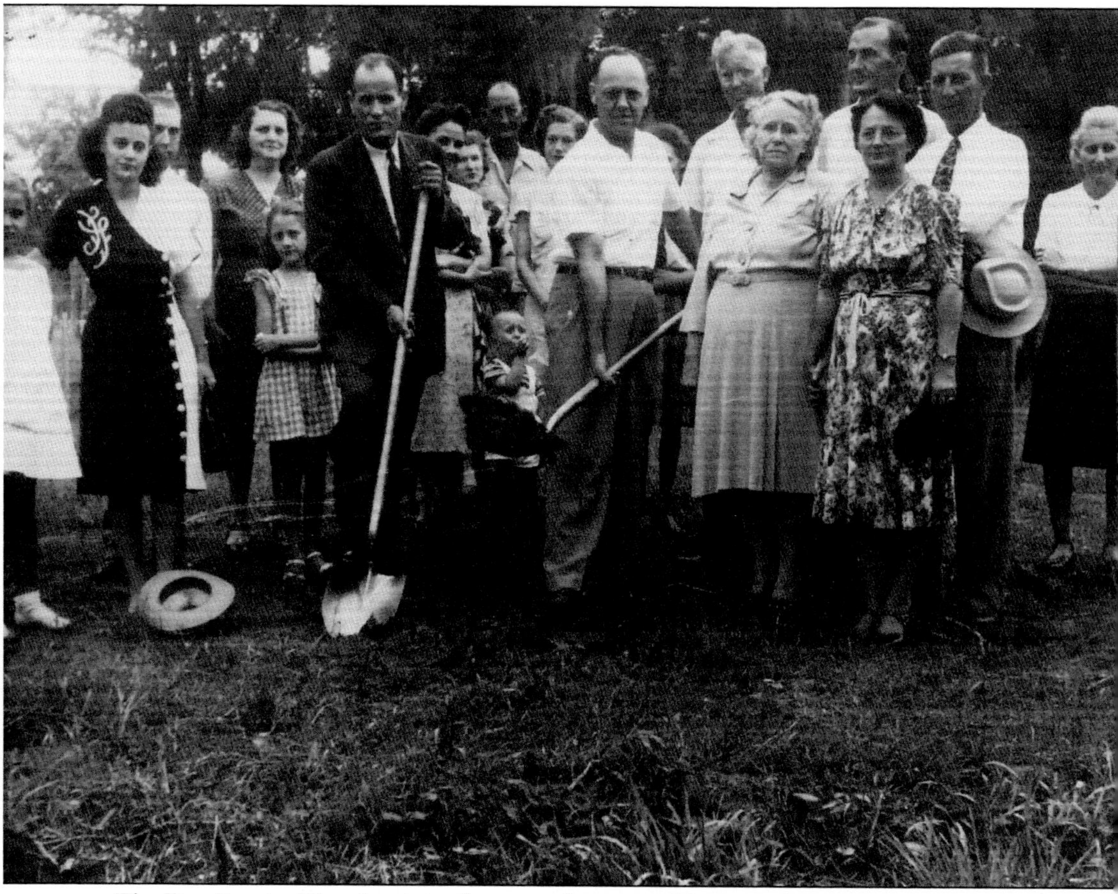

The First Baptist Church originally met in homes and later in the community center. In 1944, land was purchased from Dow Chemical Company across from Elisabet Ney Elementary School. This is the ground-breaking for the first sanctuary. Rev. Jesse Davis, in the suit, and Br. R.F. Floyd do the honors. Pictured are, from left to right (beginning with the adults), Doris Casey, Rayford Thompson, Mrs. Lucille Floyd, Carol Ann Floyd, Reverend Davis, Lorayne Swearingen, Julia May, Earl Barrow, Betty Wilson, R.F. Floyd, S.G. Marshall, Mrs. Swearingen, Joe Malone, Mrs. Jesse Davis, L.D. Monical, Mabel Barrington, and Ruth Brewer.

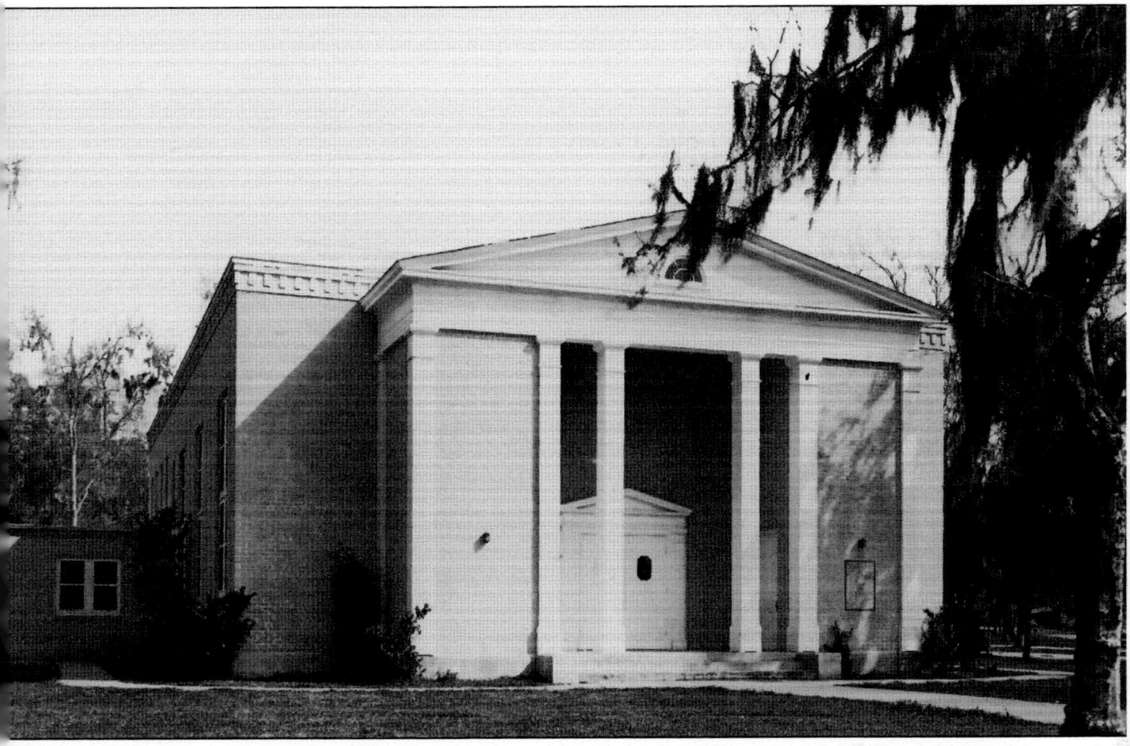

The first sanctuary of the First Baptist Church was located across the street from the elementary school grounds on Winding Way Street. The congregation began using the facility in 1947. Alden Dow planned for three churches to be located on the triangle lot. Fortunately, the Baptists had enough confidence to buy the entire tract and their campus has grown to four adjacent blocks for parking, a family life facility, and a visiting missionary's home. (Courtesy of the First Baptist Church.)

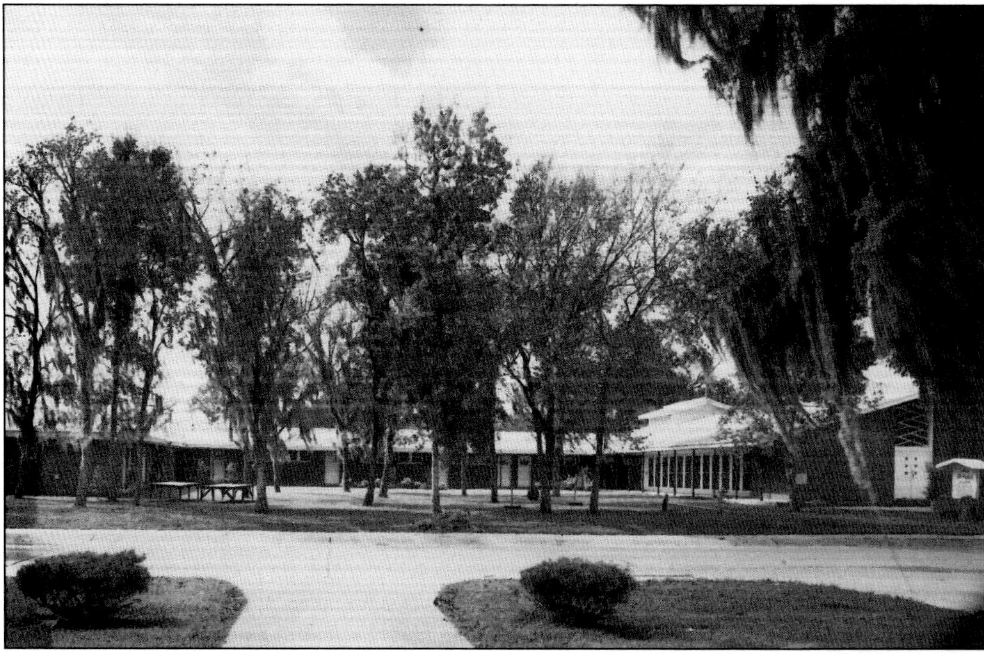

The first sanctuary of the First Methodist Church opened on Azalea Street in 1948. Volunteers under the leadership of John Stark, a Dow Chemical Company construction supervisor, built a significant portion of the building. With the shortages during and after the war, all materials received were considered gifts from God. (Courtesy of First United Methodist Church.)

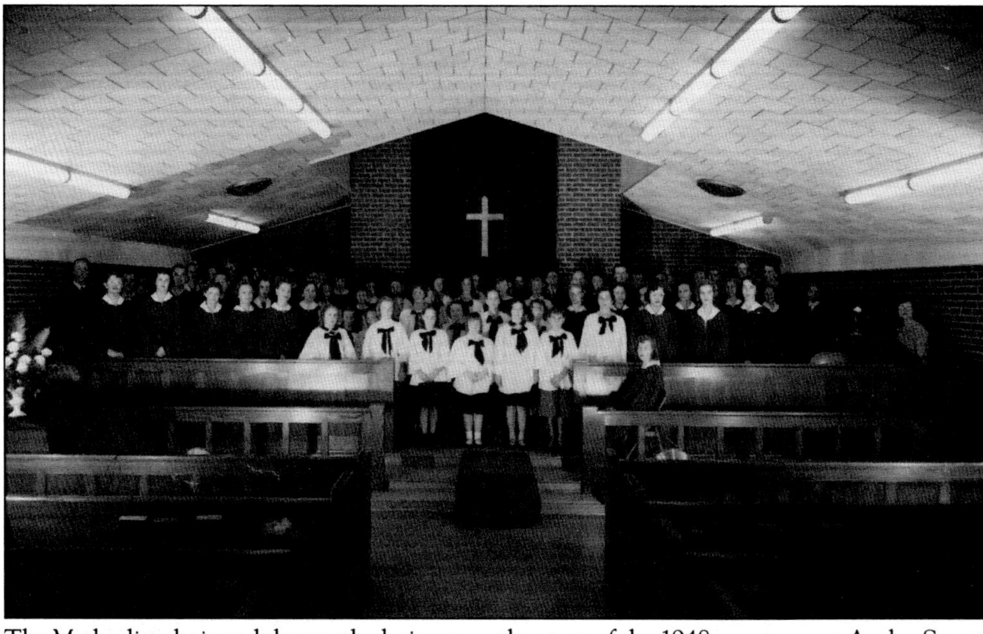

The Methodist choir and the youth choir are on the stage of the 1948 sanctuary at Azalea Street, which is still used as a reception room. The organist was Esther Jones. Ethlyn Raney is the fifth woman from the right. Laurence Epps is on the far left. Other members that cannot be enumerated are Winona Burk, Bob Johnson, Exa Galbreath, Marie Bridges, and Virginia Batchelor. (Courtesy of First United Methodist Church.)

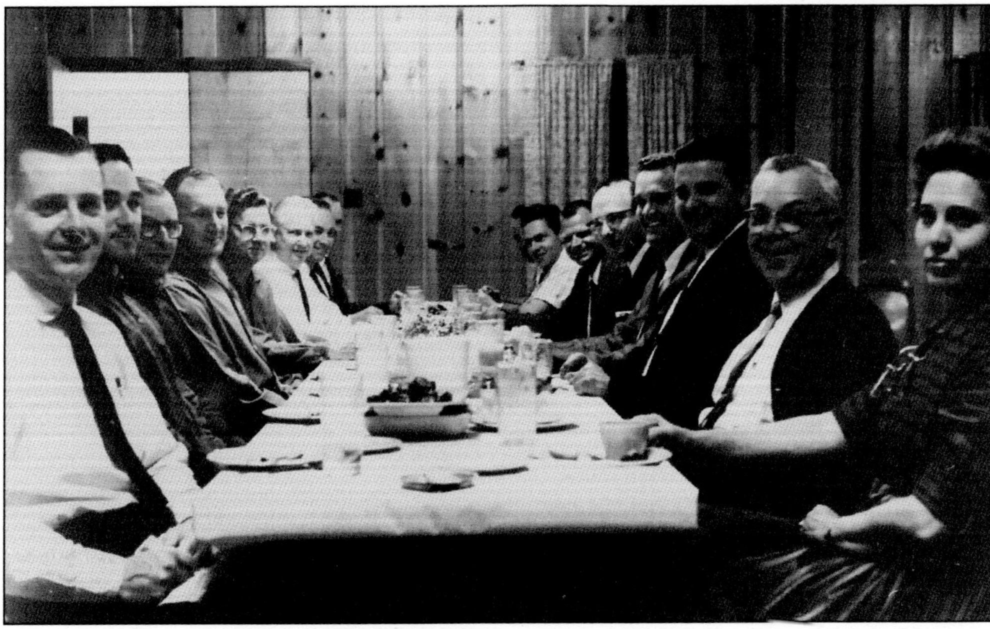

The visitation committee of the First Methodist Church eat before going out into the community seeking new members in the mid-1960s. They are, from front to back, (on the left) ? Johnson, Wiley Barton, Jim Demland, Leroy Bacica, I.J. Taska, and three unidentified men; (on the right) Bea Denton, Nig Raney, minister Carlos Davis, Bill Burk, Thurmond Munson, Bob Hackney, and A.G. Snelgrove. (Courtesy of First United Methodist Church.)

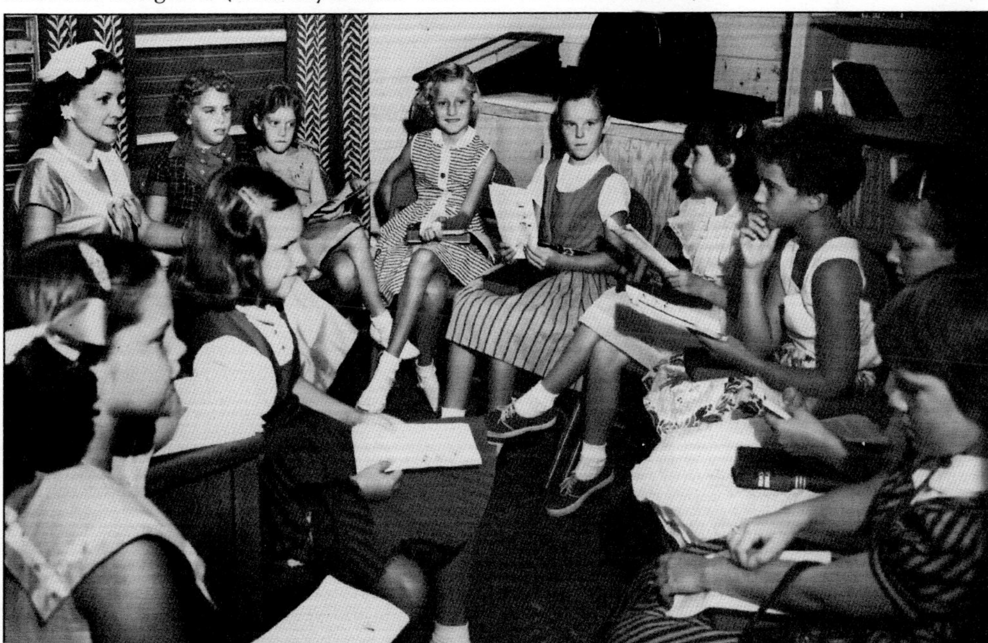

This is a youth Sunday school class at the First Methodist Church in the early 1950s. The teacher is Madeline Reichenbach, and to her left is Cherie Nowlin (McBride). Note the mimeograph machine. This was a church office serving double duty. This became part of the kitchen in 1958. (Courtesy of First United Methodist Church.)

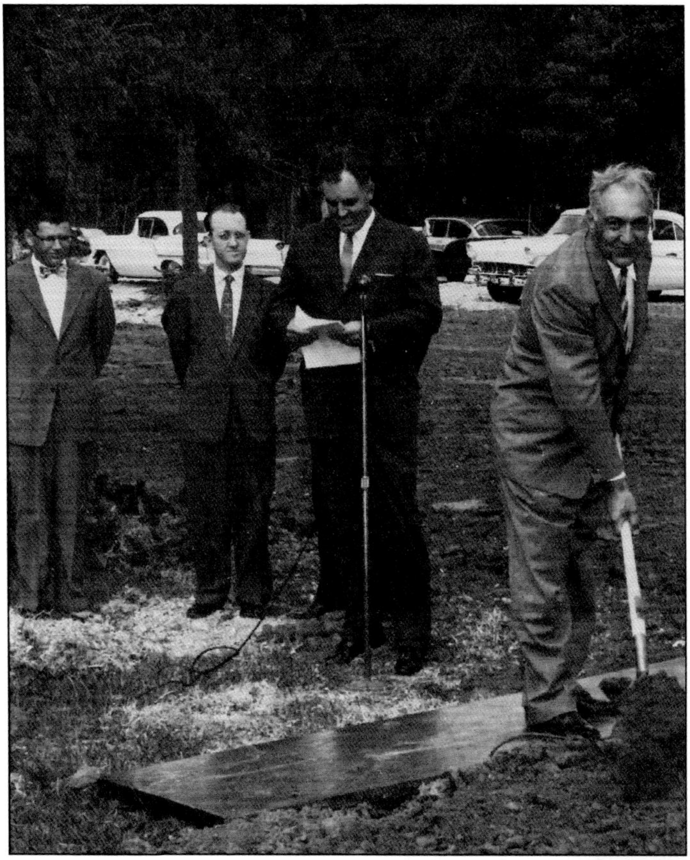

The ground-breaking for the First Methodist Church sanctuary on the corner of Azalea and Yaupon Streets was in 1957. Pictured here are, from left to right, Richard Clemens, Frank Carter, Rev. Weldon Morton, and John Stark. Notice the heavy vegetation in the background (Courtesy of First United Methodist Church.)

The First Methodist Church opened its new sanctuary in 1958. The congregation grew so quickly over the next 12 years that it chose to start another Methodist church, Chapelwood, rather than continue to expand on Azalea Street. (Courtesy of First United Methodist Church.)

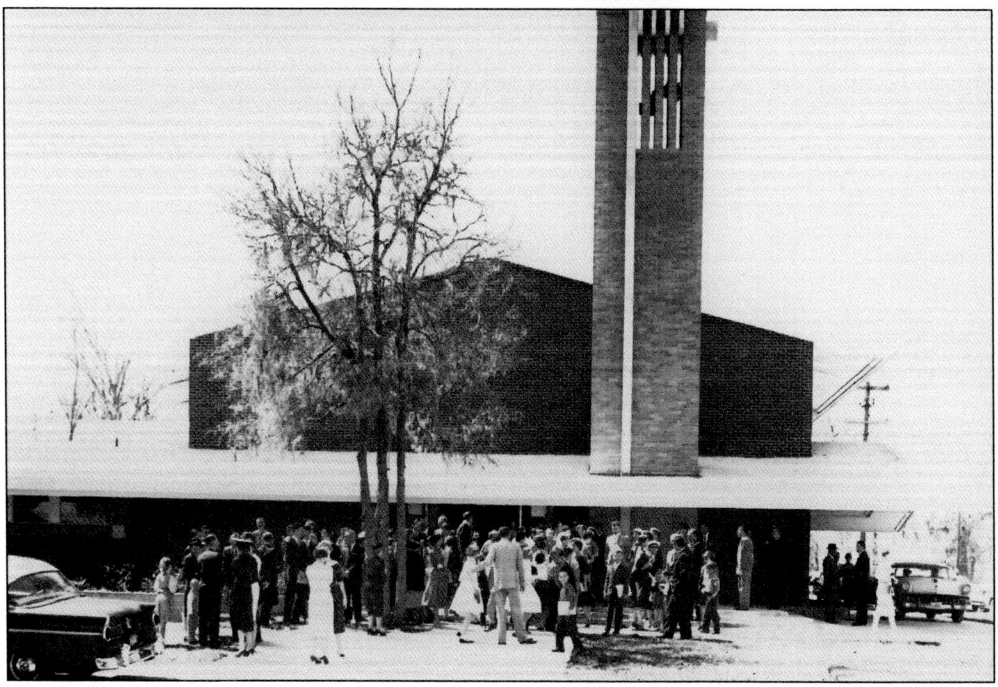

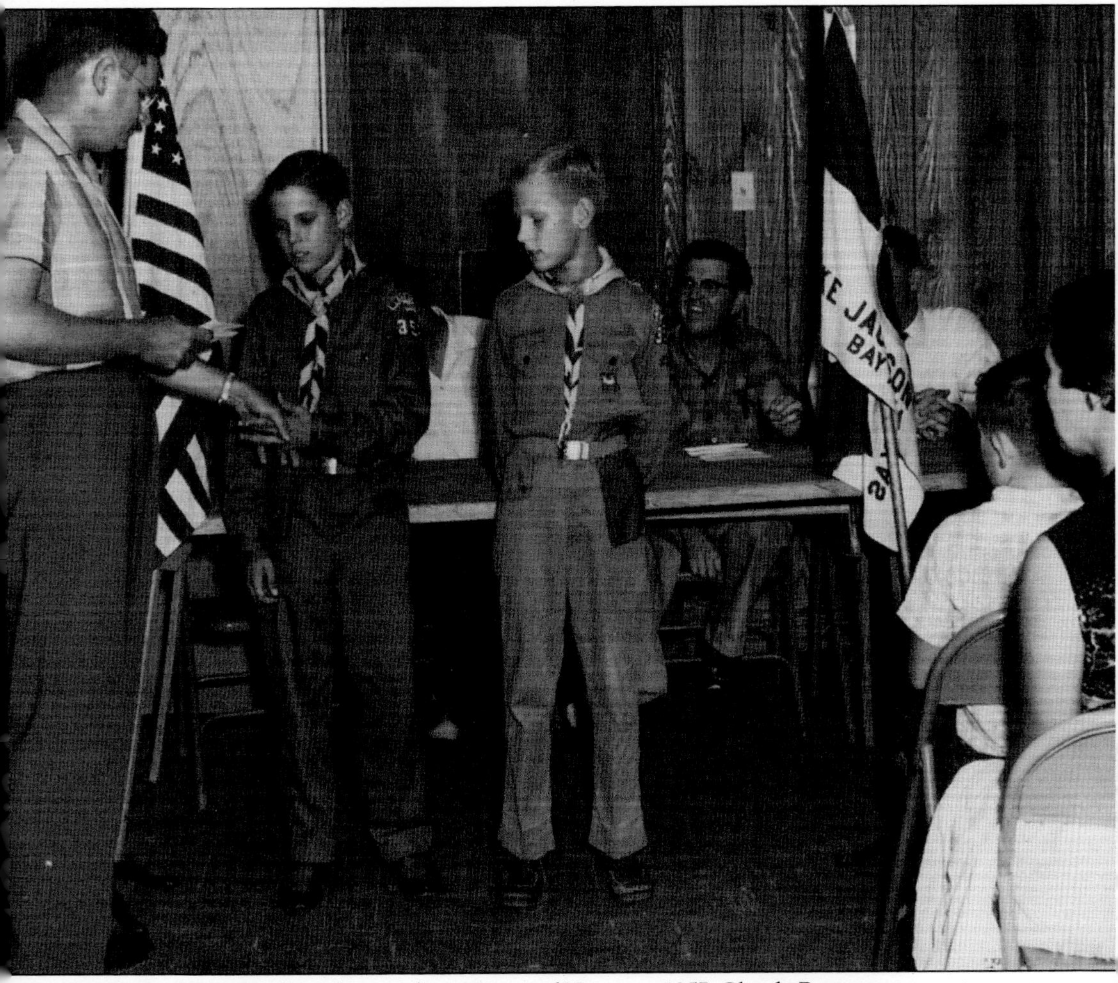

Ric Snyder and Ross Kroll are honored at a Court of Honor in 1957. Claude Bagget, a committee member, sits at the table. Troop 325 was the first Boy Scout troop in Lake Jackson, formed in 1943. It was troop 25 in the beginning and was sponsored by "concerned citizens." The Jaycees then sponsored it until sometime in the 1950s. The First Methodist Church became the sponsor around 1958. The Scouts met in a Scout house on the creek side of Oyster Creek and Yaupon Streets. Early Scoutmasters were D. Matthews, 1943; R.E. Barron, 1944; Raymond Walley, 1945–1948; Richard Bloomfield, 1949; Clyde Parish, 1950–1951; and Jack Knight, 1952. (Courtesy of First United Methodist Church.)

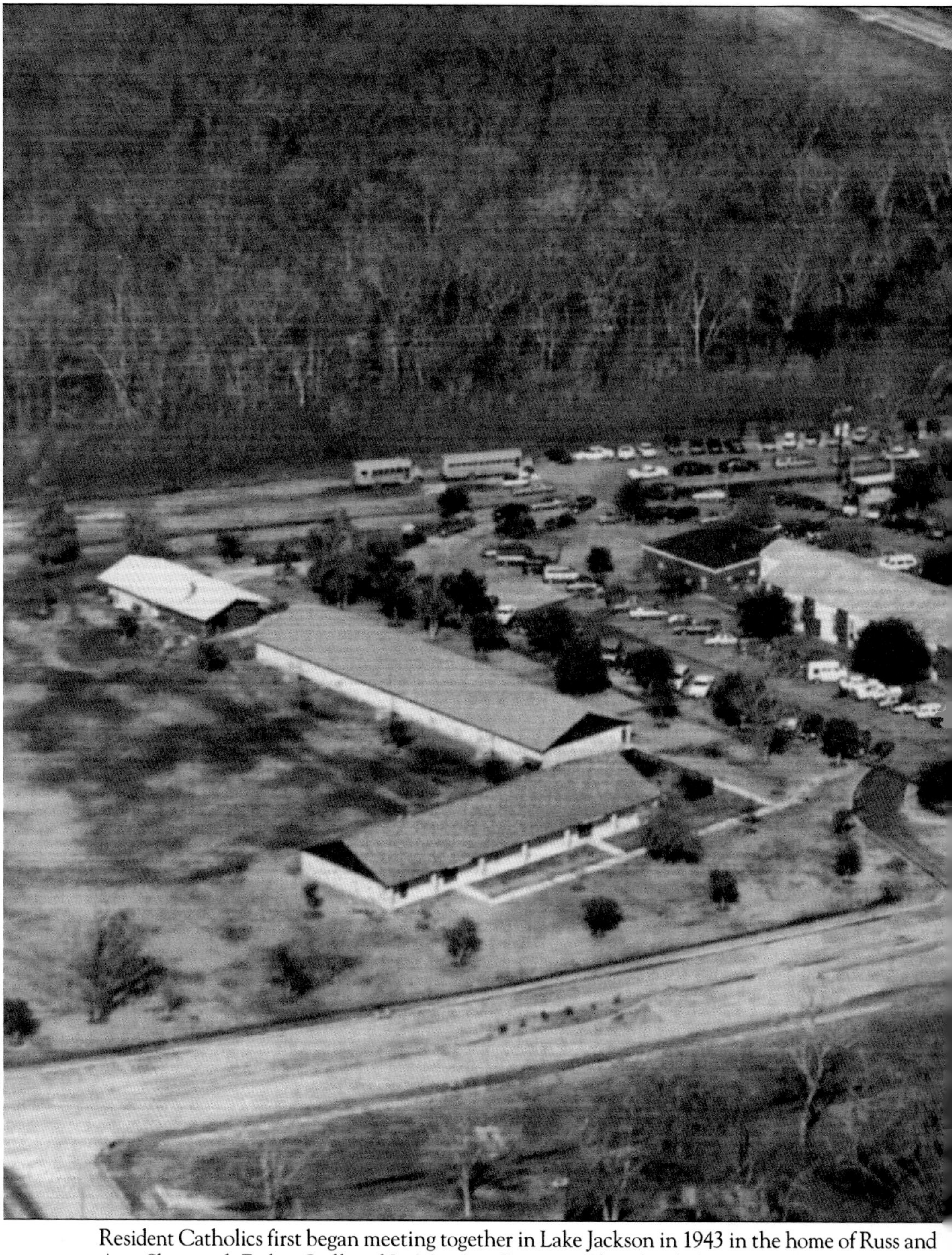

Resident Catholics first began meeting together in Lake Jackson in 1943 in the home of Russ and Ann Shaw with Father Coffey of St. Mary's in Freeport. They decided to move to the community center for more space. Even in the center, some of the congregants had to sit on the porch. This picture is of the current campus at Highway 288 and Oak Drive in the 1980s. The center building

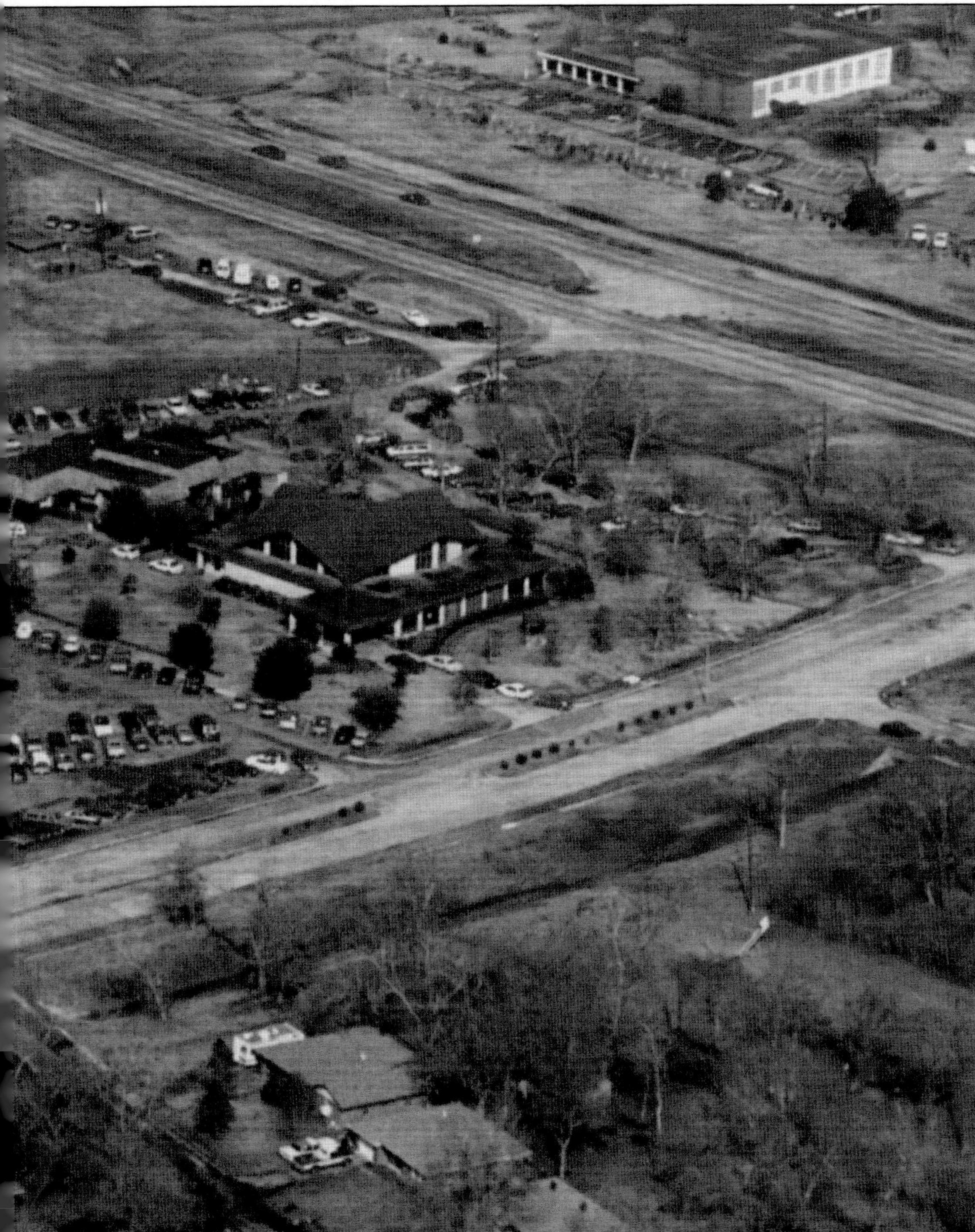

was the original sanctuary occupied in 1958, while still a mission of St. Mary's. The parish was established in 1966. In 1970, the current sanctuary, the structure on the right, was consecrated. (Courtesy of St. Michael's Catholic Church.)

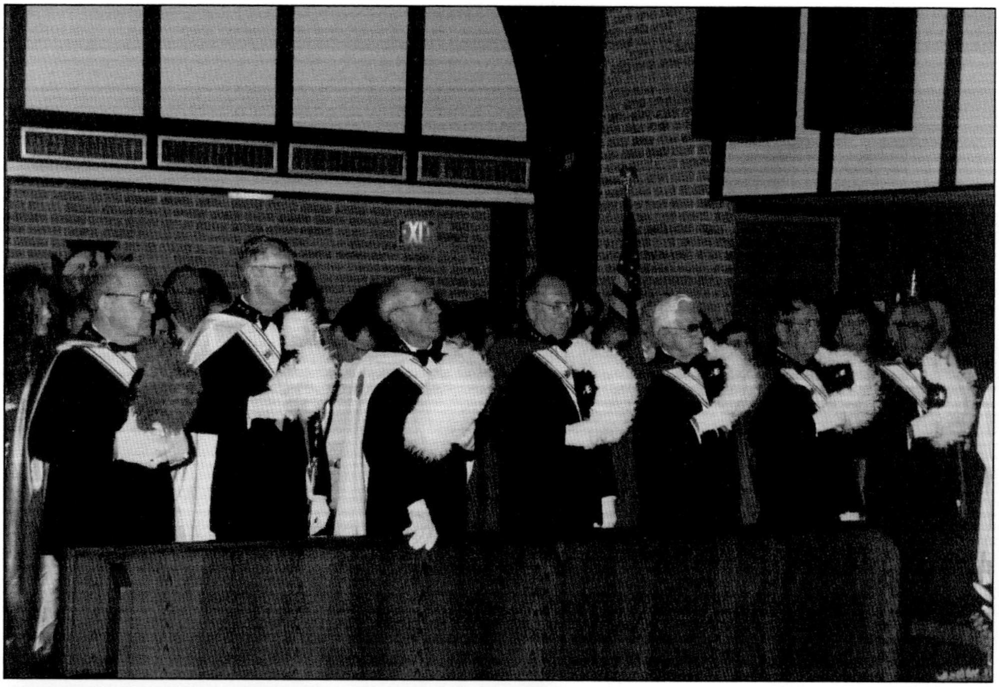

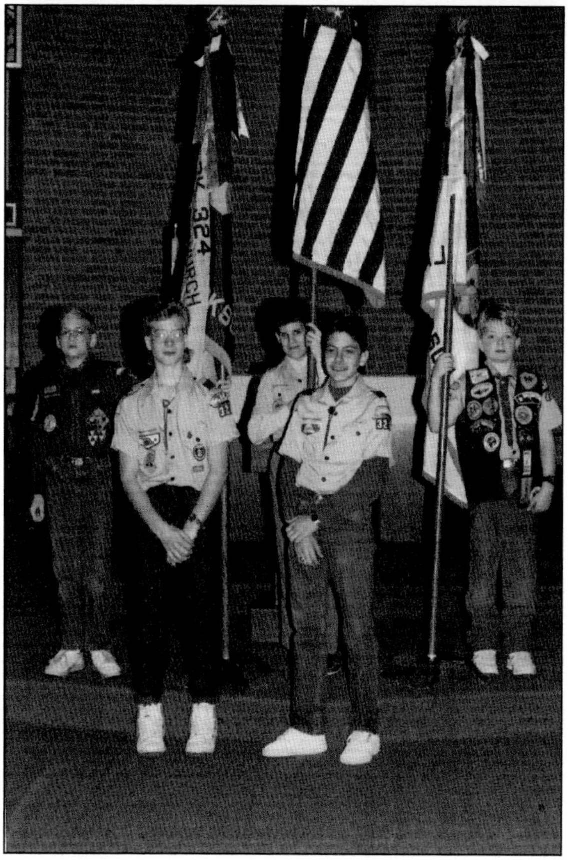

The front row of the congregation is filled with area Knights of Columbus. This tradition is held for all funerals of Knights of Columbus members. This is in the current sanctuary of St. Michael's Catholic Church. (Courtesy of St. Michael's Catholic Church.)

Troop 324, sponsored by St. Michael's Catholic Church, was formed in 1960. This photograph was taken on Scout Sunday around 1986. The members are, from left to right, Eric Jacklitsch, Cub Scout; Nick Granelli, a Life Scout; Bryan Castille, Boy Scout; Brian Bartos; and Kevin Kelleher, Cub Scout. All five Scouts ultimately earned their Eagle Scout Rank. (Courtesy of St. Michael's Catholic Church.)

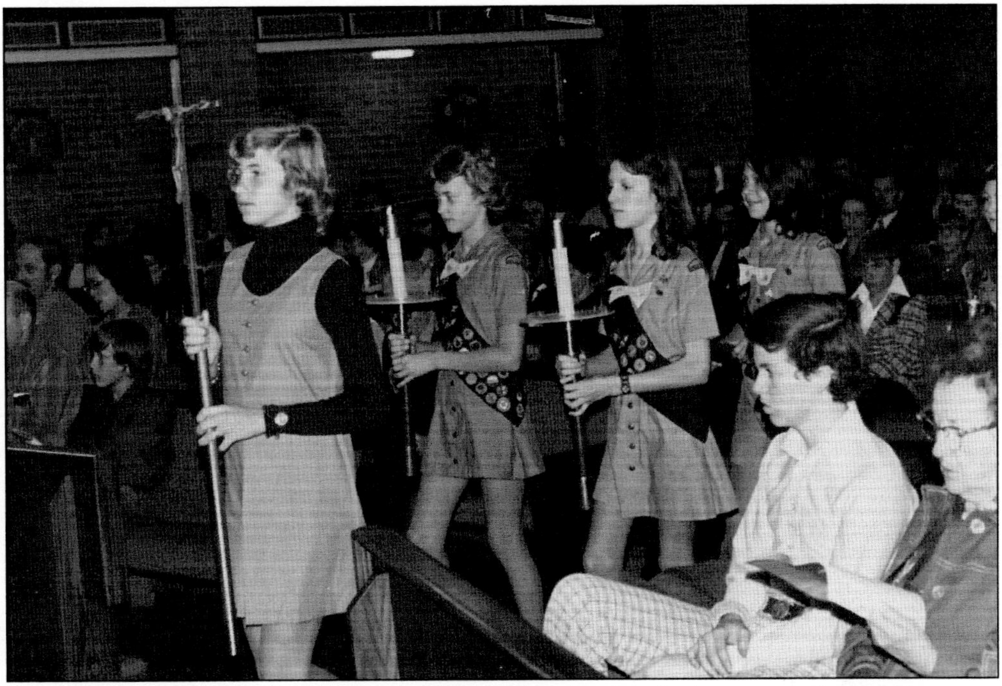

The Girl Scouts of St. Michael's Catholic Church helped with the service. Pictured here are, from left to right, Amy Grether, Maureen Stover, Rosemary Longoria, and Kay Della Mea. This photograph was taken around 1970. (Courtesy of St. Michael's Catholic Church.)

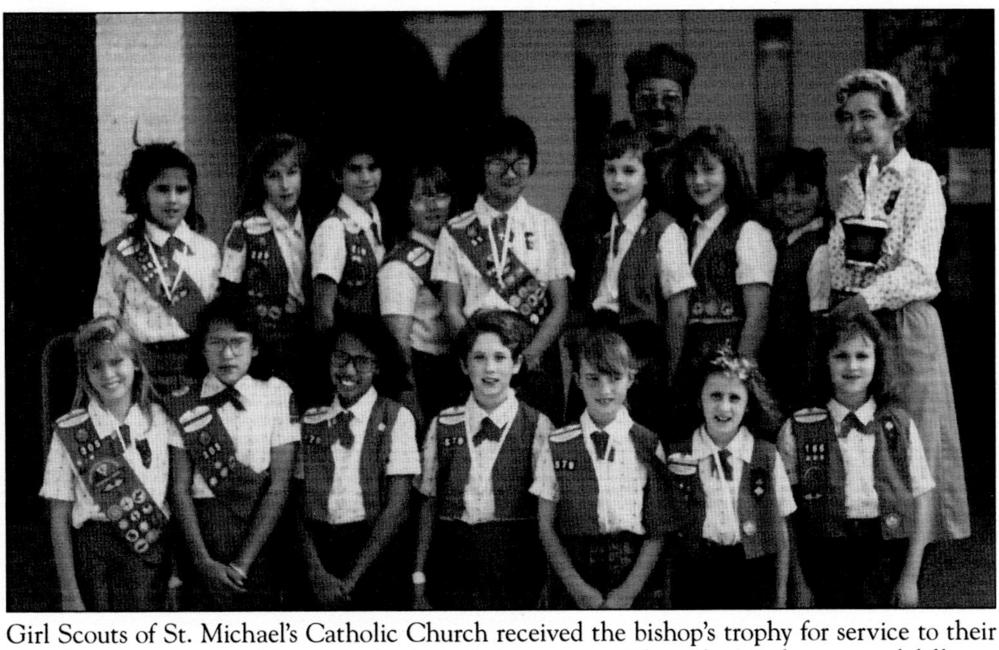

Girl Scouts of St. Michael's Catholic Church received the bishop's trophy for service to their church and community. The Scout leader is Coletta Stover. The girls were from several different troops. (Courtesy of St. Michael's Catholic Church.)

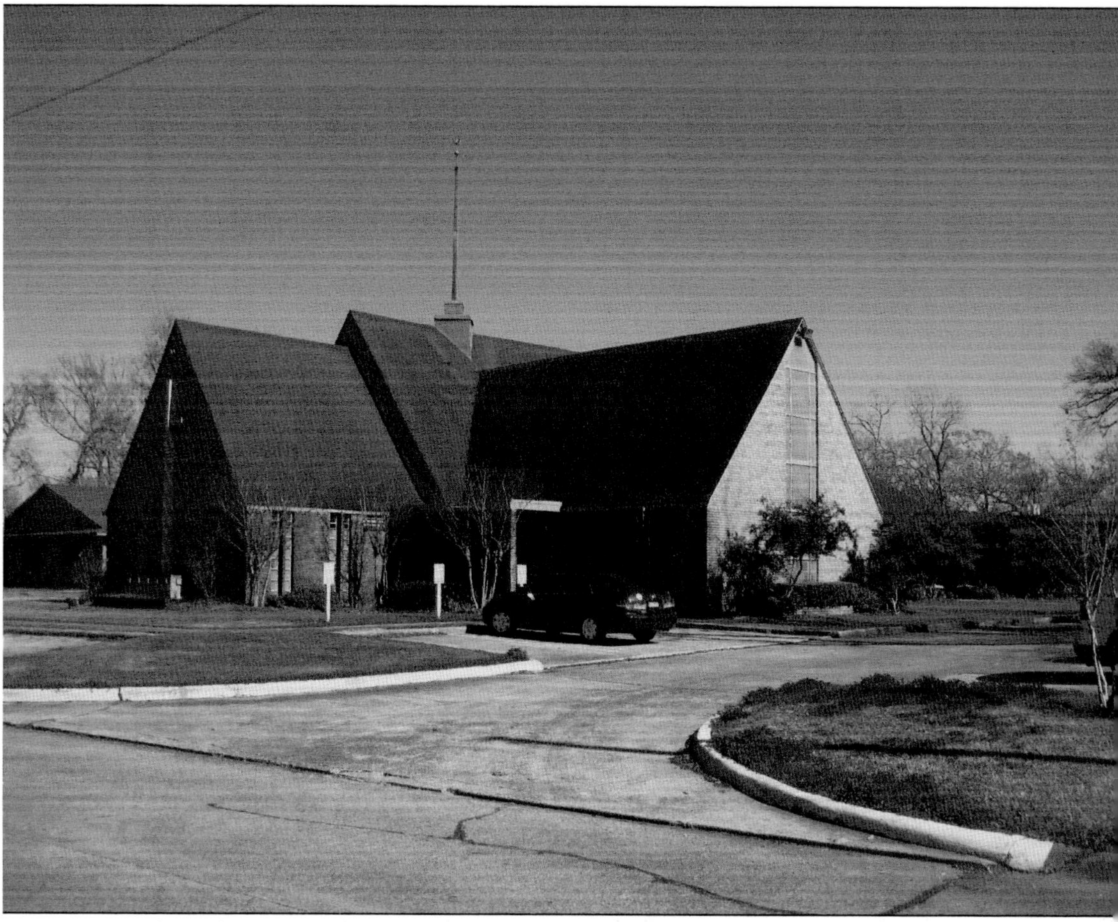

In the early 1950s, Rev. Stanley Wilson and a committee of laymen from St. Paul's Episcopal Church in Freeport acquired a six-acre tract on the corner of Oyster Creek Drive and Circle Way in Lake Jackson. On October 10, 1954, Father Wilson conducted the first services on the new site, blessing the lot and holding an outdoor celebration of the Holy Eucharist. The first regular service in Lake Jackson was on July 17, 1955, with Father Swope officiating. The name St. Timothy's was chosen, signifying the relationship to St. Paul's, which was so instrumental in bringing this new mission into being. (Timothy accompanied St. Paul on his travels and was his mentor in the first century.) Until the building was completed, services were held at the Lake Jackson Junior High School cafeteria across the street from the site. The parish hall and church school building was completed on Easter eve, 1956, and the first service, Holy Baptism, was conducted that afternoon. Easter services the next day filled the new building to capacity. The new building was formally dedicated by Bishop Goddard on June 3, 1956. (Courtesy of the author.)

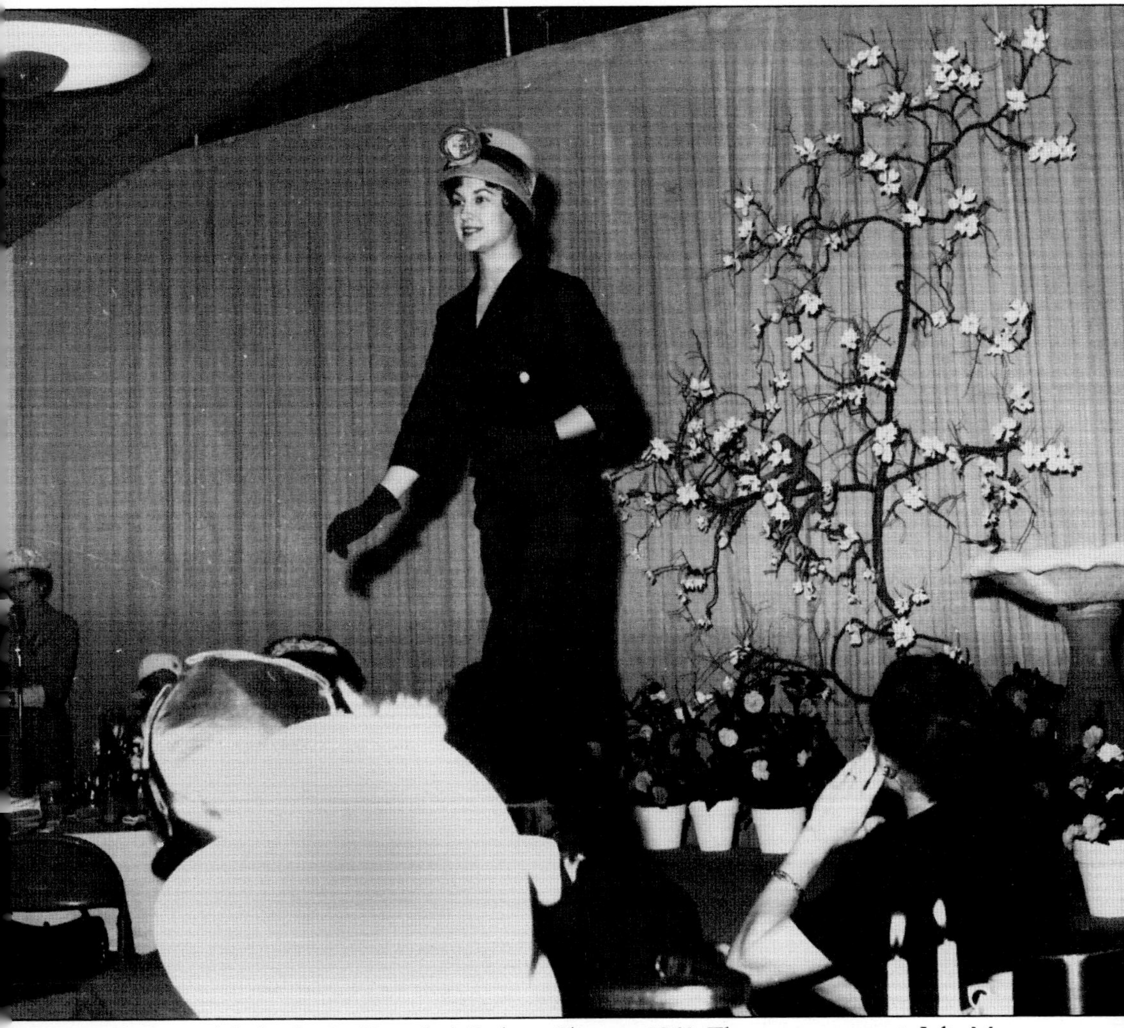

Sharon Suggs models for the St. Timothy's Fashion Show in 1960. The commentator is Julia May. The fundraiser was an annual event of the church. (Courtesy of Sharon Suggs White.)

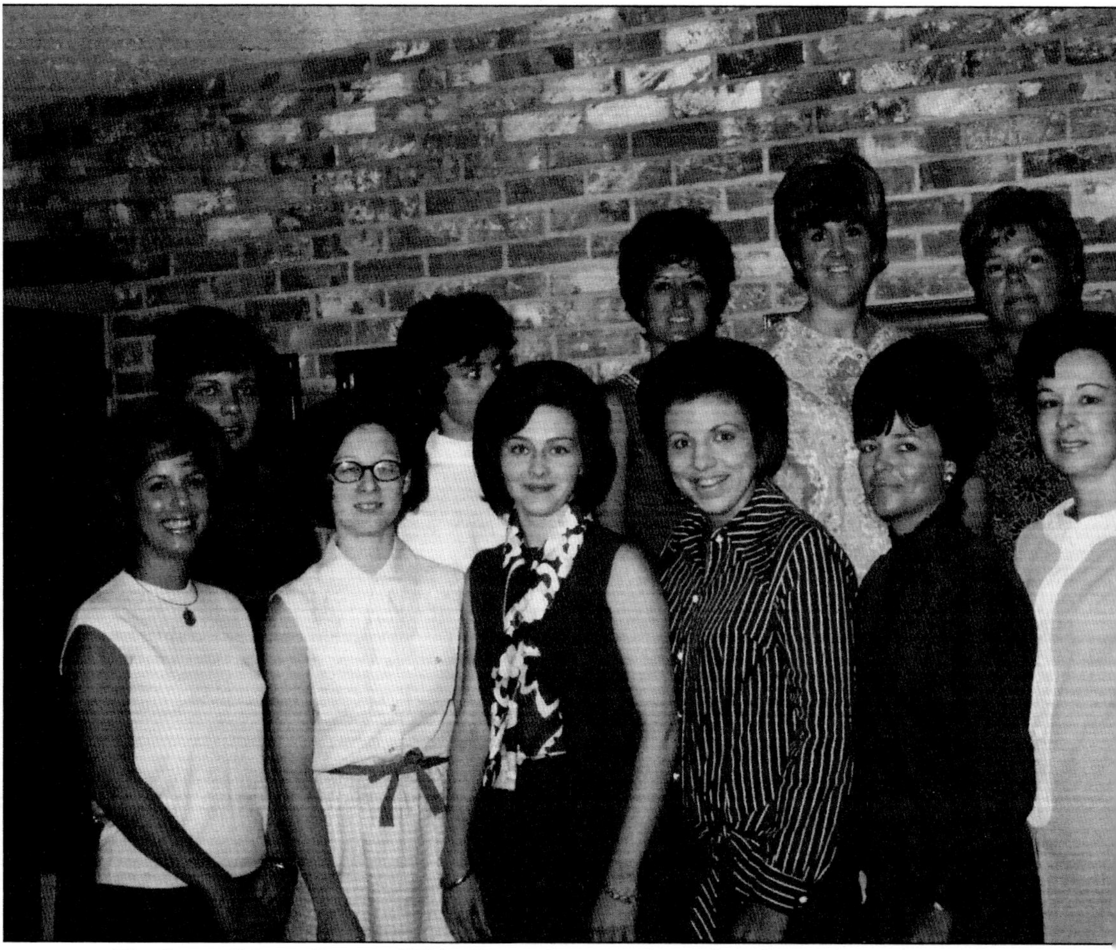

The Junior Service League (JSL) of Brazosport was formed in the summer of 1970. It provided a group of young women ages 21 to 40, who were trained in a program of education and volunteer service, to participate effectively in the community. Susan Pope, seen in the first row on the left, was the first president to the 1971 board of directors. Pictured are, from left to right, (first row) Susan Pope, Alida Fry, Jill Brown, Marcie Holt, Martha Jo Bennett, and Becky Dusek; (second row) Dorothy Ann Davis, Linda Cragar, Nancy Olefke, Glenda Ransom, and Nan Gorsuch. Over the years, the group has contributed to Lake Jackson with many events and projects such as the JSL city park on Yaupon Street, the Emergency Room Hosts, the Bargain Box, the Children's Safe Driving School, and more. (Courtesy of the Junior Service League.)

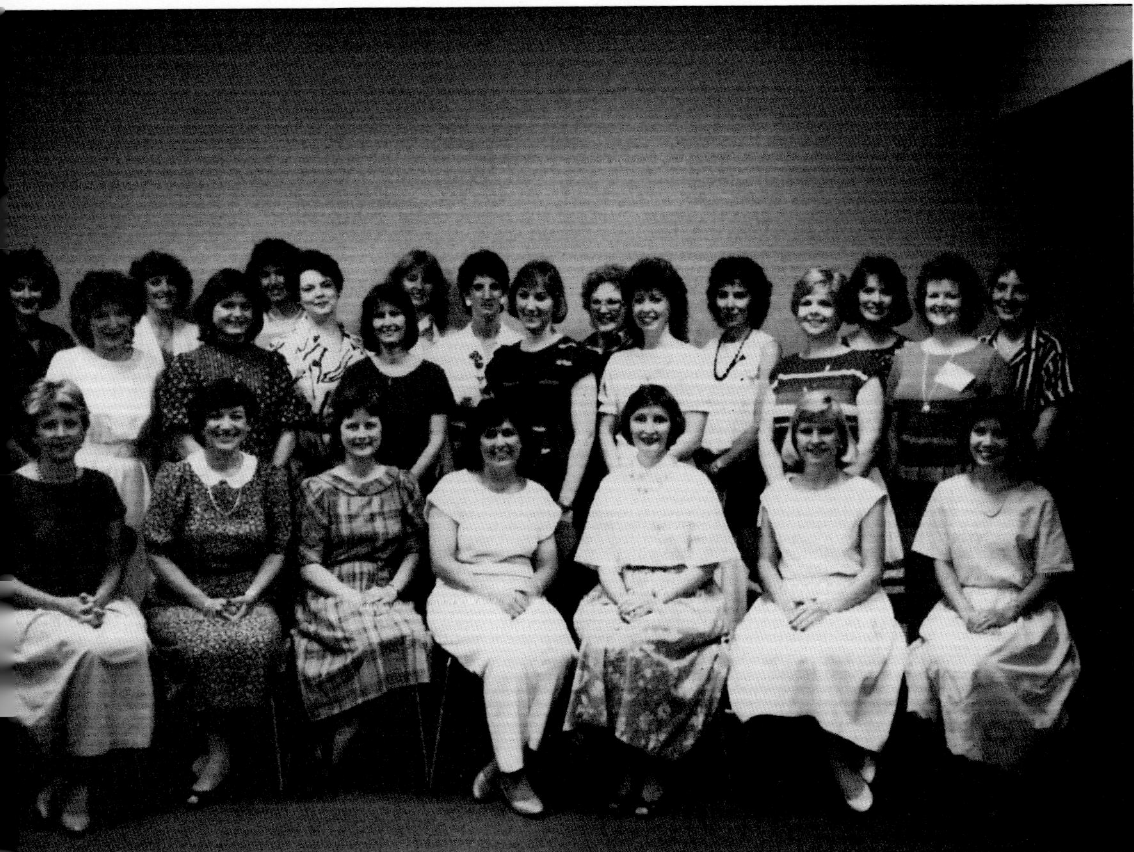

The 1986 Junior Service League Provisional Class members are, from left to right, (seated) Binnie Bauml, Marilyn Woody, Jonsi Elam, Georgia Huff, Delores Smith, Jo Ann Brown, Ann Moon; (standing) Peggy McKnight, Bonnie Corbett, Connie Ralston, Cindy Carhcart, Kay Hoffman, Jane Ray, Jan Davis, Kendal McDaniel, Alice Campbell, Betsy Travis, unidentified, Karen Moran, Janis Warny, Marilyn Mathews, Olivia Suazo, Suzanne Stofer, and Tami Blevins. (Courtesy of the Junior Service League.)

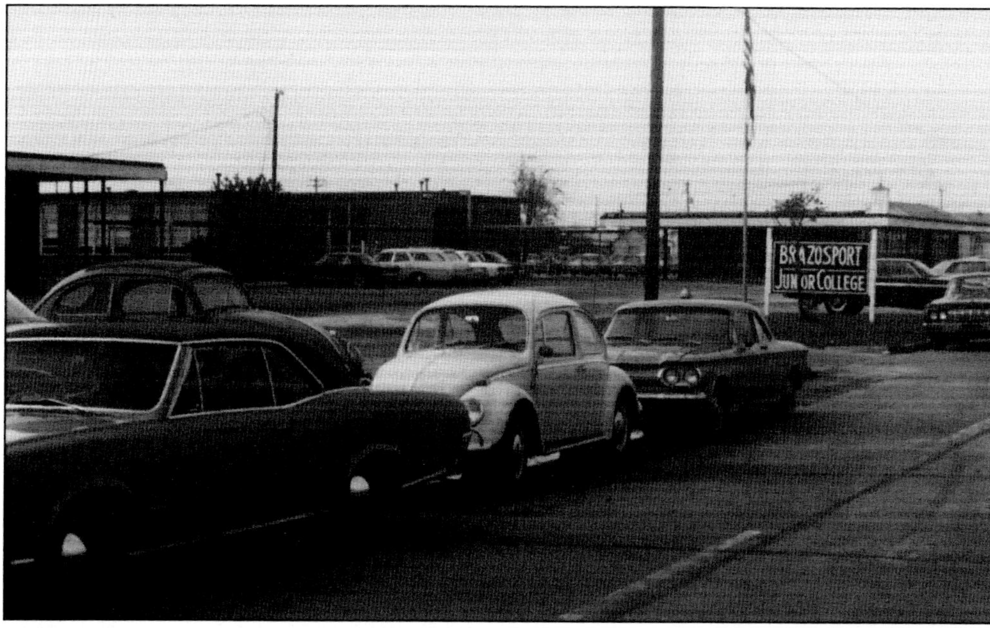

The Brazosport Independent School District voters approved Brazosport Junior College in 1948. Voters authorized a tax to support the maintenance of the college in 1967. The college admitted its first class of 879 students in the former Lanier High School in the fall semester of 1968. After the citizens approved a bond issue, a 156-acre site at the Lake Jackson and Clute city limits was chosen to construct a permanent facility. (Courtesy of Brazosport College.)

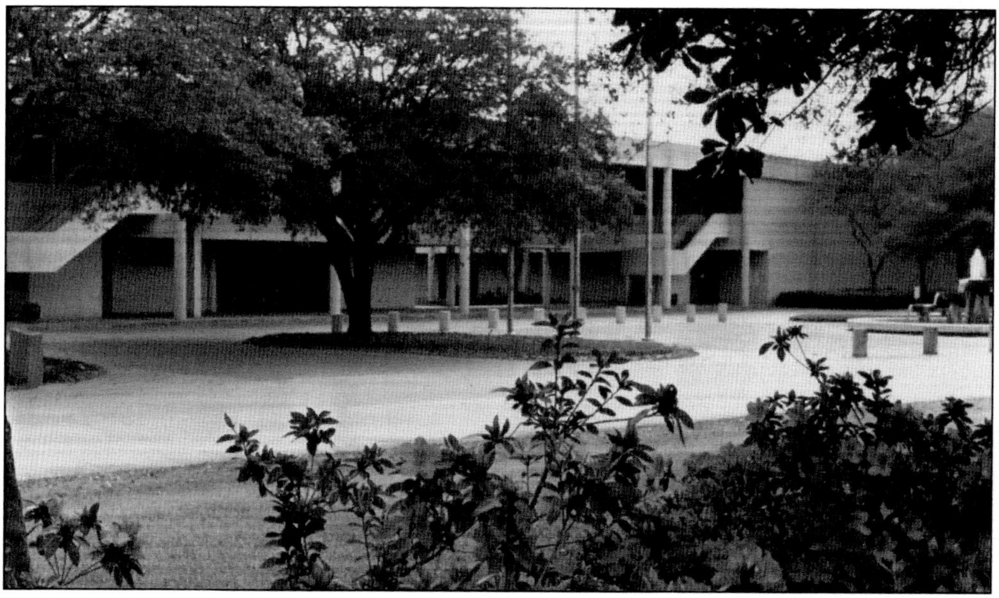

The college's permanent facility in Lake Jackson was initially a single structure that allowed students to move between classes while being sheltered from wet weather. Staff offices, a library, a bookstore, a cafeteria, and a student center are all in the primary structure. Separate buildings were added for the day care facility and the Clarion Performance Hall and music department. In 2011, new classrooms were added in the BASF and Dow buildings, along with an impressive front entry suitable for the campus complex. (Courtesy of Brazosport College.)

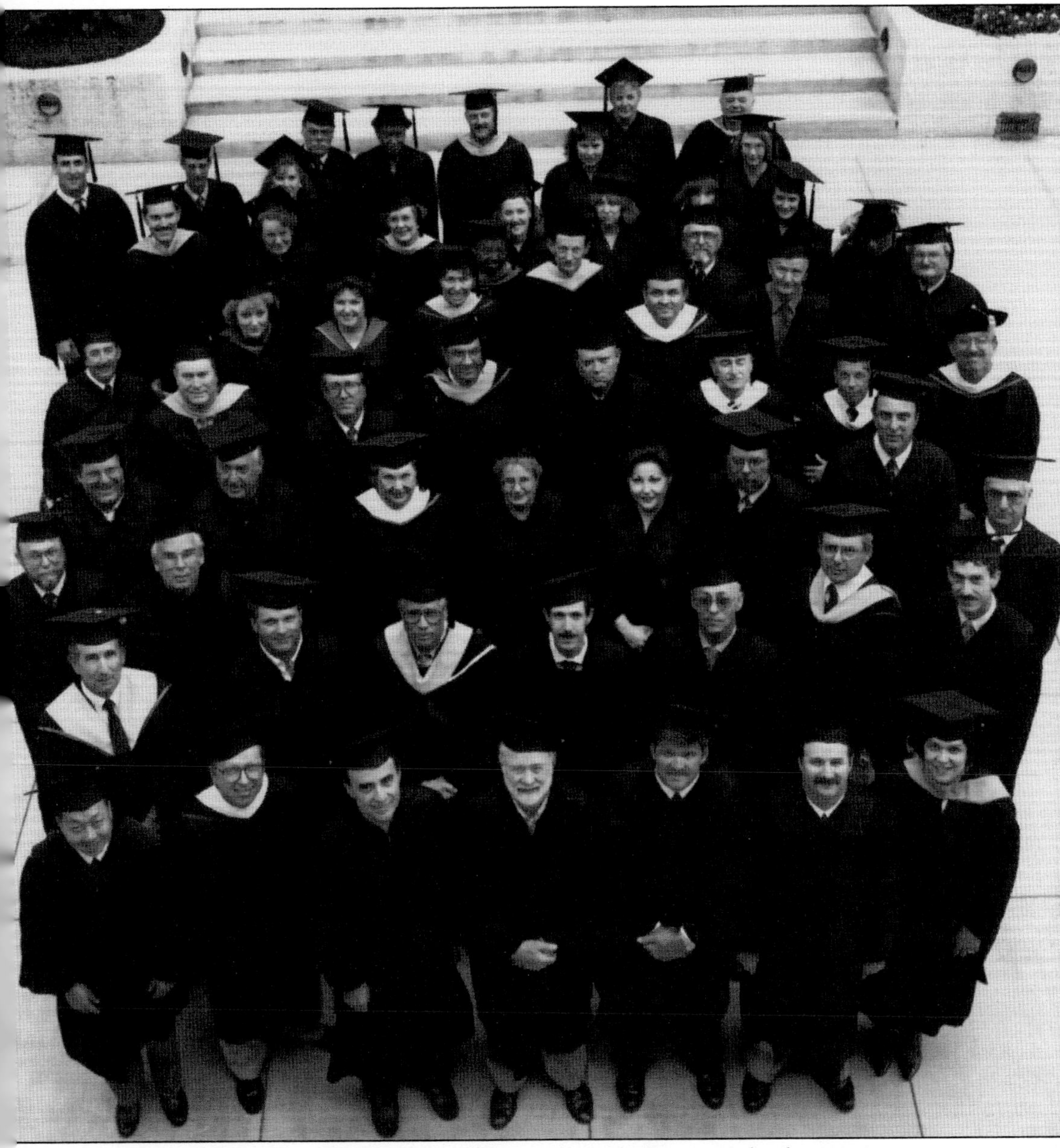

The Brazosport College faculty members gather in their academic regalia for a group picture before a commencement exercise. (Courtesy of Brazosport College.)

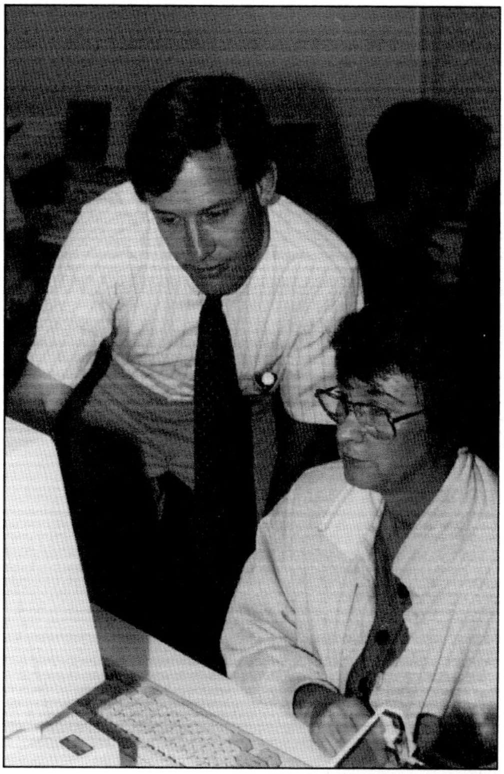

Andy Smith, faculty member at Brazosport College in the computer technology department, gives guidance to a student in a college computer lab. These facilities are also used for adult learning programs twice a year and business training sessions for various local industries. (Courtesy of Brazosport College.)

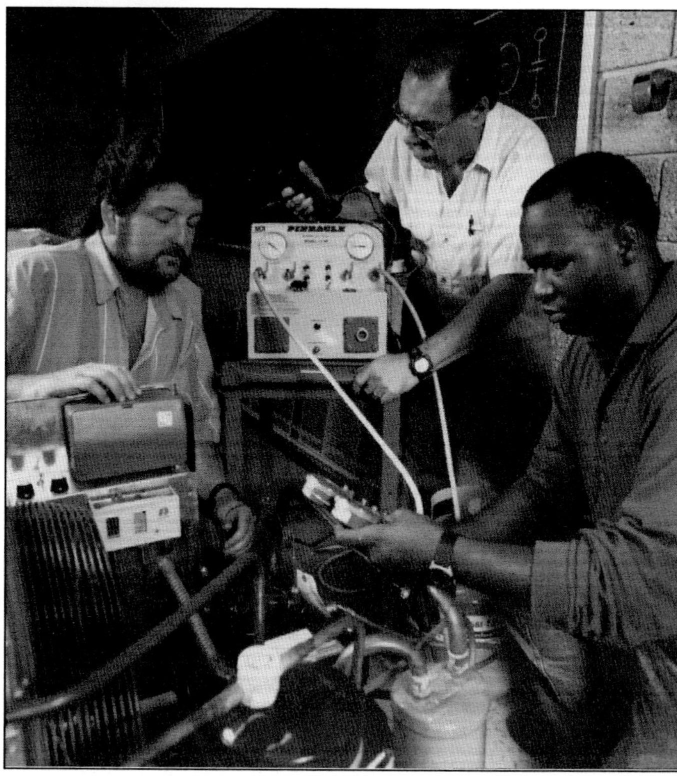

Walt Fitzpatrick, a faculty member at Brazosport College in air-conditioning and refrigeration, instructs students in pressure readings. This is one of the vocational training areas providing technicians for local industry. Other vocational fields include nursing, law enforcement, welding, electricity, chemical plant operations, laboratory, automotive, construction, computers, instrumentation, pipefitting, and others. (Courtesy of Brazosport College.)

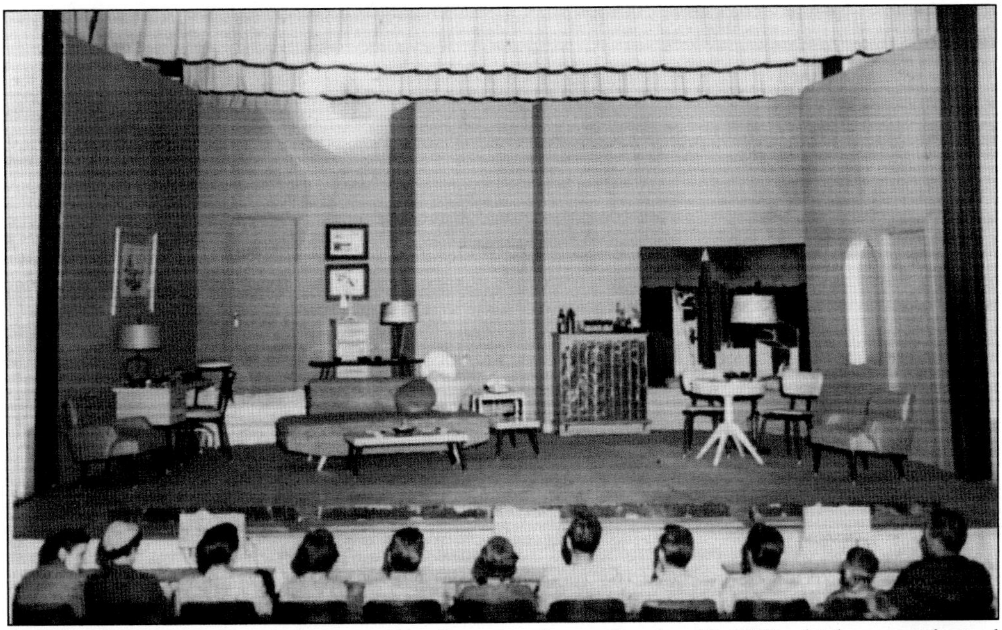

Little Theater for Brazosport began with a three-act play on October 29, 1943, which was performed on the High School Stage. It was such a success that the actor participants contributed $10 each to prepare for the next performance. They would perform several two-night runs at the high school by carrying sets to the stage from a storage building. In 1952, they moved into their own facility in a refurbished house in Velasco. (Courtesy of the Brazosport Center for the Arts and Sciences.)

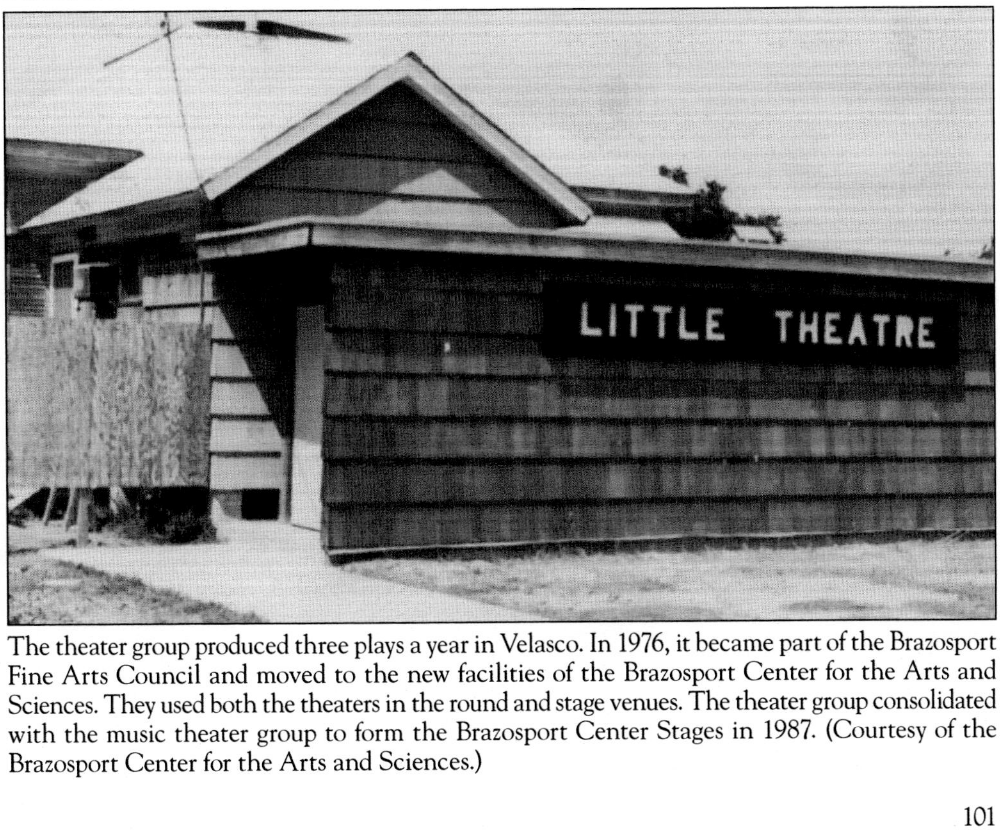

The theater group produced three plays a year in Velasco. In 1976, it became part of the Brazosport Fine Arts Council and moved to the new facilities of the Brazosport Center for the Arts and Sciences. They used both the theaters in the round and stage venues. The theater group consolidated with the music theater group to form the Brazosport Center Stages in 1987. (Courtesy of the Brazosport Center for the Arts and Sciences.)

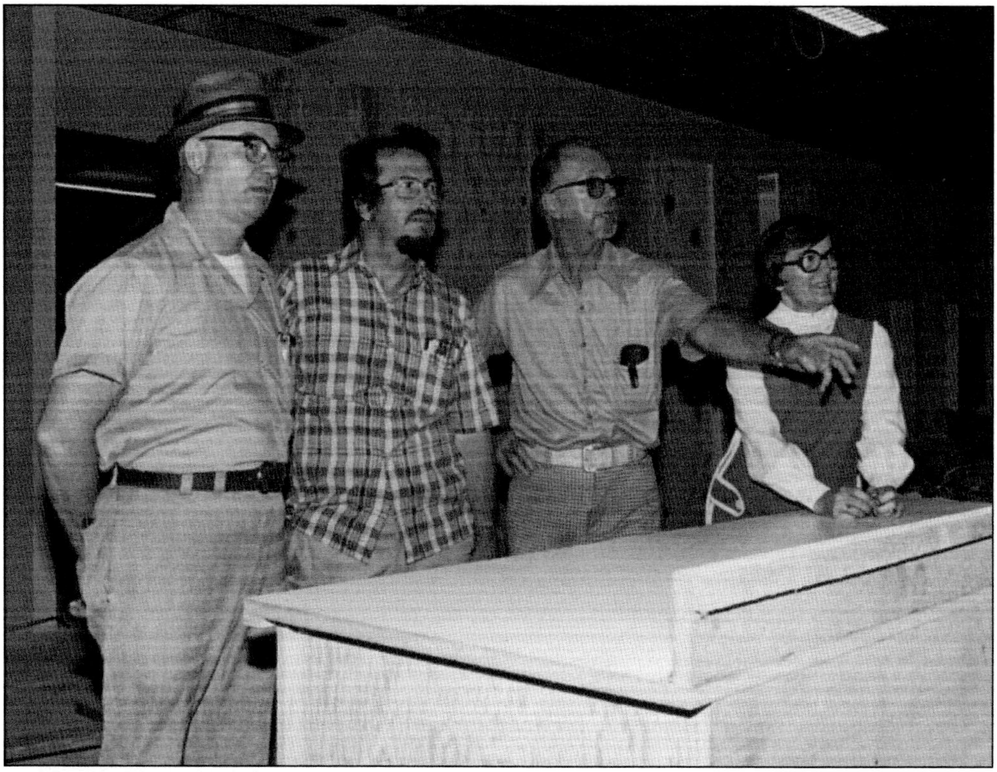

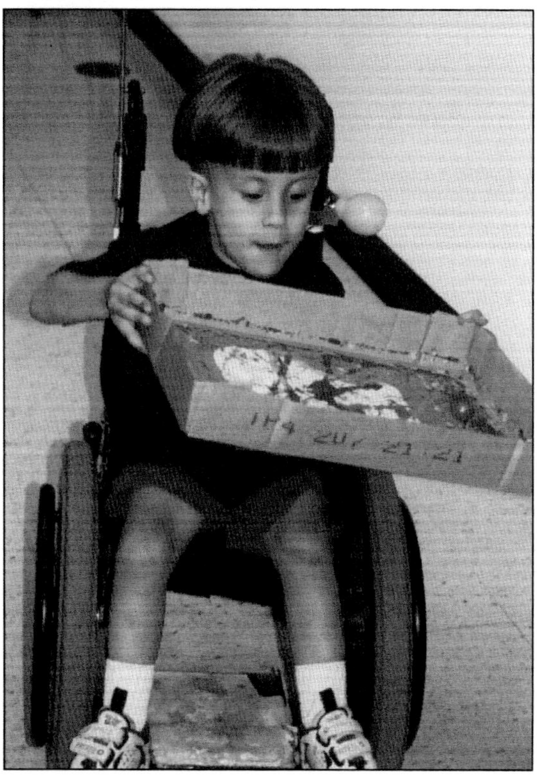

The Brazosport Art League moved into the new Center for the Arts and Sciences in 1976. Before the gallery was completed, the officers inspected the new facilities. The officers are, from left to right, Clell Sechrest, Bob Hayden, Ed Greene (president), and Arlene Baker. They try to envision the finished room. (Courtesy of the Brazosport Center for the Arts and Sciences.)

Susan Chester was the chairperson for the Brazosport Art League's Any Kids Kan program in 1997, which twice a year offers an art opportunity for local special children. The art league also began offering Art Odyssey to elementary school children in two sessions each summer beginning in the late 1970s. (Courtesy of the Brazosport Center for the Arts and Sciences.)

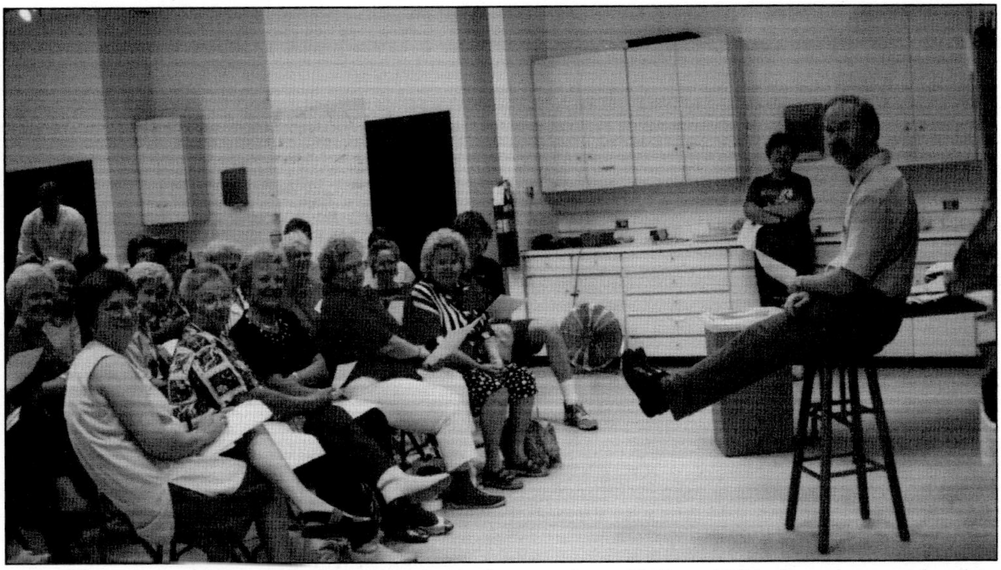

John Grotte, president of the Brazosport Art League from 1991 to 1994, directs a membership meeting in 1993. The members are, from left to right, (first row) Lil' Anna Klein, three unidentified women, and Julia Sikes; (second row) Peggy Mungerson, Joannie Covell, three unidentified women, Doris Munson, Dot Salisbury, Patty Schulte, and Carolyn Tunnel. Brenda McNinny is standing to the right. (Courtesy of the Brazosport Center for the Arts and Sciences.)

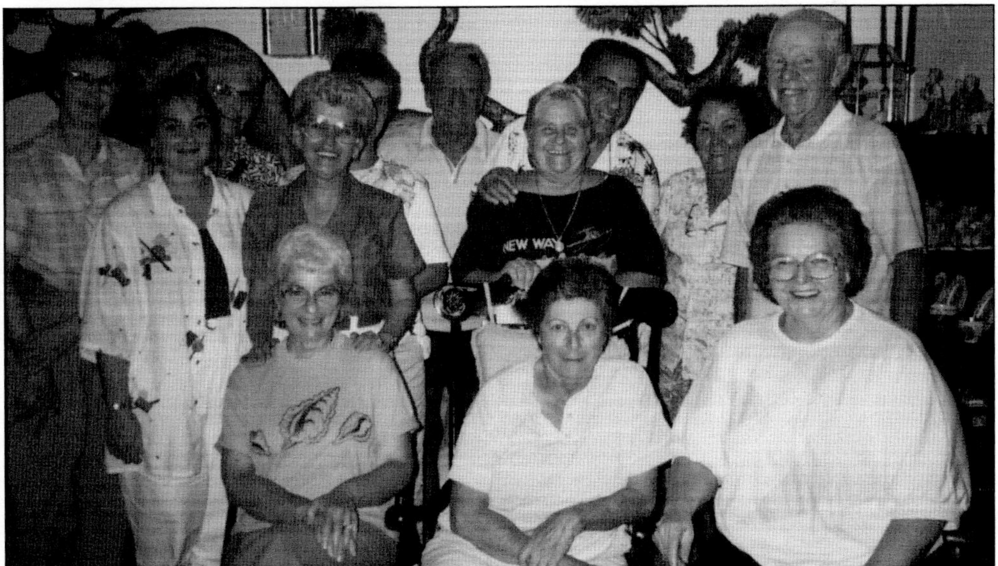

Mildred Tate and A.P. Beutel started the Brazosport Museum of Natural Science in 1964 as the Brazosport Youth Museum in Lake Jackson, adjacent to the Ben Franklin store. In 1969, the scope increased and the name changed to the current BMNS. A key to this group is several small, special interest groups. The 1989 shellers are, from left to right, (first row) Mary Rogers, Bea Sanchez, and Ester Billick; (second row) unidentified, Marinelle Jones, and Hulio Santiago (a Venezuelan guest); (third row) Freida White, Mildred Brothers, Dean Woodard, Don Brunner, Rudolpho Santiago (a Venezuelan guest), Betty Bickham, and Joe Rogers. (Courtesy of the Brazosport Center for the Arts and Sciences.)

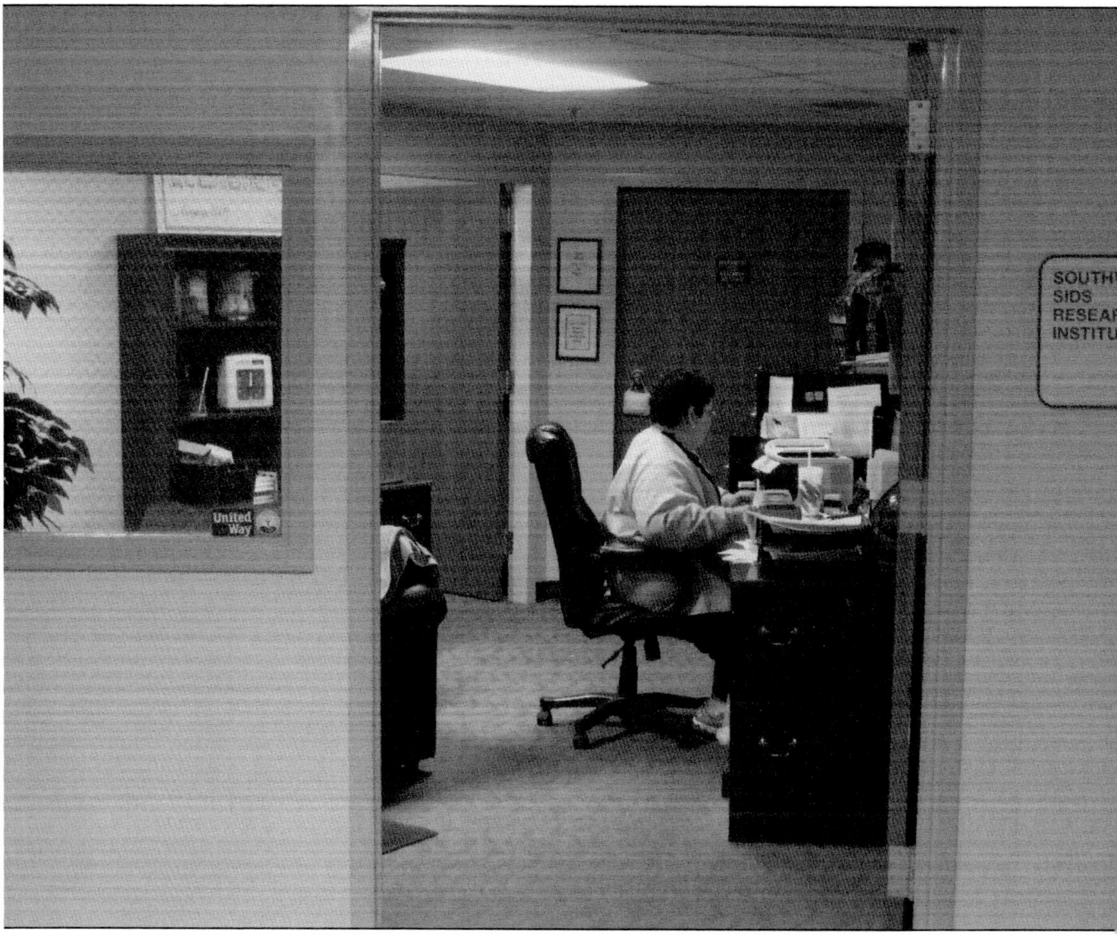

The Southwest SIDS Research Institute is located on the second floor of the Brazosport Regional Hospital. This organization was among the first clinics to address sudden infant death syndrome. Thanks to major contributions from Dow Chemical Company, the Rollin M. Gerstacker Foundation of Midland, Michigan, and United Way, it has provided sleep studies for tens of thousands of patients in this region of Texas.

Founded by Richard A. Hardoin, MD, FAAP (Fellowship of American Academy of Pediatricians), and Judith A. Henslee, LMSW (Licensed Master Social Worker), the Southwest SIDS Research Institute, opened in November 1984. In September 2007, they helped author *The Voice Within*, a book written to comfort families who have experienced premonitions and then have lost their babies to SIDS. (Courtesy of the Southwest SIDS Research Institute.)

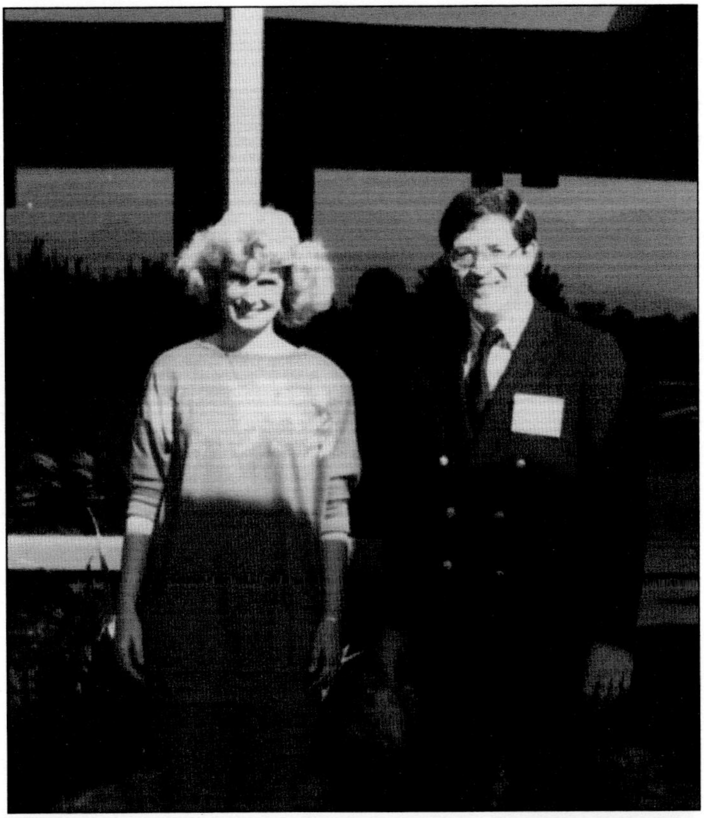

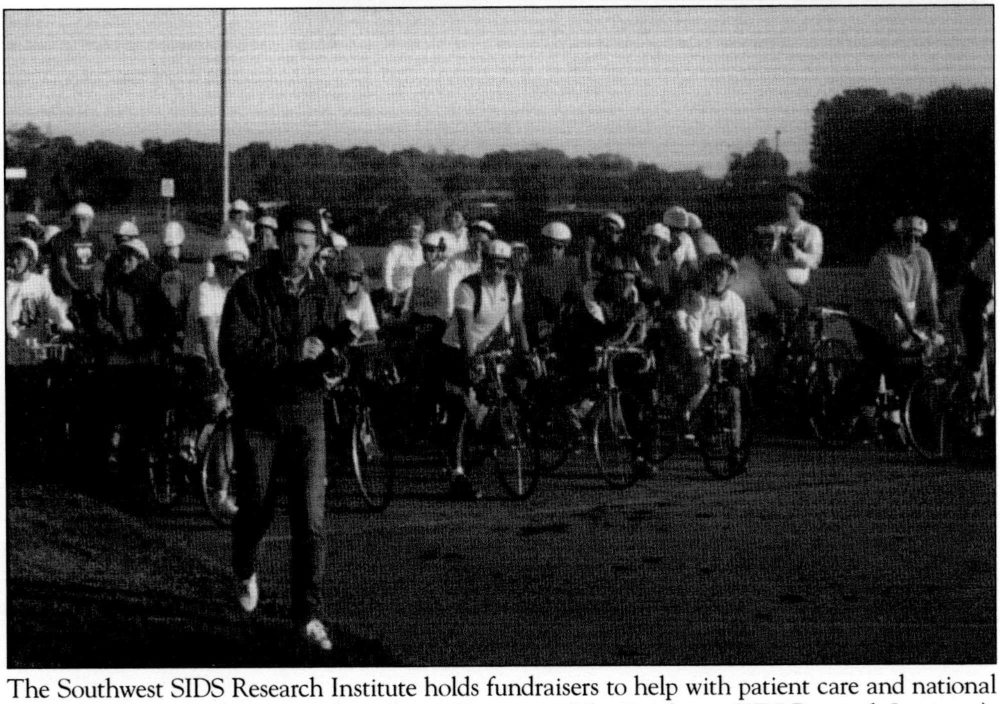

The Southwest SIDS Research Institute holds fundraisers to help with patient care and national research programs. This was a bike-a-thon. (Courtesy of the Southwest SIDS Research Institute.)

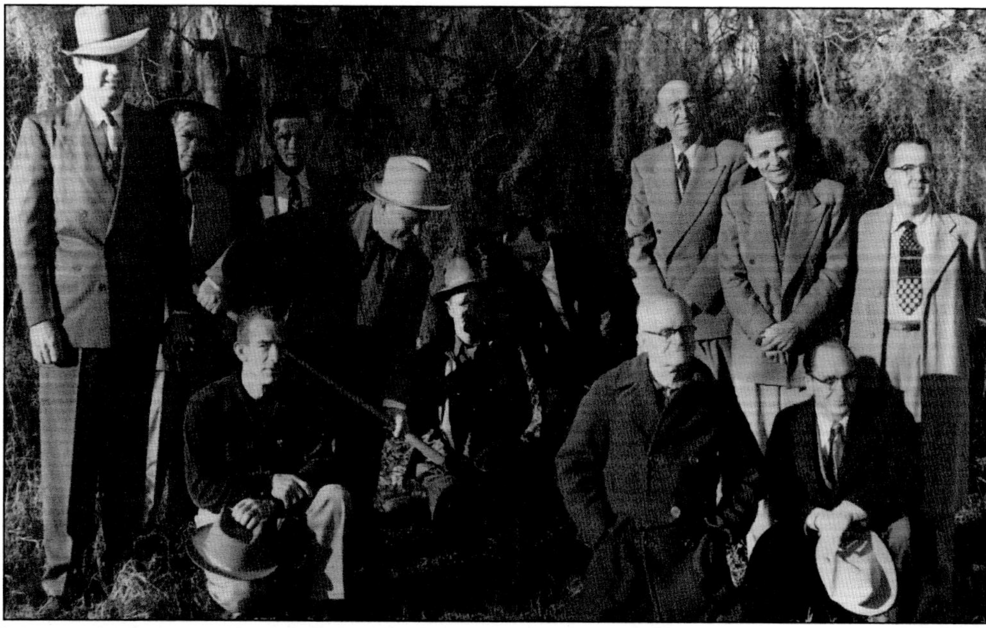

Masonic Lodge No. 1317 AF & AM (Ancient Free and Accepted Masons) first met in Brazoria in 1948. The Masons follow the vision to "take good men and make them better." The Clute Masonic Lodge No. 1334 discontinued meeting in 1953 and consolidated with Lake Jackson. In 1952, the Masonic lodge broke ground for its lodge in downtown Lake Jackson. W.D. Colegrove is using the shovel. Pictured are, from left to right, (first row) J.Q. Bennett, J.S. Strother, and G.F. Reichenbach; (second row) W.D. Skaggs, F.M. Sanders, H.S. Efird, B.C. Stevens, D.M. Stovall, H. Slife, M.O. Kavanaugh, and J.E. Chism. (Courtesy of Masonic Lodge No. 1317.)

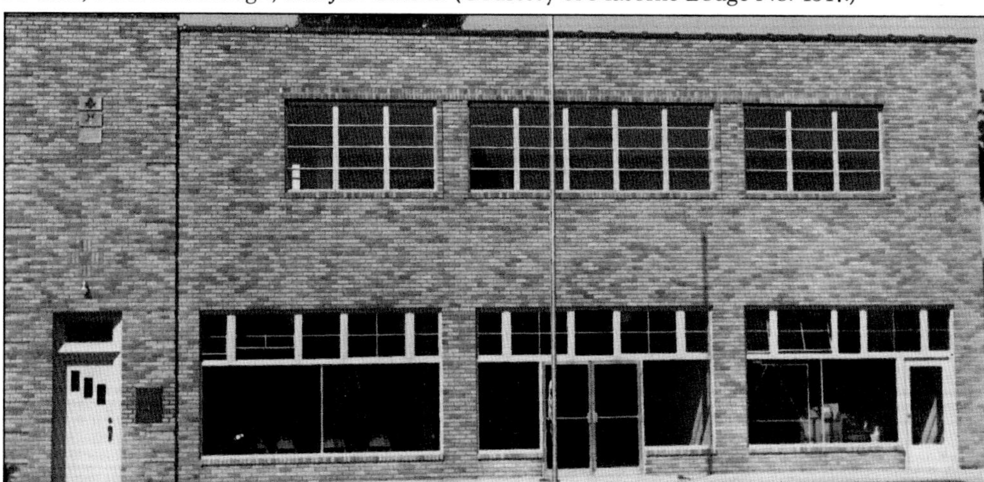

The lodge was dedicated in 1953. Charter members in 1949 were (by last name) Bechtel, Barnes, Bennett, Beutel, Bowles Jr., Brown Jr., Brumbelow, Cason, Chism, Colegrove, Condit, Cone Jr., Christian, Crout, Cutshall, Davidson, Davis, Dearman, Denton, Dickerson, Dunn, Efird, Ewing, Fisher, Floyd, Franklin, Frederick, Glenn, Goodyear, Guinn, Glenn Harris, Hibbetts, Hood, Kavanaugh, Lewis, Lindveit, McKibbon, Malone, Marshall, Morrison, Nance, Perryman, Pevey, Raney, Rawlins Jr., Rawlins Sr., Reichenbach, Richardson, Robbins, Roddy, and Sanders. Downstairs offices were rented by the post office and Bob Franklin's Insurance. (Courtesy of Masonic Lodge No. 1317.)

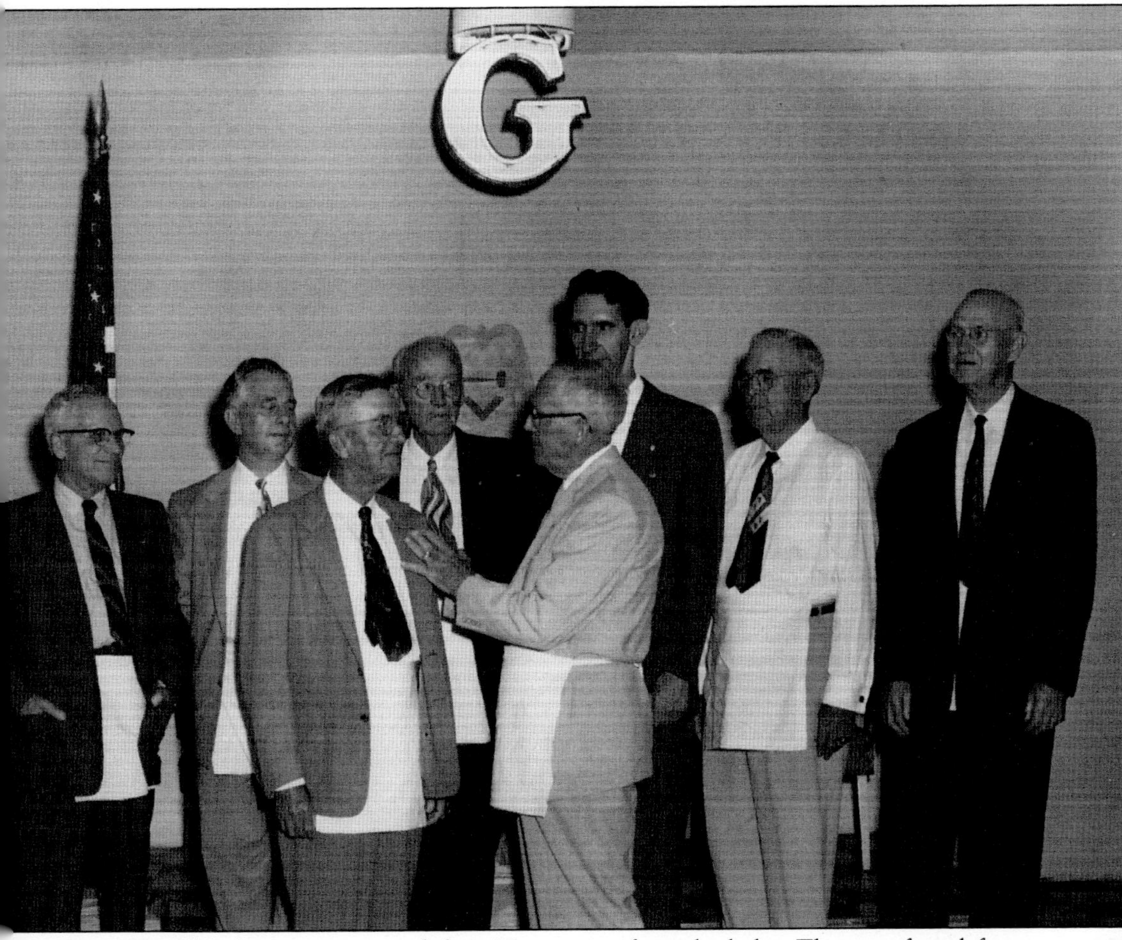

On May 18, 1956, these men received their 25-year pins from the lodge. They are, from left to right, A.P. Beutel, G.M. Lindveit, J.P. Warren, A.C. Rawling Sr., R.E. McBride (past District Deputy Grand Master, 31st Masonic District), E.L. Perryman, R.O. Harper, and E.W. Nance. (Courtesy of Masonic Lodge No. 1317.)

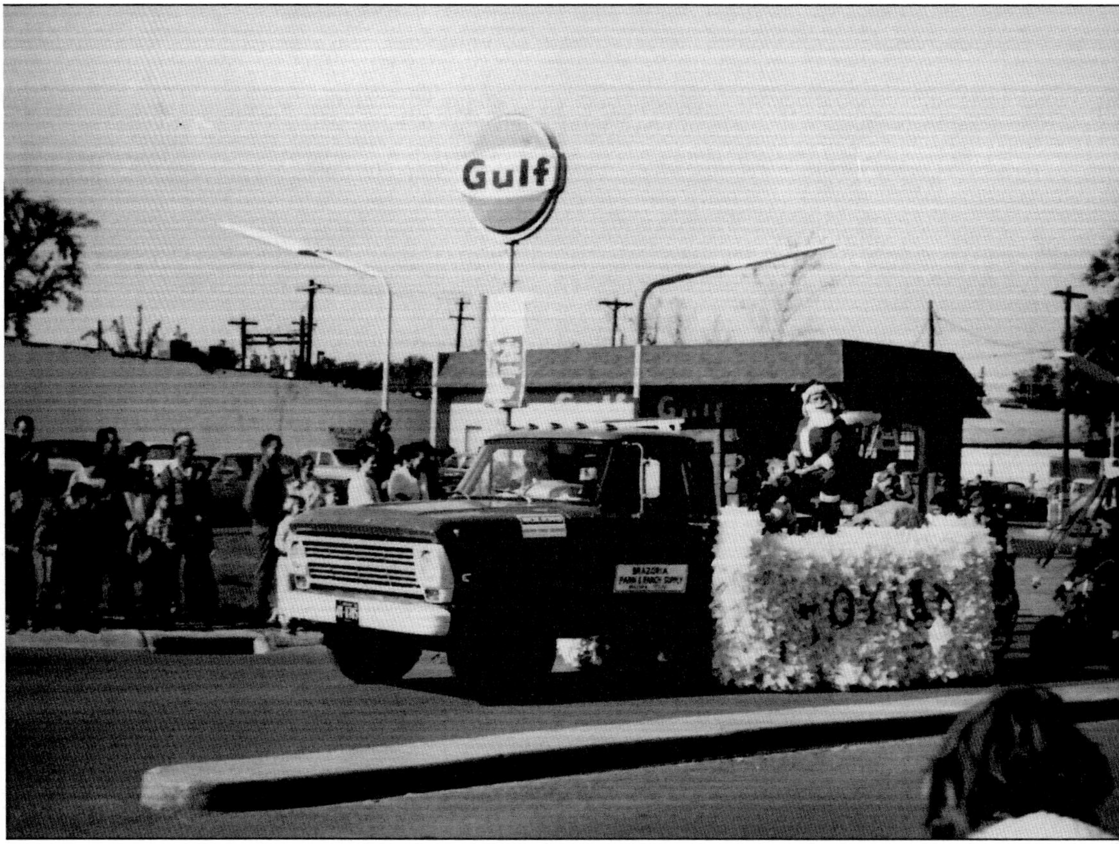

The Jaycees organized a Christmas parade in 1968, and the Jaycettes prepared the fire truck for Santa to arrive in town.

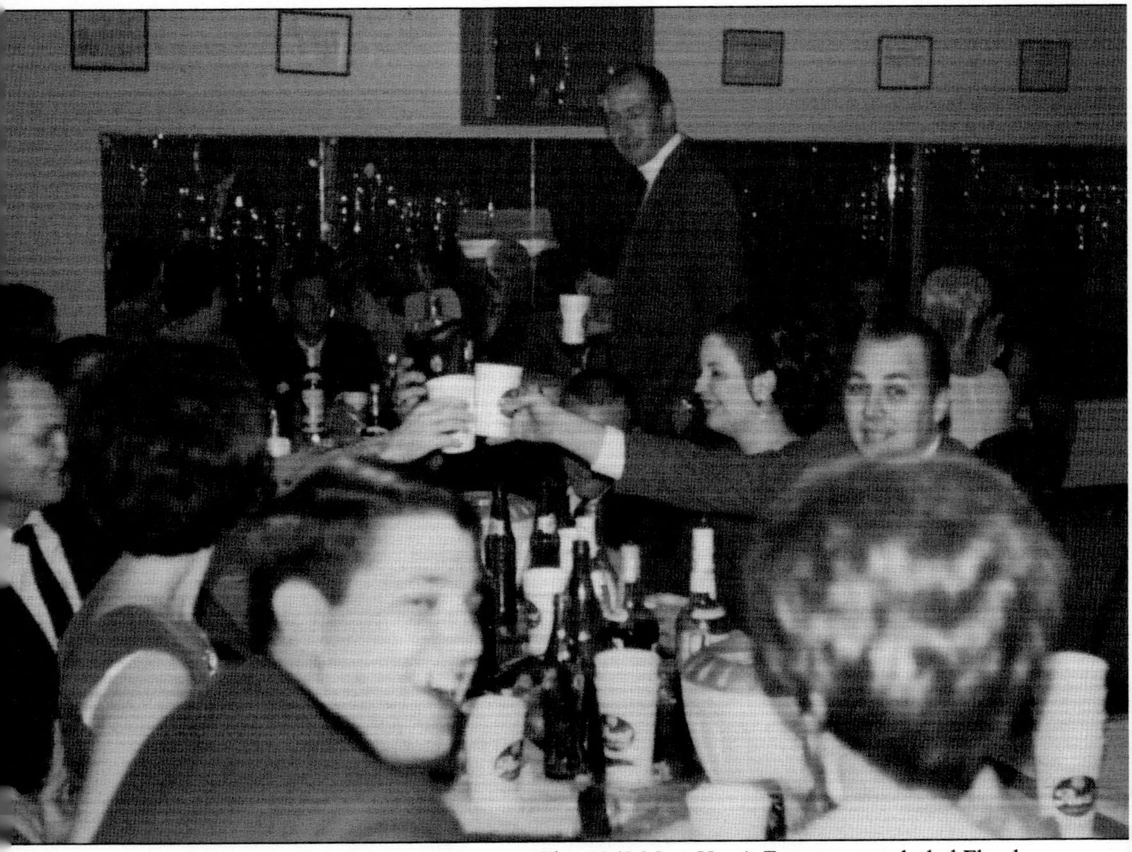

The Jaycees served a social and service purpose. The 1969 New Year's Eve party included Floyd Johnson on the left next to Suzanne Burnett. Franz June is standing. John Laundry is toasting on the right next to his wife, Claudia. Jim and Susie Huber are closest to the camera.

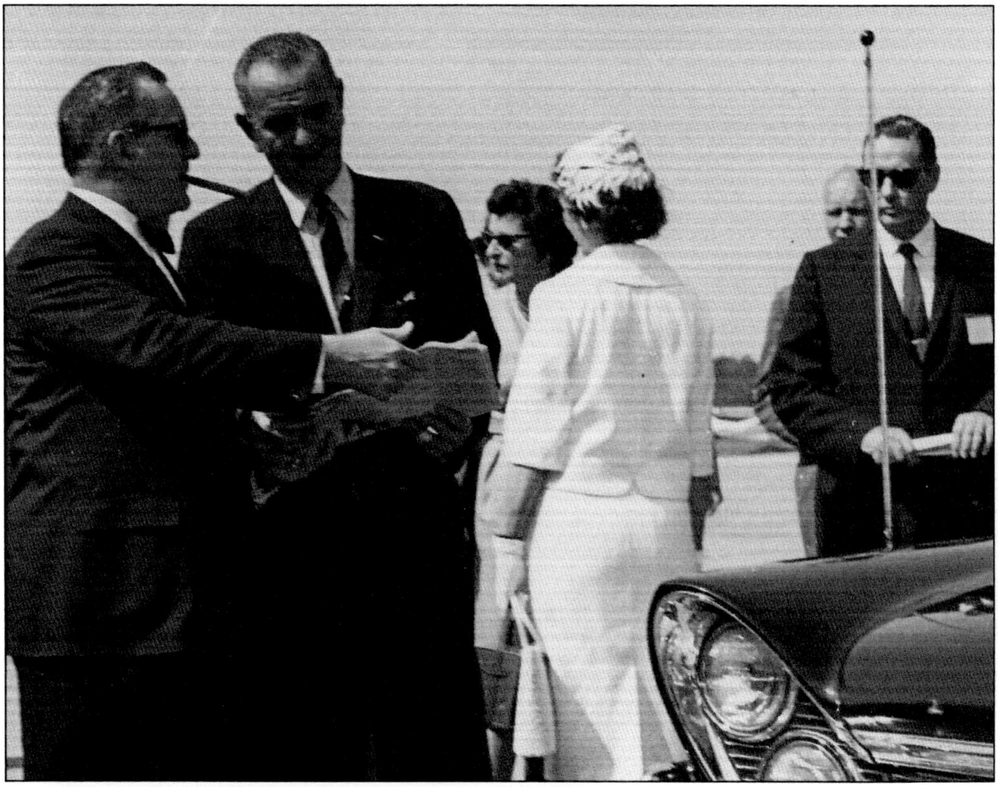

Vice President Lyndon Johnson visited Brazosport in the early 1960s. A local Democratic leader shows a copy of the town's newspaper. Johnson toured Dow Chemical Company during his visit.

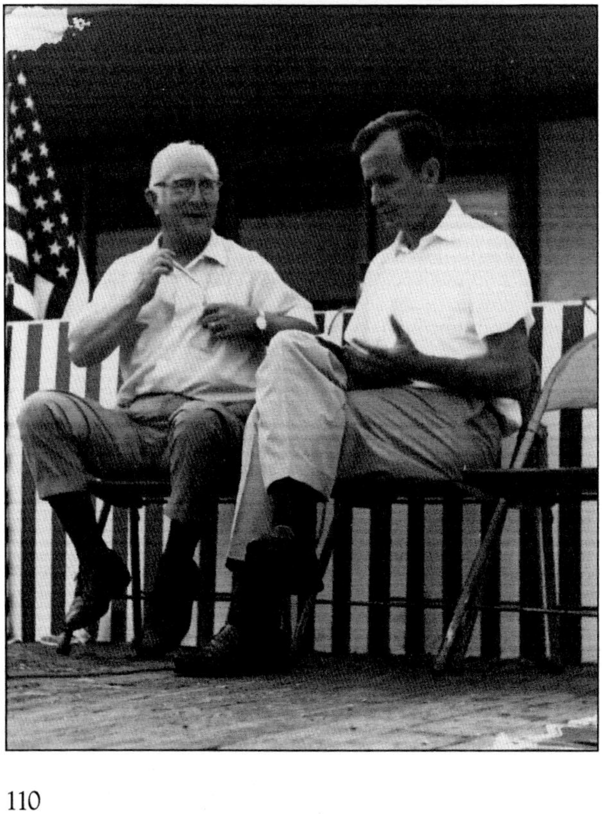

The Jaycees planned the Fourth of July celebration each year. They invited Senate candidate George Bush to speak in 1964. Here, Bush visits with Shep McKeithen—an early employee of Ethyl-Dow, local banker, entrepreneur, and GOP activist. Bush was not successful in his campaign but was later elected to the House of Representatives. He served many federal positions ultimately serving as vice president for Ronald Reagan and as the 41st president.

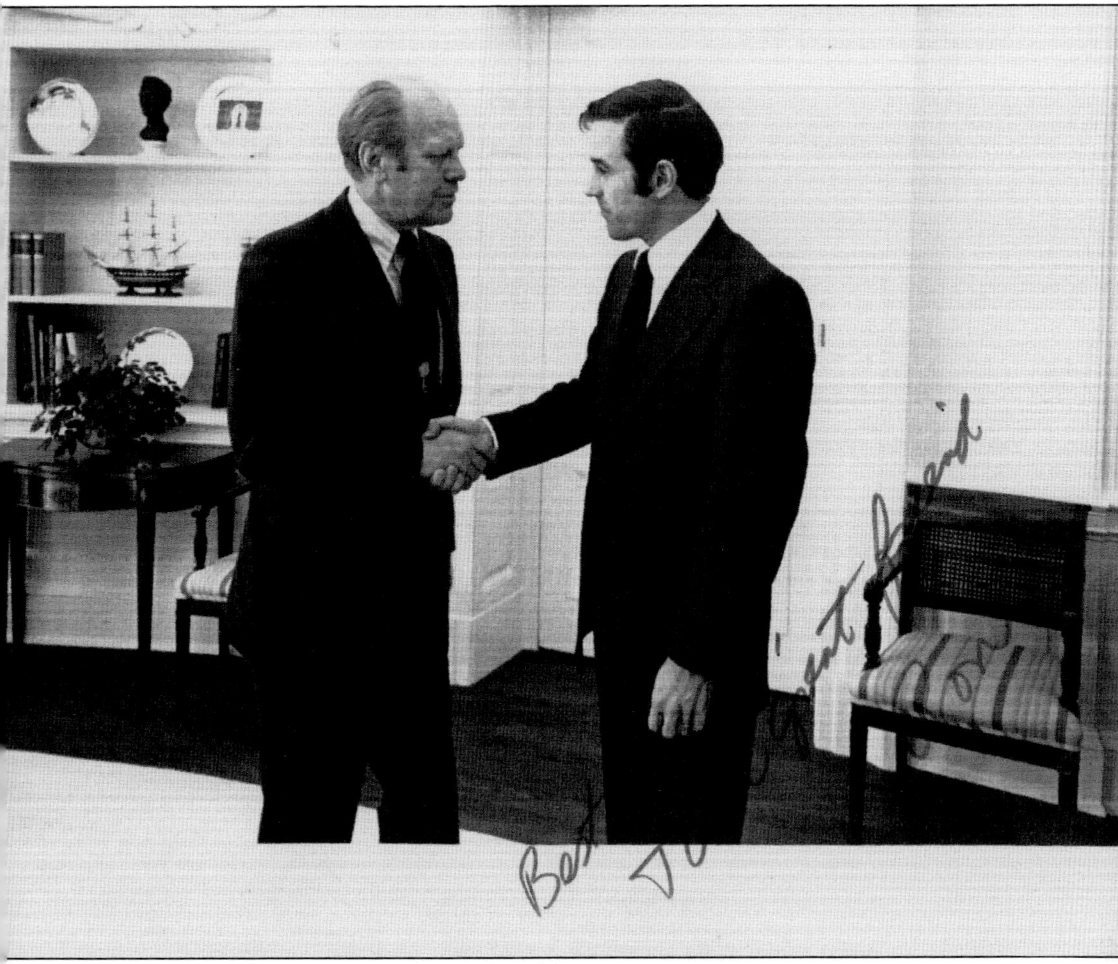

Ron Paul (right), a local obstetrician, was elected to the House of Representatives in a special election in 1976. Initially, he represented a district including Surfside and Austin. This 14th Congressional District was redistricted and Paul's district then included Lake Jackson. He is shown with Pres. Gerald Ford during Paul's first term. Paul also became known nationally during three campaigns for president in 1988, 2008, and 2012.

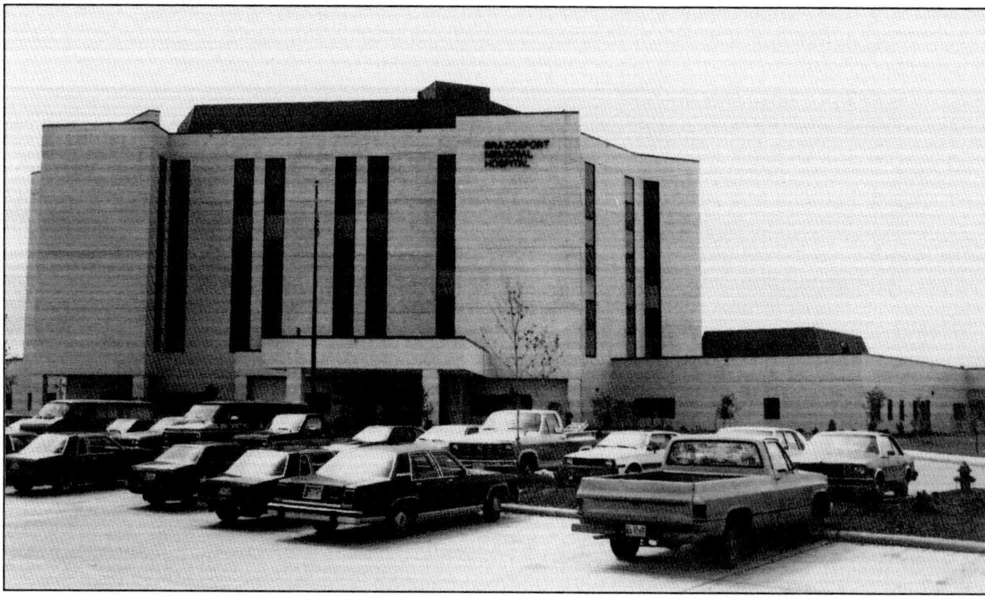

The Brazosport Community Hospital had been located at the chemical plant. Dow Chemical Company bought the hospital building and contributed land which was previously a portion of the airport in Lake Jackson. The new hospital building also received a name change to Brazosport Memorial Hospital in 1984 when it opened. There was a short public protest at the time of the move for it to become a publicly funded institution. The name was changed again to the Brazosport Regional Hospital in the 2000s.

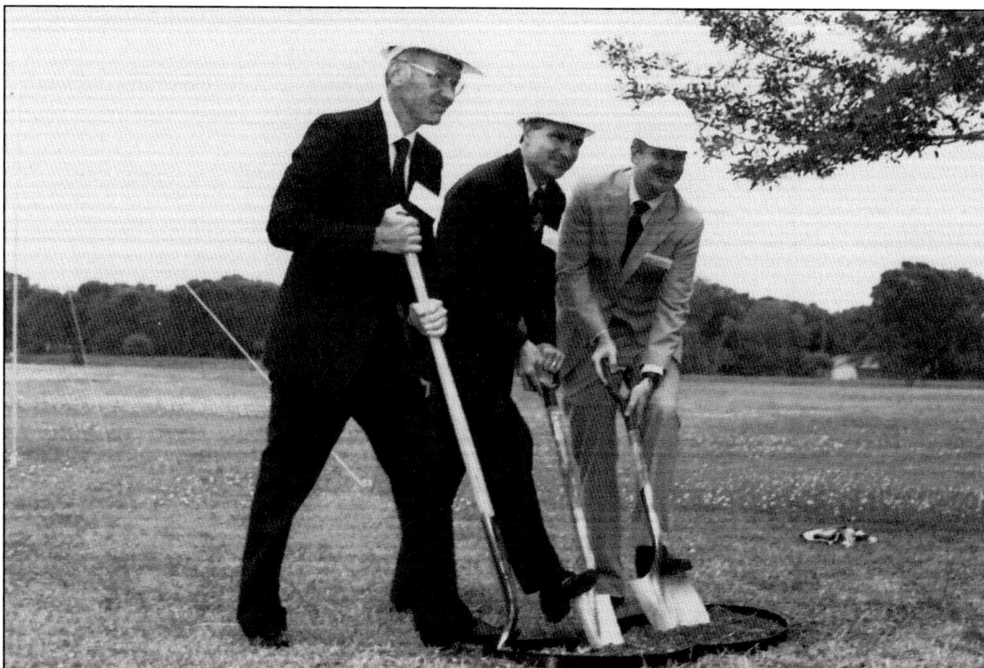

In 1991, the Brazosport Memorial Hospital Board broke ground for a cancer center. Wes Oswald (left), the hospital's chief executive officer, performed the duties with T.C. Selman (center), a health foundation board member, and Dr. Bruce Meyers, the health foundation president.

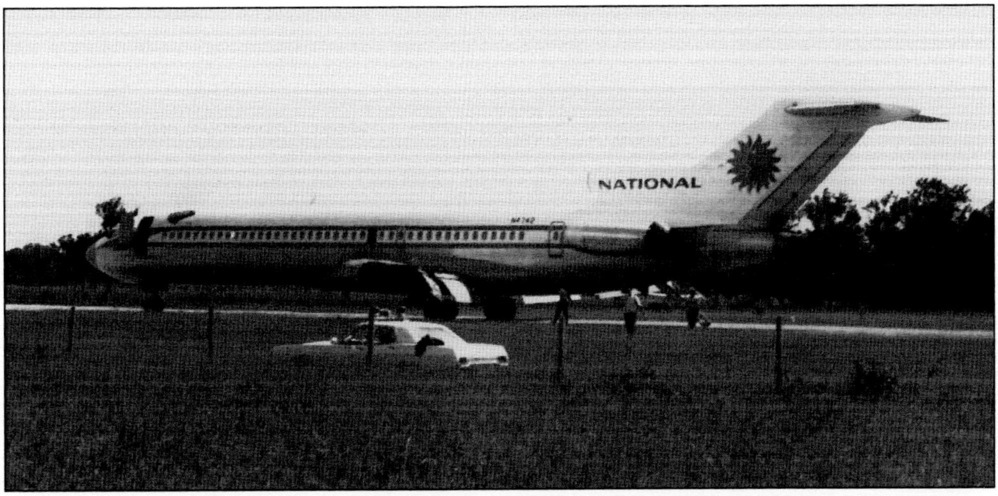

In June 1972, a National Air Lines plane was hijacked in Philadelphia. The flight path was into the Gulf of Mexico. Short of fuel, the plane landed at the Lake Jackson Airport. The summer heat ended the threat after two days of hostage holding. No one was injured.

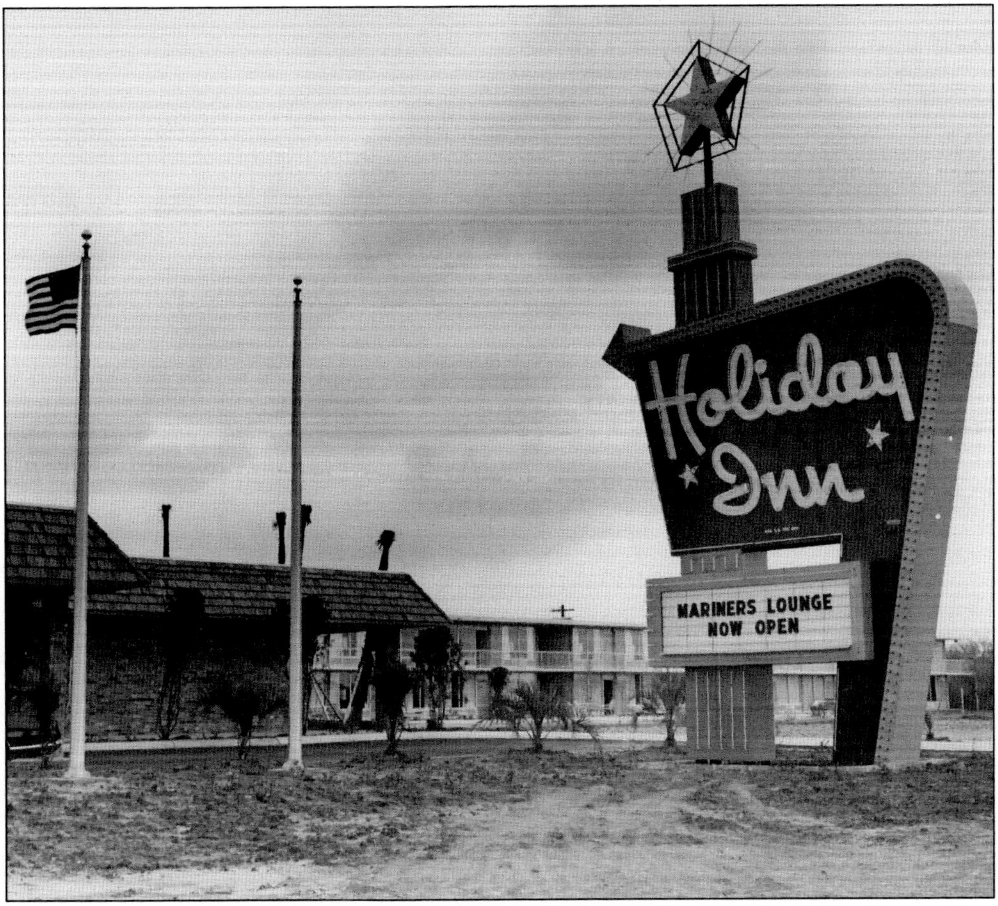

The first hotel in Lake Jackson, the Holiday Inn on Highway 332, opened in 1970. Along with it came the hotel restaurant, which added to the short list of places to eat.

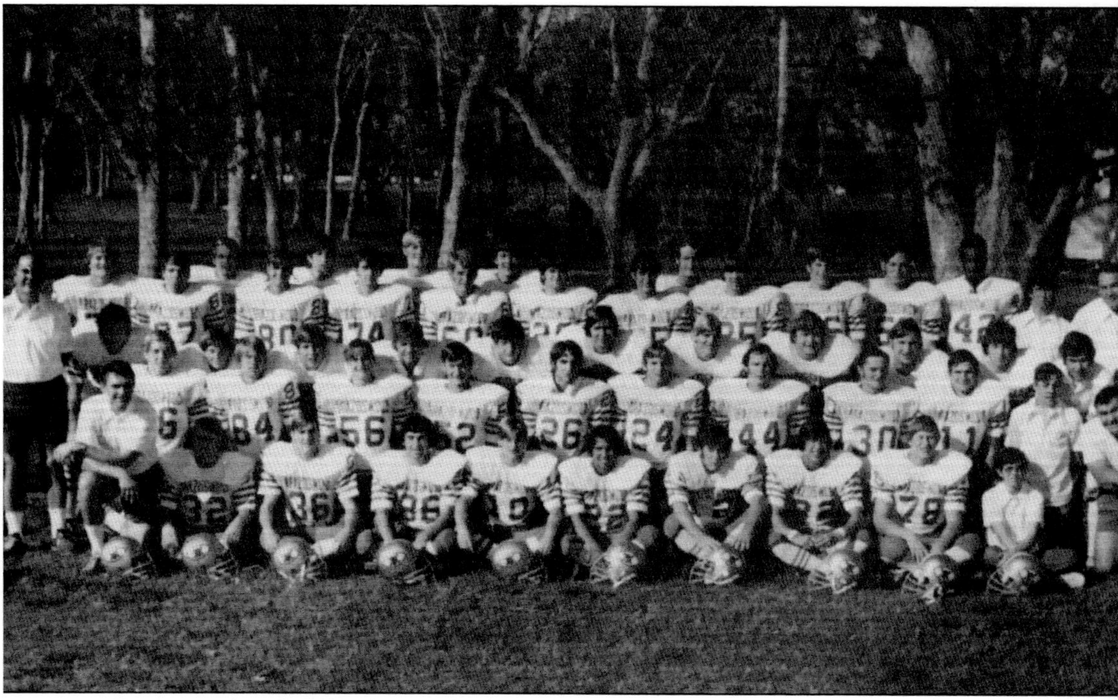

Brazoswood High School was split from Brazosport High School in 1969. In 1974, the football team won the state championship. Players are, from left to right, (front row) Coach Cuba, S. Cope, S. Simpson, P. Taylor, T. Wiggins, M. Blevins, T. Spoonemore, C. Ross, F. Barton, and R. Vera (manager); (second row) R. Patton, R. Mays, C. Faulkner, G. Rosnovsky, R. Lewis, A. McWilliams, C. Marchall, D. Bass, B. Skinner, C. Young (student trainer), and Coach Matthews; (third row) Coach Bryan, A.M. Mardis, R. Wise, R. Collins, J. Fourrier, A. Williams, C. Smith, M. Ainsworth, G. Keathley, C. Zeitler, C. Rasco, J. Ripple (student trainer), and Randy Day (athletic trainer); (fourth row) K. Kirk, D. Reimer, J. Salisbury, J. Martin, M. Wessels, D. Jouett, S. Jones, M. Baringer, S. Smith, G. Bryant, D. Benson, G. White, D. Browning, D. Jones, R. Drake, D. Hodge, H. Vera (manager), and Coach Koonce. (Courtesy of Jim Martin.)

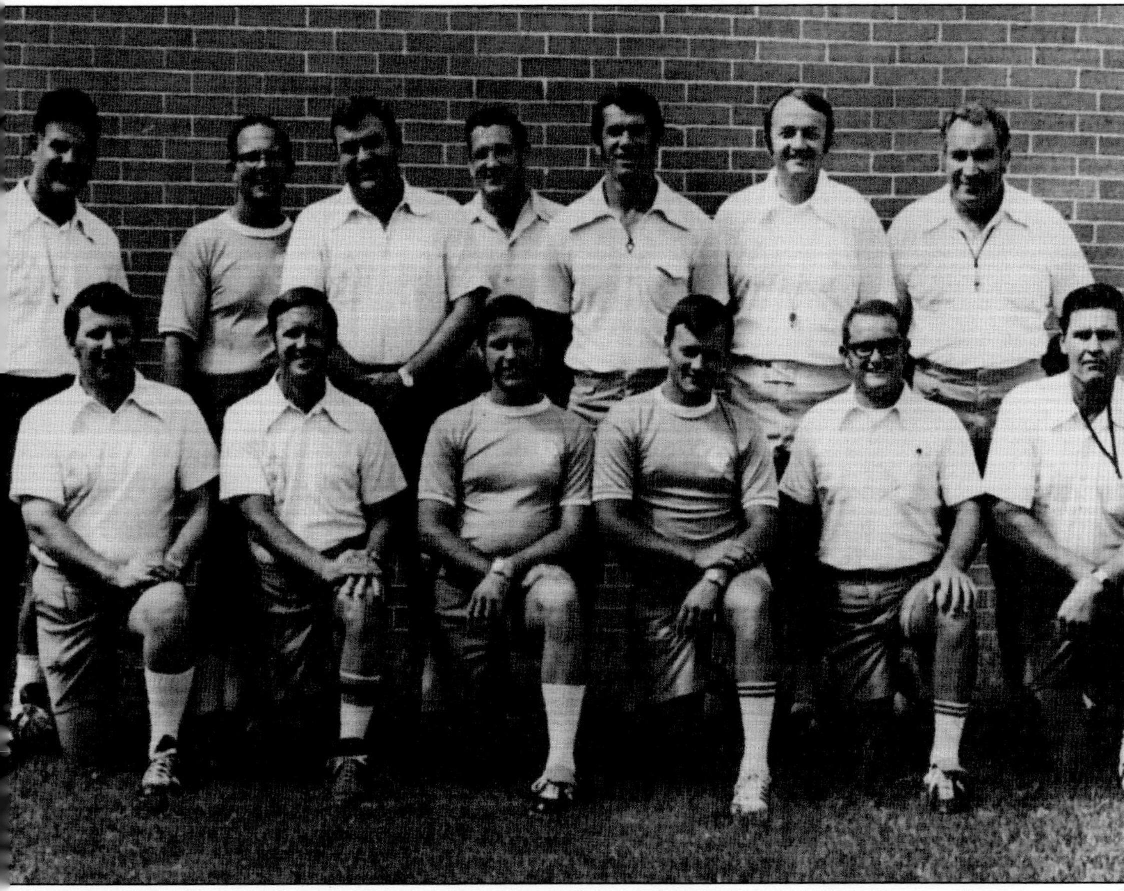

The 1974 Brazoswood football coaches are, from left to right, (front row) Billy Rogers, David Middleton, Jimmy Dodd, Jacky Mayfield, Randy Day (trainer), and Tommy Cuba; (second row) L.Z. Bryan (head coach), James "Bo" Lander, Johnny Mathews, James Davis, Benny Sorgee, Shannon Spears, and Phil Koonce. (Courtesy of Jim Martin.)

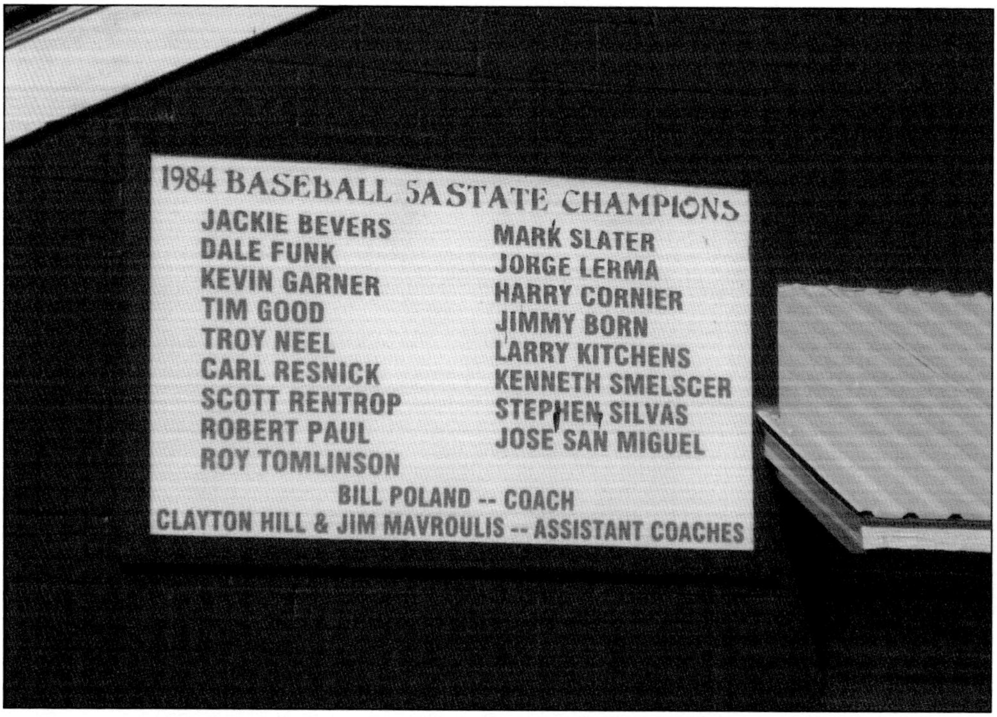

The Brazoswood baseball team won its first state championship in 1984, under the coaching of Bill Poland. Dale Funk and Kevin Garner went on to college and professional careers.

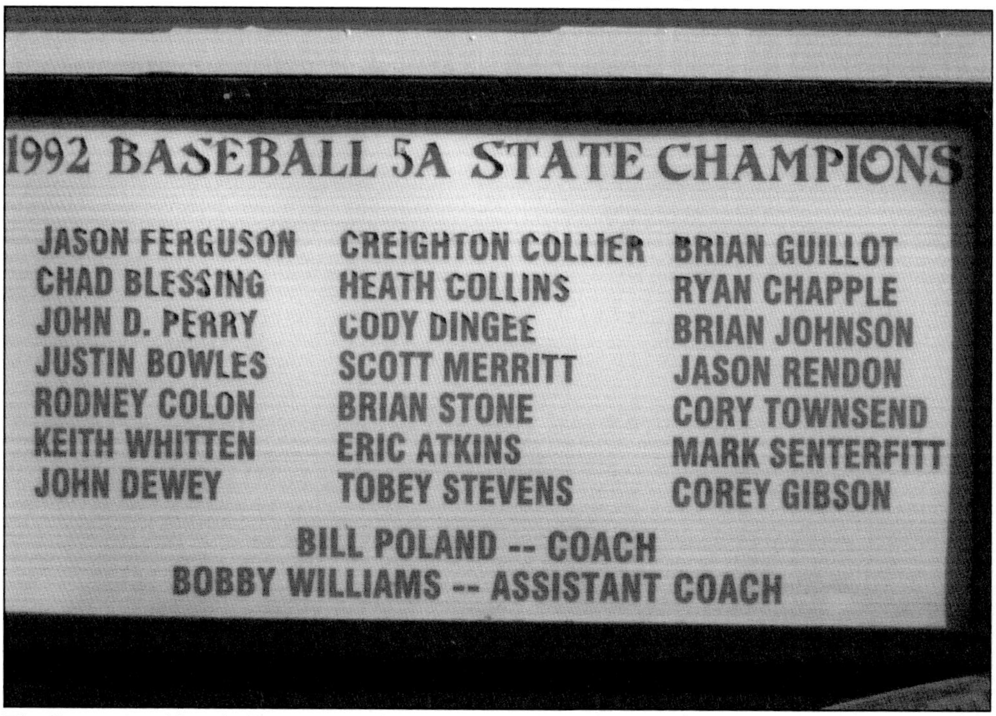

The Brazoswood baseball team won the state championship again in 1992, under the same coach, Bill Poland. This second marker was added to the field house at the stadium.

The Brazoswood girls' softball team experienced the pinnacle of achievement in 2000, when it won the state championship and was declared number one in the nation. A granite monument was erected at the new field next to Slade Field.

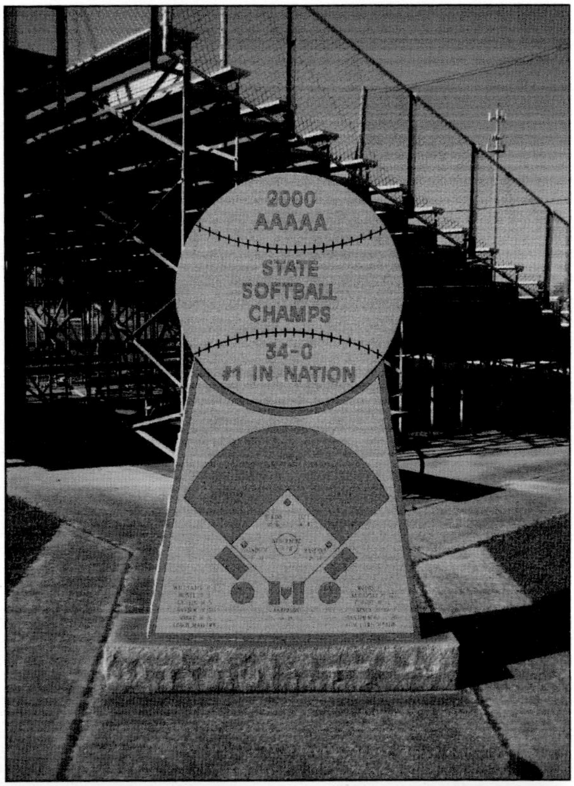

Jenna Pisarski, a junior, won the state wrestling competition in 2011. She is the first wrestler to win state in the school's short history of University Interscholastic League wrestling. Her season record was 29-0. Wrestling at Brazoswood began for girls in 2003. (Photograph by Ryan Evon; courtesy of the *Facts*.)

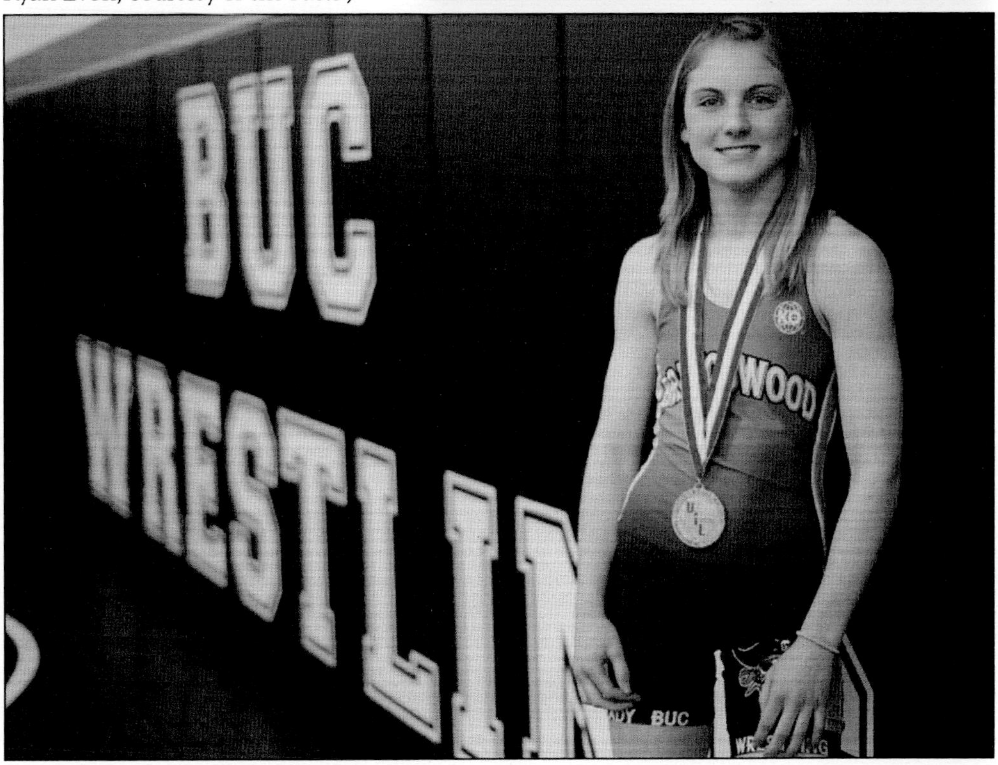

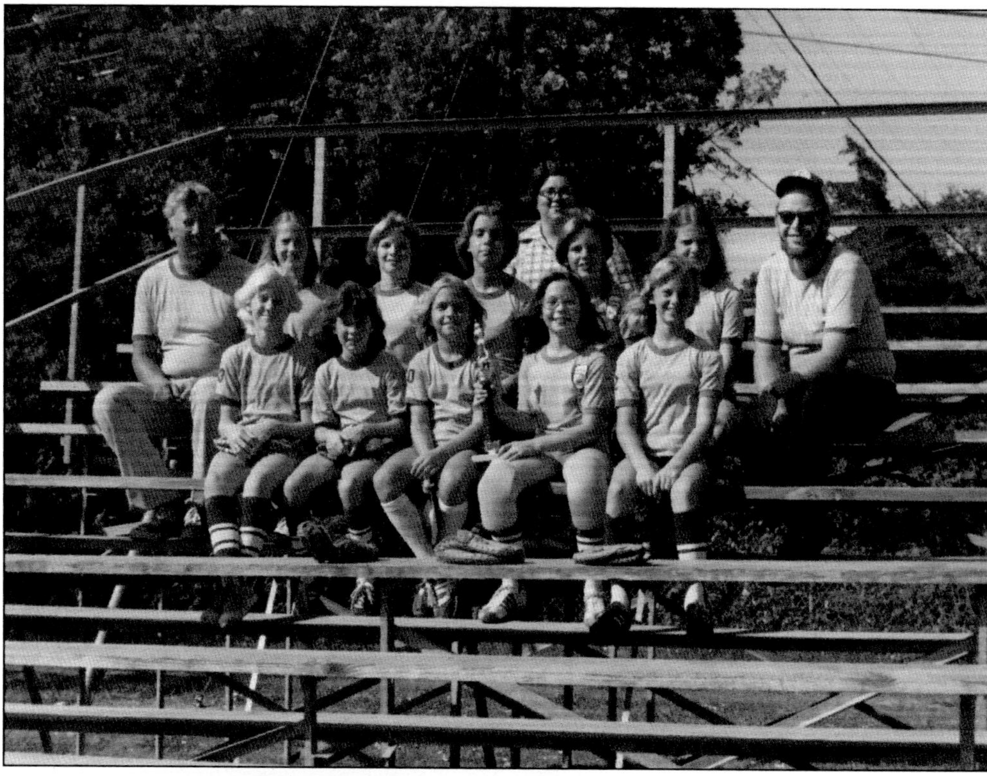

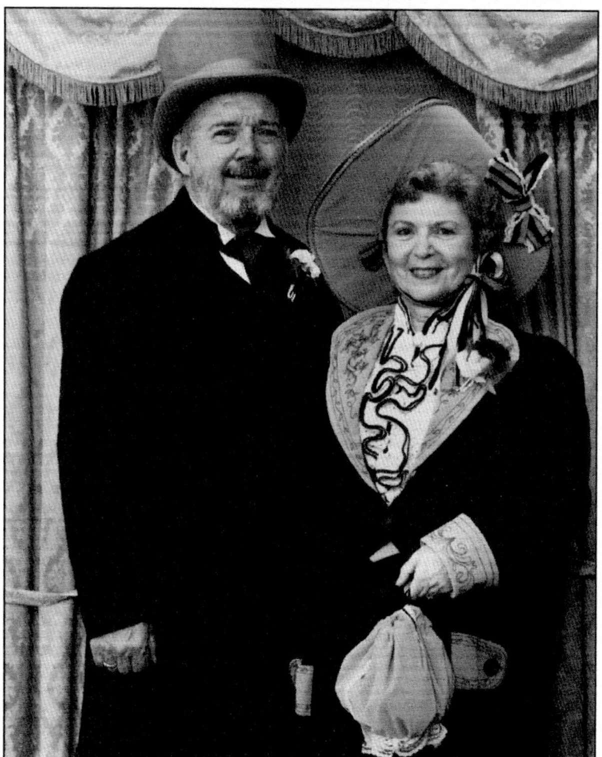

Girls' softball was and is a major program. Softball fields were on the Elisabet Ney Elementary School campus and on Circle Way. A major new complex was built by the city in MacLean Park after 2000. This 1976 team is shown with its trophy. Players are, from left to right, (first row) Bonnie Whitmire, Jean Furney, Paige Sparks, Susie Bertram, and Patrice Terresa; (second row) assistant coach Bob Davidson, Amelia Davidson, Andrea Eratt, Mary Jo Stoerner, Robin Bartow, Ceresa Bartek, and manager Eugene Whitmire; (third row) team mother Phyllis Bertram.

Mayor and Mrs. Vic Vickers dress for the Texas Sesquicentennial Celebration in April 1986.

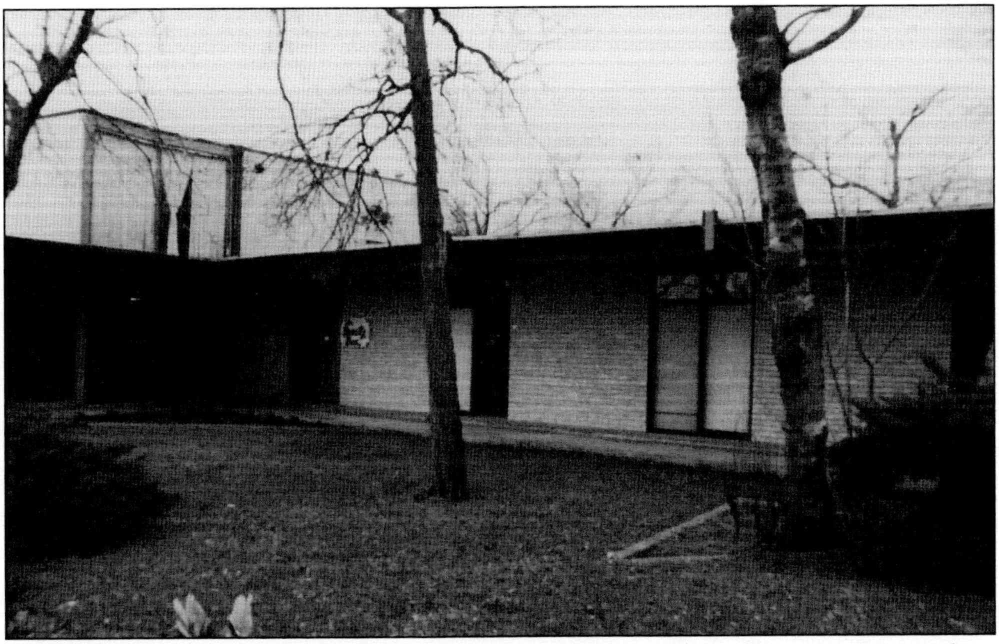

The Lake Jackson Historical Association was formed in 1982. Its museum opened at 122 S. Parking Way in January 1985. The building was previously an unused medical office. The museum was open to the public from 1:00 to 2:00 p.m. on Thursdays. Items on display were a 1940s room with A.P. Beutel artifacts.

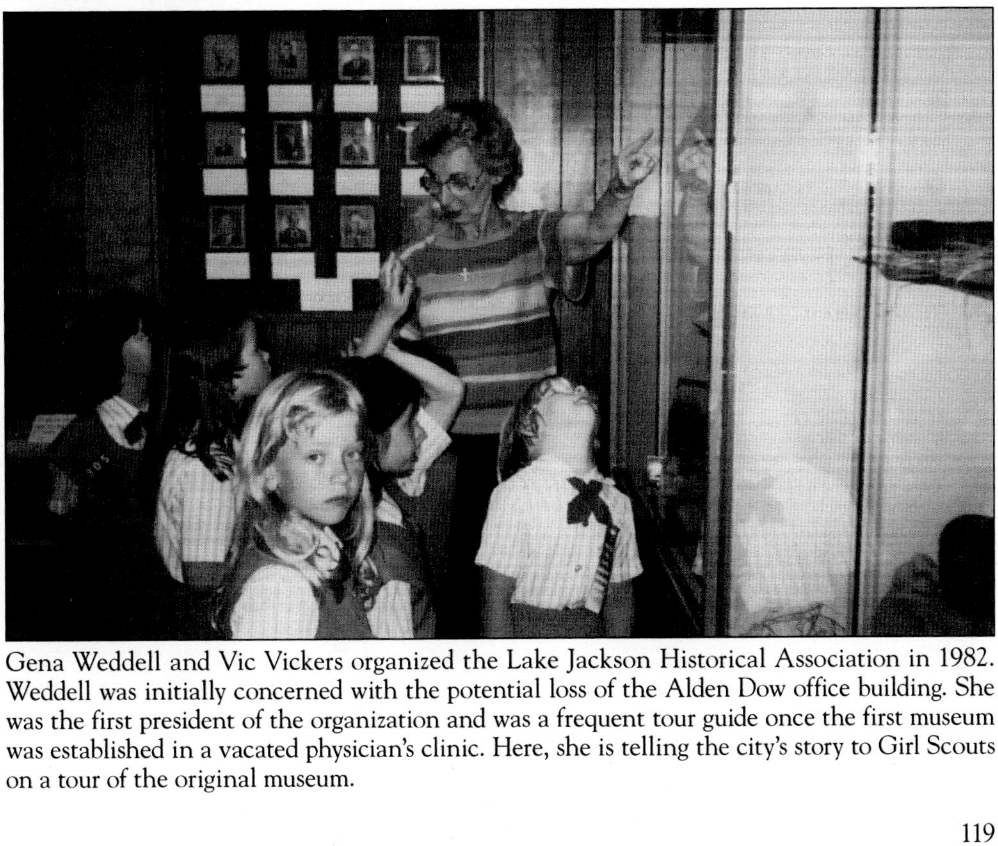

Gena Weddell and Vic Vickers organized the Lake Jackson Historical Association in 1982. Weddell was initially concerned with the potential loss of the Alden Dow office building. She was the first president of the organization and was a frequent tour guide once the first museum was established in a vacated physician's clinic. Here, she is telling the city's story to Girl Scouts on a tour of the original museum.

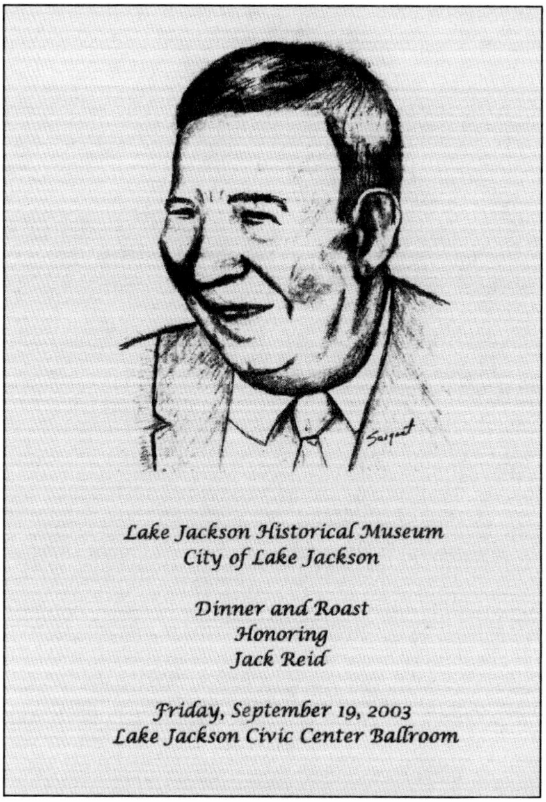

Jack Reid was the honoree of the first dinner and roast for the Lake Jackson Historical Association (LJHA) organized by Sharon Suggs-White. Reid was the mayor from 1968 to 1972 and was also a businessman. Many friends came to both poke fun at and honor him. Reid came to the city in 1948. He was a brick mason, lumberyard employee, and appliance dealer, which led to becoming a city leader.

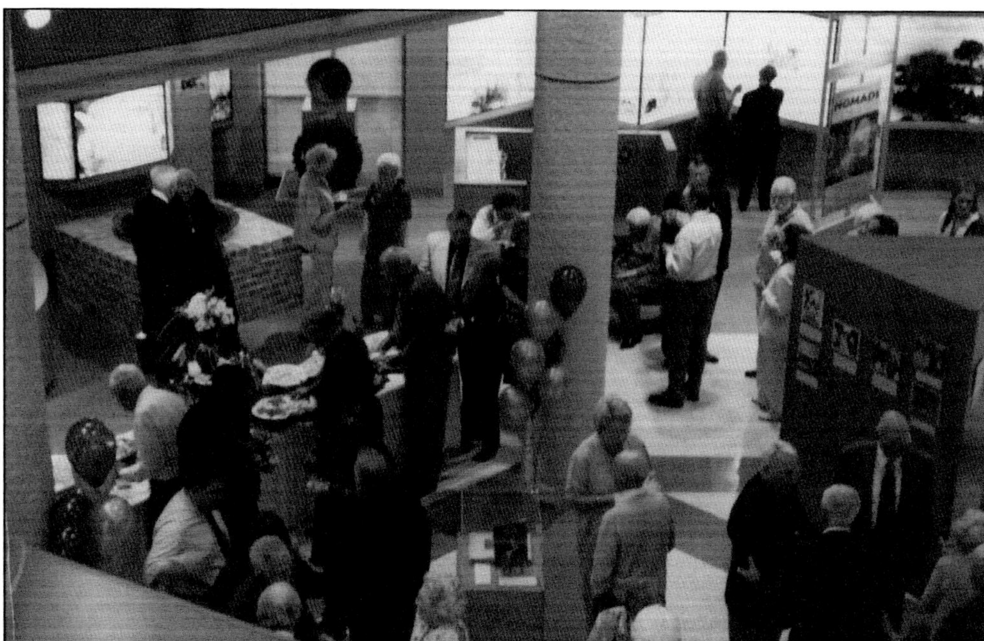

The city museum held a Lake Jackson 60th anniversary display and reception in 2003. A temporary exhibit of Lake Jackson pictures and milestones throughout the decades with captions brought back memories to visitors.

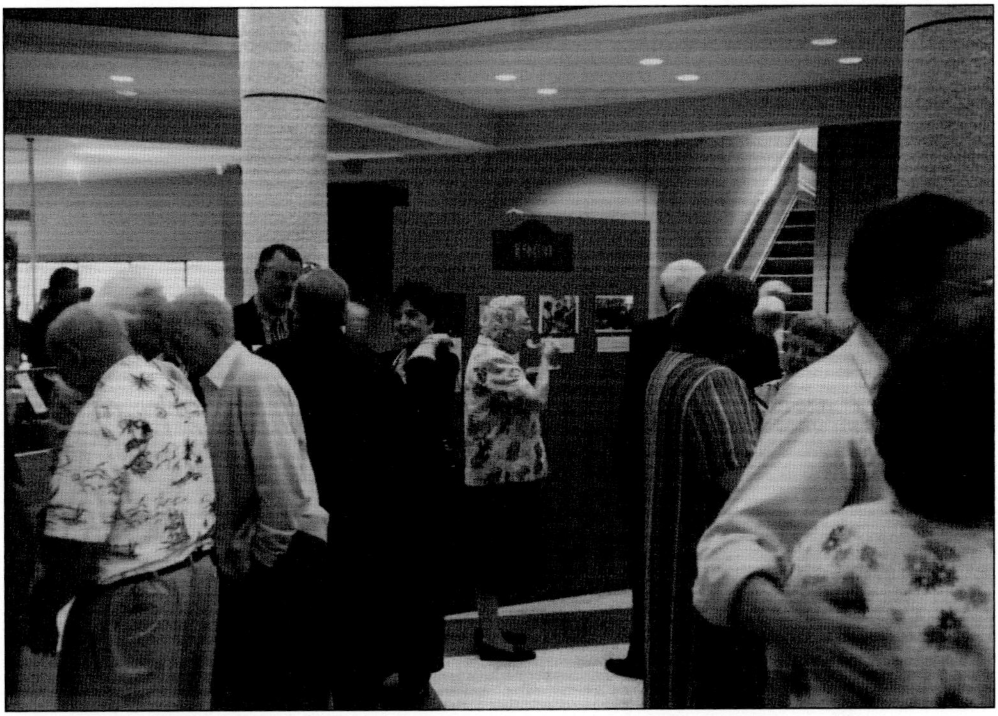

Past mayor and LJHA board member Doris Williams is visiting with Sean Pirtle, also a past mayor. Joe Denton, a longtime resident, is in the sweater on the left.

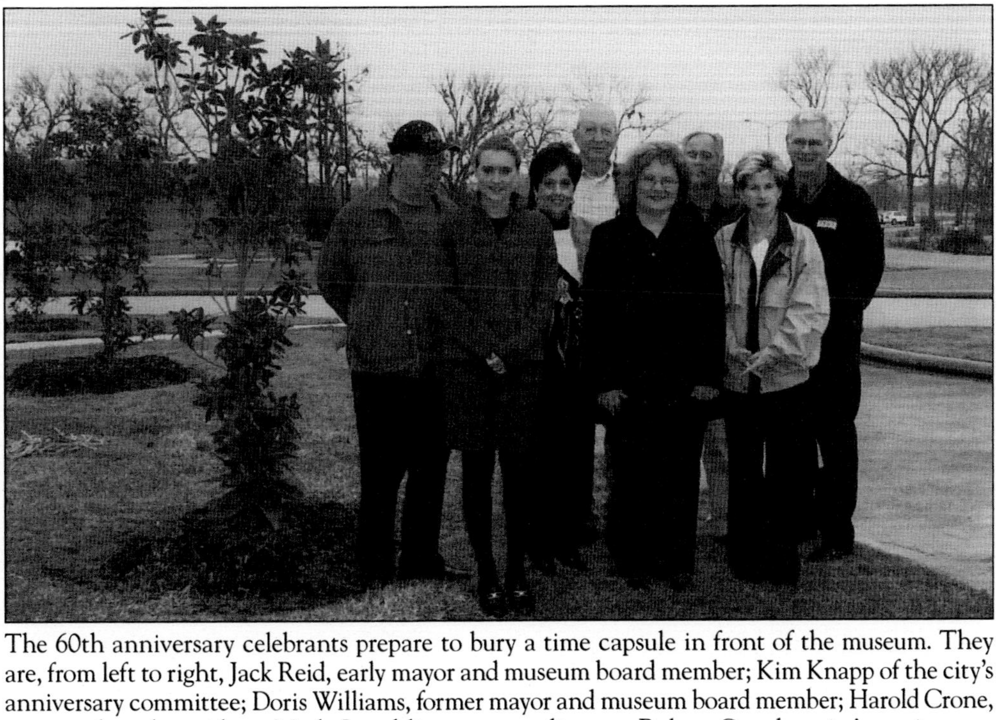

The 60th anniversary celebrants prepare to bury a time capsule in front of the museum. They are, from left to right, Jack Reid, early mayor and museum board member; Kim Knapp of the city's anniversary committee; Doris Williams, former mayor and museum board member; Harold Crone, museum board president; Marla Laughlin, museum director; Robert Canalas, city's anniversary committee; Sandra Oliver, Lake Jackson Civic Center director; and Bill Yenne, city manager.

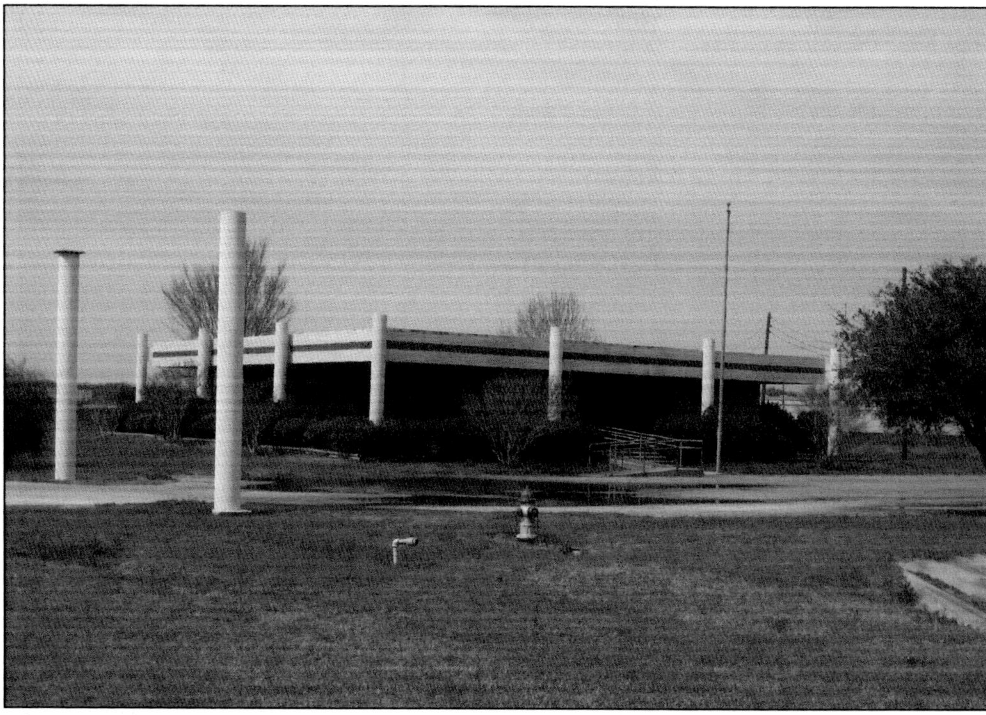

The Brazosport Chamber of Commerce was formed in 1945 in Freeport. The concept of Brazosport included the cities of Freeport, Lake Jackson, Clute, Jones Creek, Oyster Creek, Quintana, Surfside, and Richwood. The chamber of commerce moved to this building on Highway 332 in Clute in the 1960s. The organization promoted local businesses, including tourism.

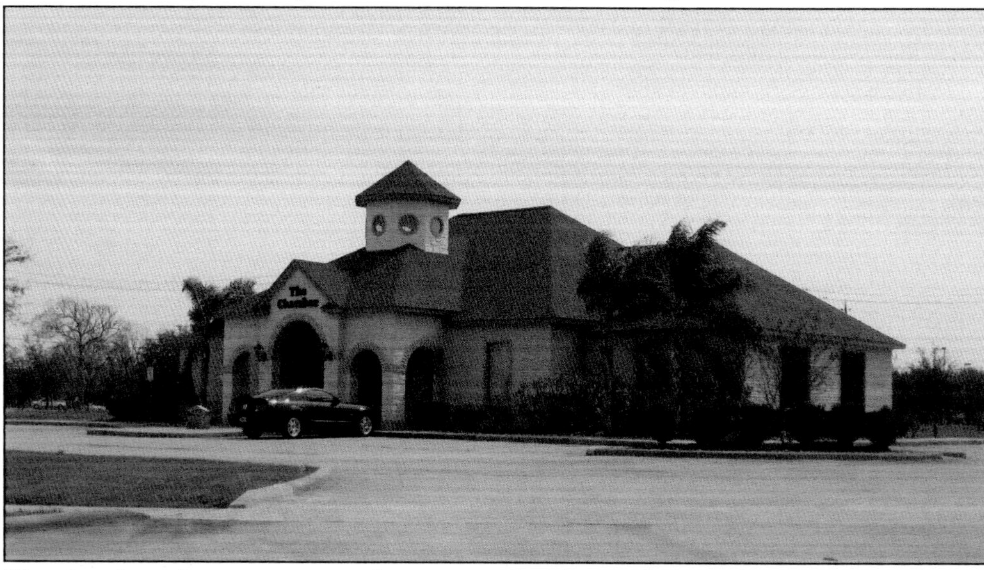

The chamber of commerce moved to its new building in Lake Jackson in 2008. The top employers of the county in 2011 are the Dow Chemical Company with 4,570 employees; the Texas Department of Criminal Justice with 2,440 employees; the Infinity Group with 2,413 employees; the Brazosport Independent School District with 2,015 employees; and WalMart Associates, Inc., with 1,880 employees.

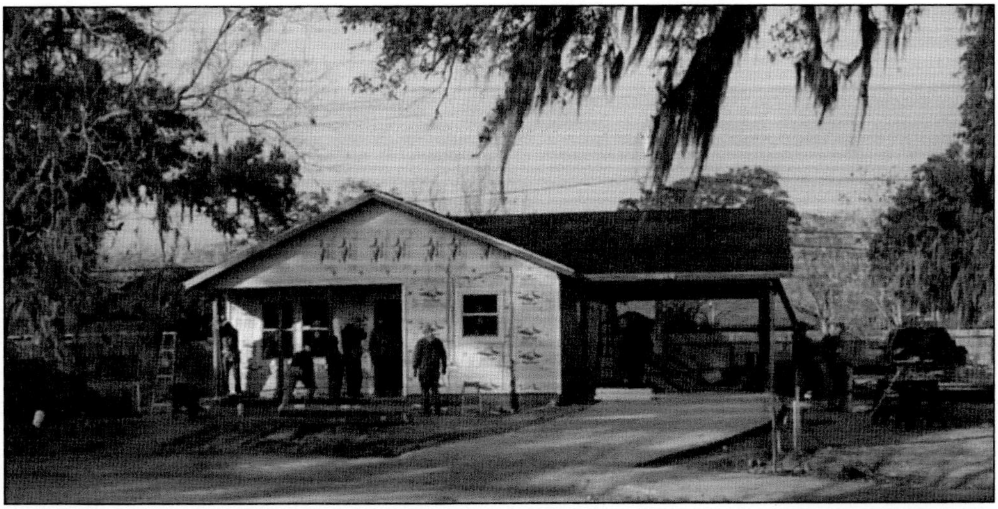

Brazoria County Habitat for Humanity began in 1990 to build homes for families in Brazoria County who have qualified through interviews and by performing sweat equity hours. This house was built in Lake Jackson on Fern Court in January 2005. It was house 48. The goal is to build five to six houses per year with volunteers. They are frame homes with extensive Gulf Coast windstorm elements of construction; there are variations of six basic plans. Vinyl siding gives a maintenance-free exterior. Texas Department of Correction trustees volunteer with on-site construction, truss construction, and cabinet construction. The homeowners purchase the buildings with a no-interest loan. The first homeowner completing the mortgage payment took place in 2010. (Courtesy of Southern Brazoria County Habitat for Humanity.)

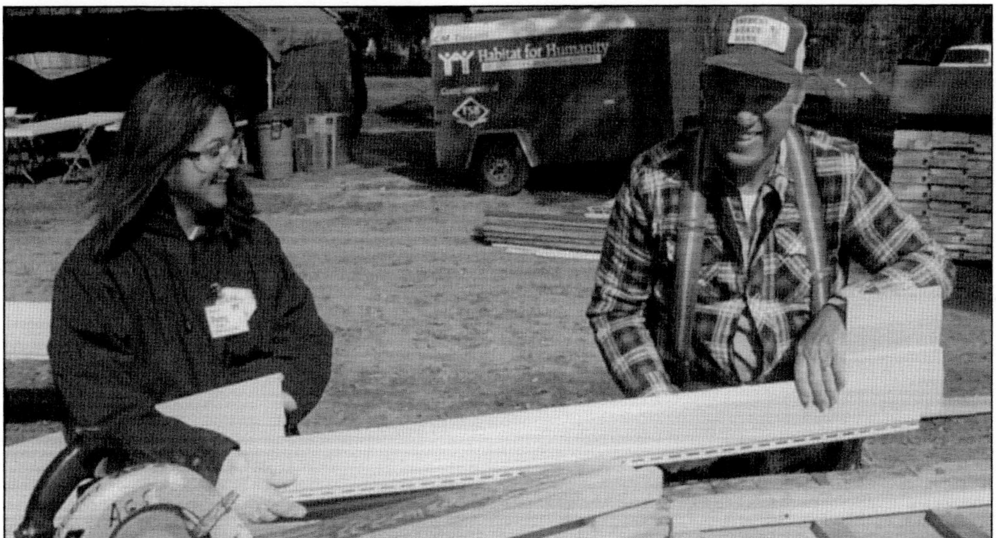

Henry Turner is shown working on vinyl installation with Patty Chavez, a Habitat for Humanity future homeowner. In January 2011, house number 77 was constructed. Home construction takes about 14 days. Home expenses have been contributed for by Dow Chemical Company, the *Facts* newspaper, Galaxy Roofing, Brazosport Art League, Lake Jackson Presbyterian Church, Lake Jackson First United Methodist Church, the Texas Department of Corrections, and more, plus individuals. Mary Ruth Rhodenbaugh was one of the organization's founders and long-term executive director. (Courtesy of Southern Brazoria County Habitat for Humanity.)

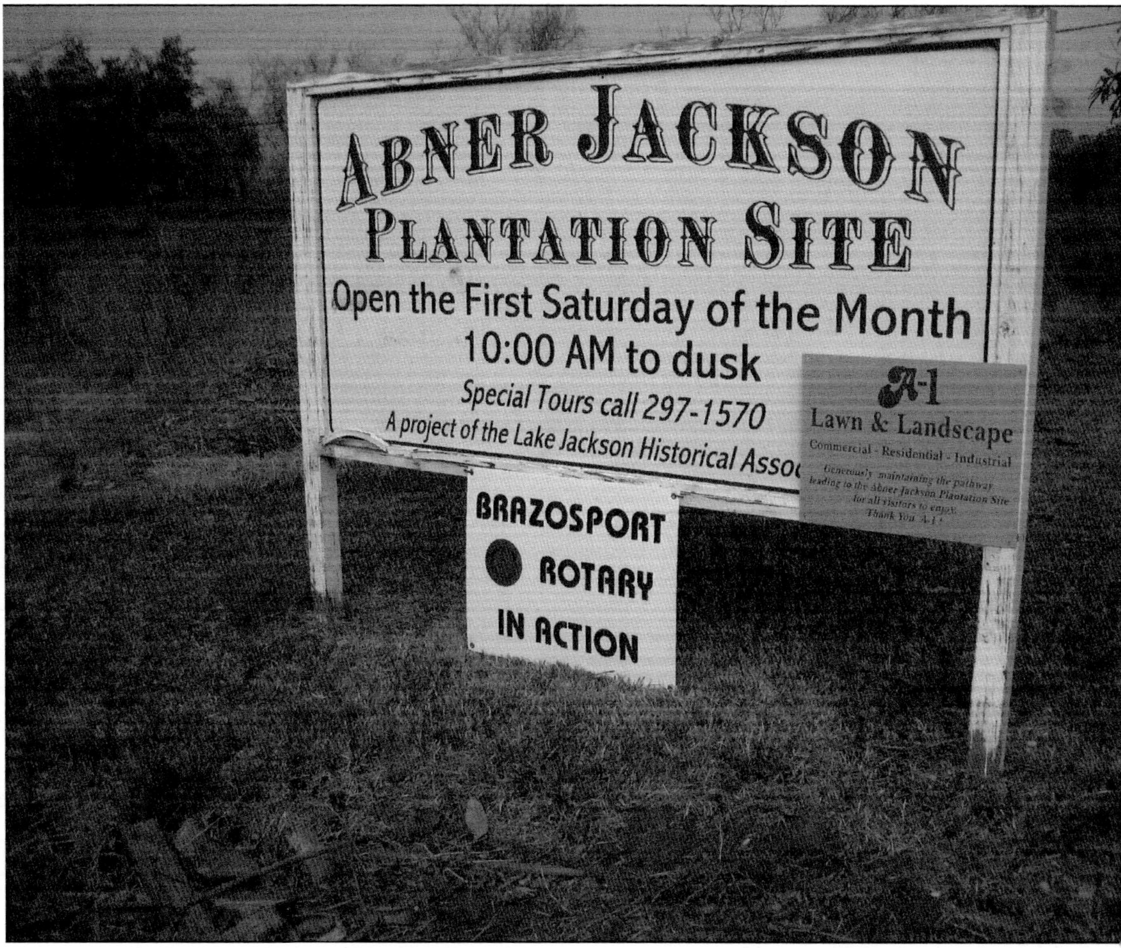

The Brazosport Rotary, an organization of community leaders, began in 1953, serving the community both with funds and labor. Its annual shrimp boil is a major event and income source. It also has work teams under Brazosport Rotary in Action. This sign at the front of the Lake Jackson Historical Association Plantation site is only a small indication of its support over 15 years. Its contributions include installing the memorial brick pathway, landscaping with automatic watering and area lighting, and, in 2011, assisting in restoring the bridge for access to the site.

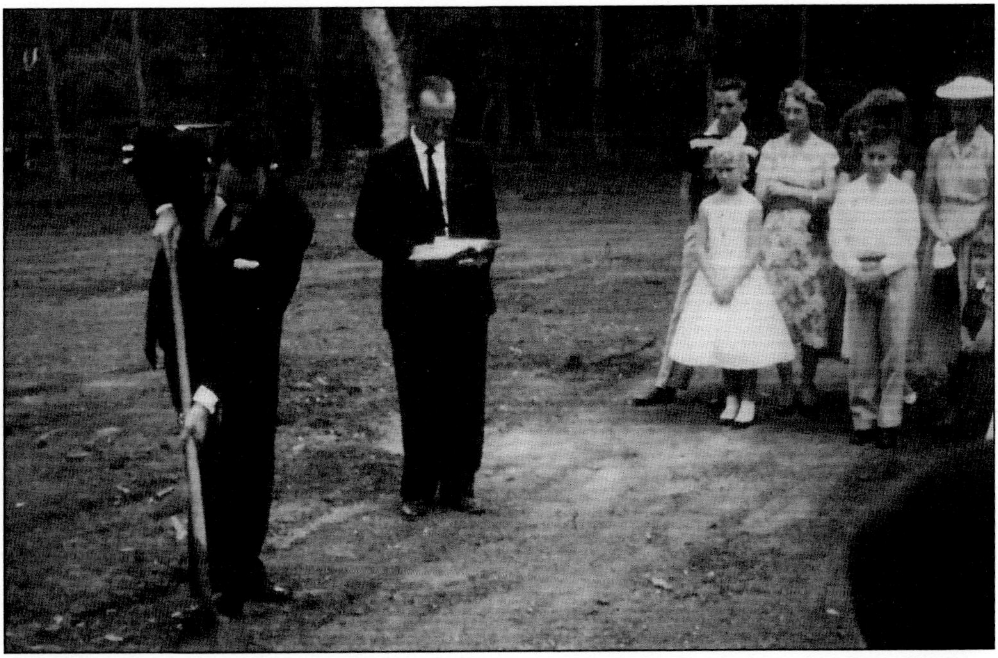

Rev. John Schulz led the ground-breaking ceremony for a modernistic new church building on Willow Drive at Oyster Creek. The ceremony, held on April 13, 1958, began a series of building projects for St. Mark's Lutheran Church–Missouri Synod. Grace Lutheran Church of Freeport originally began the church. (Courtesy of St. Mark's Lutheran Church.)

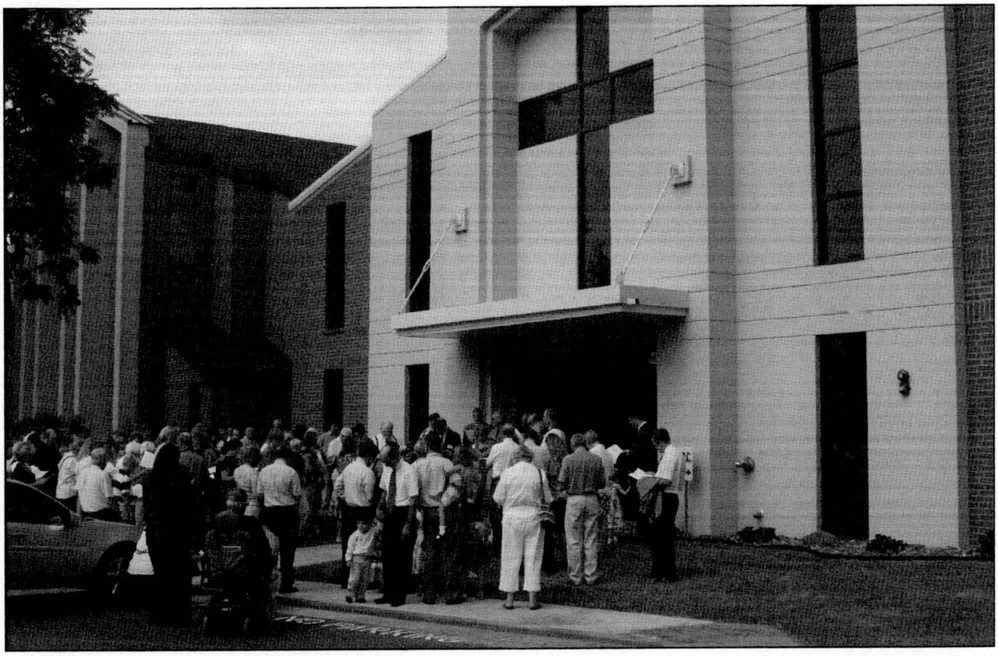

In 2009, the congregation of St. Mark's gathered for the dedication of the new fellowship hall located on the site of the original 1958 church building. In addition to church activities, the fellowship hall also holds community events such as film night and the annual fall festival. (Courtesy of St. Mark's Lutheran Church.)

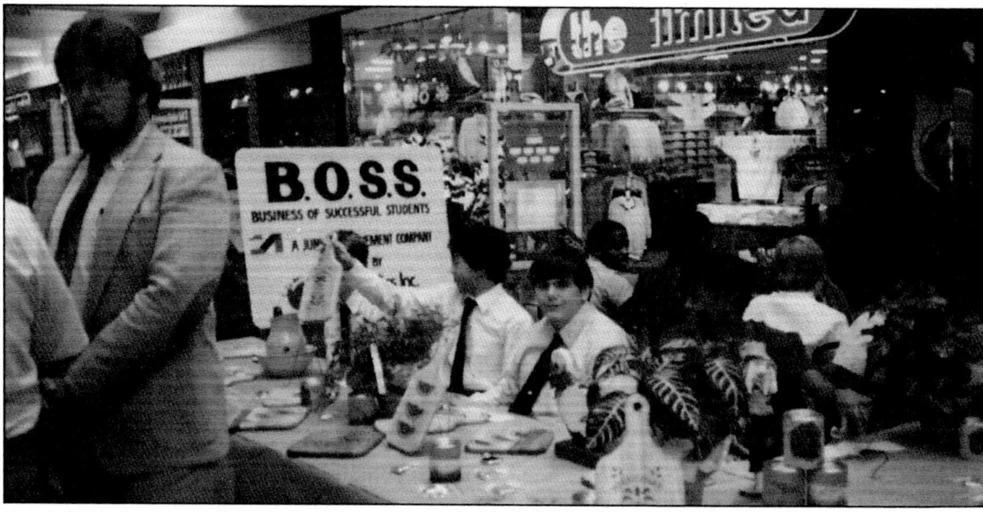

Brazosport Junior Achievement was formed in 1956. It allowed high school students to learn American economic principles by forming companies to plan, manufacture, and sell products to the local community. These students are selling their products in the mall. A.P. Beutel, of Dow Chemical Company, formed a committee of local business leaders to start a Junior Achievement company for Brazoria County. That original committee consisted of O.L. Bass, Beutel (chairman), Ray Charron, D.V. Collins, J.F. Crews, Horace Owings, Vernon Richards, J.C. Sanders, B.O. Smith, V.A. Thorpe, Jack W. Waltrip, and J.L. Wilson. Dow Chemical Company donated a building, across from Roberts Elementary School in Lake Jackson, for Junior Achievement. (Courtesy of Brazoria County Junior Achievement.)

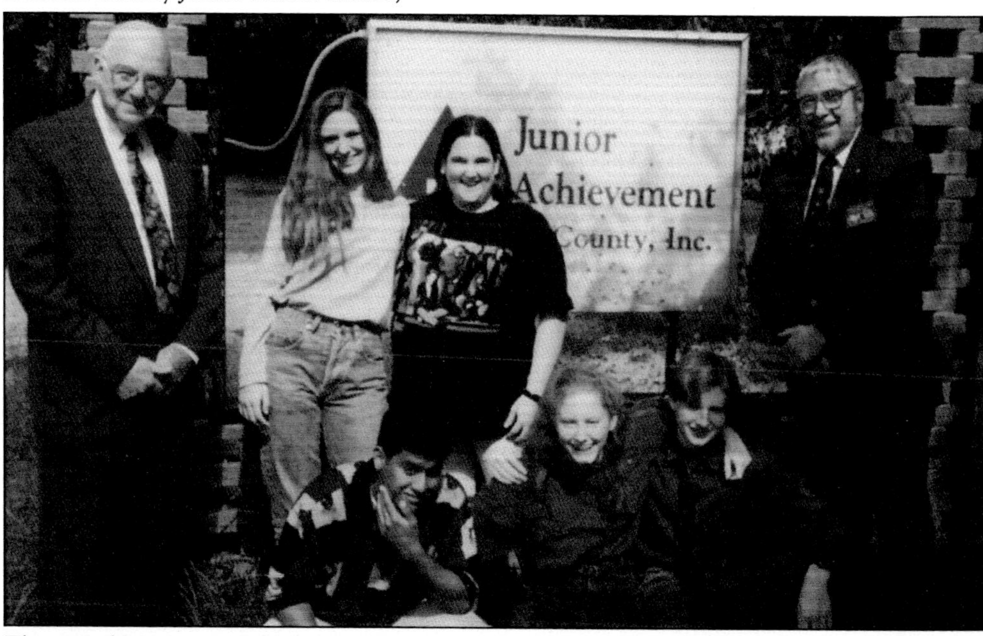

Thurmond Munson, on the left, and Kerry Magee, on the right, are shown with students at the sign for the facility in Lake Jackson. The offices moved to Angleton and the program expanded to kindergarten through 12th grade in the early 1990s. Programs include free enterprise education, basic money management, career investigation, business basics, leadership, ethics, job skills, global economics, and entrepreneurship. (Courtesy of Brazoria County Junior Achievement.)

About the Organization

The Lake Jackson Historical Association is very fortunate for the guidance and leadership it had during its critical formative years. Vic Vickers and Gena Weddell created the organization and collected key early board members and citizens who shaped the vision of the association.

H.H. "Mac" McClure, retired vice president of the Dow Chemical Company, was key in fundraising an excess of $1 million from Texas and Michigan supporters to build a museum with no debt on city property and gifting it for the city to maintain.

McClure was the first director of the museum after construction and guided its permanent display design. He also had the vision to solicit funds for a permanent endowment of $400,000, which became key to the financial stability of the organization. He worked with the city to receive seven percent of the annual local hotel-motel tax as another linchpin of the budget.

As a result, the association has a staff of three degreed historians on salary with benefits. They manage three properties: the museum, the Alden Dow building, and the Lake Jackson Archeological Site.

Few cities have such a great asset after only 67 years of existence!